Bug Swamp
Palavering

BILLIE H. WILSON

WESTBOW
PRESS®
A DIVISION OF THOMAS NELSON
& ZONDERVAN

WestBow Press books may be ordered through booksellers or by contacting:

WestBow Press
A Division of Thomas Nelson & Zondervan
1663 Liberty Drive
Bloomington, IN 47403
www.westbowpress.com
1 (866) 928-1240

ISBN: 978-1-5127-2525-4 (sc)

Library of Congress Control Number: 2016903303

Print information available on the last page.

WestBow Press rev. date: 03/17/2016

Dedication

To dear Grandma Nettie, who never tired of palaverin'.

To her sisters: Aunt Freddie, Aunt Beulah, and Aunt Gertie.

To their mother, my great-grandmother, Margaret Madora Allen Holmes.

To Madora's mother, my great-great-grandmother, Peggy Holmes Allen.

To all palaverers, from Bug Swamp to the far side of distant regions:

Thank goodness, there's a place for us all!

A Heartfelt Thank you:

To my OCAF and Southern Scribes writing buddies;

To our Robin Road coffee palaverers, open to

praising and/or disdaining a writer's work,

both appreciated!

To The Golden Glows; to Joan Humphreys; to Peggy and

Ray Neal; to our pastor, Rev. Ed Boland; to Chester and

Carol Sosebee; to all members of Milledge Avenue

Baptist Church

For your prayers and good will.

To Brother, Jack, and Sister, Marcie, my Savannah champions.

To a sympathetic ear in California, Buddy's sister and mine, Ramona.

To Harriette Austin, teacher, friend, mentor.

(To Anthony, (Donnie) Clemmons, Calabash,

N.C. vital and appreciated,

As well as to Sue and Glascow Smith, cheerleaders

and special friends for portions of my

***third** memoir, "Bug Swamp's and Other Legacies," soon to be published.)*

To my children and grandchildren, but, especially,_

<u>To God Who gives me courage.</u>

Contents

Part VII

Part VIII

Recipe for a Bug Swamp Cake

Select a main ingredient, in this case, Grandma's Little Bushy. Measure all of her five feet and three quarters of an inch. Place resulting <u>essence</u> into a blue-speckled dishpan.

Add "dry" ingredients: Daddy's sly humor, Grandma's faith, Mother's boundless energy, Jackie Boy's curiosity.

Round up the Jersey cow, Petunia. Melt her butter into Great-Grandpa Bill's homemade cane syrup. Boil down to a gooey goodness. (Daddy traded his Old Tin Lizzie for that cow.)

One at a time, beat in four brown eggs, produced by Mother's lovely Leghorn layers.

Employing clean hands and fingernails, mix into this creamy concoction the five "dry" ingredients, alternating substances with Petunia's milk. Make that eight ounces.

To this smoothly mixed batter, splash a teaspoon of Bug Swamp's Baptist flavoring, add a scoop of hope, and a pinch of Grandma's Sweet Society snuff. (You'll never know it's there.)

Pour all ingredients into a carefully greased angel food pan. Forcefully drop the filled pan onto a firm counter, granting all superfluous, airy troubles an escape route through to the mixture's surface.

In Grandma's generous iron oven, lit by God, bake six days at low temperature. No cooking on the Sabbath. Grandpa Hamp's rule: no work on the Sabbath of any kind, unless the ox is in the ditch.

Remove from oven and practice patience. Cake eaten hot swells the tummy. Don't fret, if due to love's pressures, cake falls slightly.

Place cake on plate. Slather with Grandma Nettie's unique icing, one that dispels evil thoughts, tastes like heaven on earth, smells like a fudge factory, and cracks when sliced, revealing an interior of creamy goodness you can't wait to lick off your fingers.

Oh! I almost forgot. In a single slice, one lucky diner will find Grandma's promise of a story, more tantalizing than any piece of cake.

Cup of amber coffee in hand, pour into a
saucer to cool. Sip, munch, enjoy.

Thank you, Lord, for your blessings!

Introduction

Revelations of a Bug Swamp Gal

Asked about my place of birth, my husband liked to quip, "Billie's my swamp gal."

He was right. Some might be misled, for today, proper souls call my home community Good Hope. Just sweet talk for Bug Swamp.

Grandma Nettie thought our land as nearly like heaven as God ever made. She said, if not, then why had He honored our acreage with the Venus fly trap, with pitcher plants, even 'Mary Cut Your Thumbs,' the former two, rare plants growing few places else on earth. Grandma said those insect eaters were probably God's way of gaining a tad more control over Bug Swamp's *bug* population.

To display these and other beauties He shaped islands of sand, plopping them into and around ponds, rivers, lakes. All became perfect foils for cypress trees and mossy oaks, for sweet-smelling magnolia and bay trees, for lofty pines, commingled with myriad varieties of greenery and bloom.

God created creatures: deer to dart around trees and graze grass. Today, raccoons, possums, foxes, fish, gators, wild cats, bears, birds, rabbits, squirrels, all bask in God's gifts to Bug Swamp, as does humanity, finding its way to this tidewater region later than to most "New World" habitats.

On second thought, maybe God wasn't the being who placed honey pot sloughs in beautiful Bug Swamp, for today these miss-named man or beast traps lie in wait for any unwary creature who makes a misstep. An authority on most subjects, Grandma said, "Little Bushy, if you ever get lost in the thick of Bug Swamp, make sure you have with you a long stick. Test every inch of ground before you take a step. Not until your foot sinks into one of them quick sand pits will you even know it's there." Leaves and forest debris perfectly camouflage these unseen, sneaky holes.

Our 1890's farmhouse, planted a mile from church by Grandpa Hamp, sat "right kadab as close as Bug Swamp would allow," a gnat's breath from Bay Swamp with its sweet smells, and gate-keeper to Cypress Swamp behind our house. Meanwhile, Maple Swamp lay within walking distance.

Horry is South Carolina's largest county. So, why was it our state's last area developed? Its rivers: Big and Little Pee Dee Rivers with their swamps, marshes, and muck. And that circuitous Waccamaw. Snaking from head waters in North Carolina, it winds through Horry County, it meanders past Conway, then glides to the Atlantic Ocean via Georgetown County.

Speaking of the Pee Dee, originally Stephen Foster wrote his song, "Way down upon the Suwanee River," as "Way down upon the Pee Dee River." I guess Foster, or someone influential, decided Suwanee flowed more smoothly over the tongue.

Nature's priceless obstacles gave prospective road builders headaches. Thus, hardy souls swimming faster than alligators, and running more swiftly than mosquitoes fly, they settled our area. Today, when I peruse the obituary column of our Horry Independent newspaper, I know well the names of Horry's natives: Todd, Allen, Fowler, Causey, Buck, Thompson, Gore, Gause, Powell, Rabon, Holmes, Bryan, Lundy, Hardee, Williams, Royals, Sarvis, Skipper, Hucks, Anderson, Cartrette,

Baker, Vereen, Bellamy, Frink, Singleton, plus others I'd recall, reading those death notices.

People from parts of our U. S. of A. joke about southern in-breeding. In "early days," when a body living in Horry County reached the age of fourteen or fifteen, and the only nearby folks *not his or her kin* housing marriageable offspring disputed over boundary lines, if they stole horses, if they made bootleg whiskey, a body's own respectable, God-fearing cousins began to look plumb good. Anyway, most people found mates somewhere within walking distance.

Take for instance Grandma Nettie's parents. Her dad, Hezekiah Benjamin Holmes, married Margaret Madora Allen, his dad's niece. It went thusly: Hezekiah's dad, Christopher Holmes, was brother to Madora's mother, Peggy Holmes Allen, making Mr. and Mrs. Hezekiah Holmes first cousins. Sharing one set of grand-parents, they were not alone. Suffice it to say, many people in Horry County, if native to the area, call each other "Cud'n."

The exception to that statement had to be my Mama Todd. Her mom and dad, Callie Royals and George Williams, spawned five children. Their four daughters and one son all married Todds, and not a branch of either Todd family, but for the siblings and their offspring, claimed kin. Wonder why?

In 1933, with The Great Depression at full tilt, Mother sprang me onto the scene. Like others in Daddy's time and space, to get to Adrian, or Arthur's store, maybe to Conway, my dad hitched up Old Pet, or Old Mary to a wagon. Little more than a toddler, I remember climbing aboard Daddy's creaking transport, along with Mother, Grandma, and after 1937, my baby brother, Jack. With a flick of his reins and a "Giddyap," Daddy shepherded us off to whatever destination beckoned. Occasionally we forded swamps. On our scariest excursions snakes dropped from trees, sometimes into a lap.

Going to church early-on, mostly we walked, since God's house sat a mere mile from Grandma's Hampie-built, cypress farmhouse. Grandpa Hamp, Grandma's dearly beloved, died thirteen years before my birth.

Old Pet and Old Mary occupied their own barn stalls; but, our "modern" means of transportation, "Tin Lizzie," hunkered underneath Grandma's needle-shedding cedar tree. I remember with soreness rattling down our county's Potato Bed Ferry Road in that black, square Model A. Corrugated, undulating bumps along that washboard thoroughfare created a bounce I've encountered no place else. Talking and riding at the same time went "Wah, wah, wah." Back then few of our county roads wore asphalt.

Most every trip Daddy made to town, he proudly stepped onto Tin Lizzie's running-board. He'd crank up that noisy old car, step on the gas, and take off, chug-chugging up our church road. Frowning at Daddy, Mother shook her finger, "Rass, don't you dare drive over thirty-five miles an hour." She needn't have worried. "Faster could plumb jar the lard out of a fellow." That was Daddy's brother-in-law, Uncle Homer Powell's declaration.

Memoir # One, *Bug Swamp's Gold,* plops this writer back into a childhood a'swim in history. Our family, like others, fought our way through The Great Depression as well as World War II, whether on the home front or battle field.

With barely a pause, Memoir # Two, *Bug Swamp Palavering,* talks its way through the life and times of Bug Swamp's and Grandma Nettie's Little Bushy. She attends, then completes high school … college. Finding a career in teaching, she also finds a husband. Their family is blessed with children. Encountering life on earth, God, family, relationships, love, salvation, Venus fly traps, danger, bears, birth, cancer, death, jobs, creatures, visions, Christmases, cemeteries, memories, … happiness, … Billie's stories, partial to, and, hopefully, steered by the love and direction of God's Holy Spirit, may they never end.

Part 1

Highlights of Billie Hamilton's experiences

from high school through college . . .

Interspersed with palavering about and

by Grandma Nettie and others.

Isaiah 42: 9 King James Version

Behold, the former things are come to pass, and

new things do I declare: before they spring

forth, I tell you of them.

Chapter 1

Goodbye Bug Swamp, for a While

(Continued from Billie's memoir, Bug Swamp's Gold)

Eyes still shut, awareness struck my brain. Today, yours truly, thirteen year-old Billie Faye Hamilton, could legally enter Conway High School's teen club, not to mention the ninth grade!

I shivered, then opened my eyes. Yep. Here I was, plopped into mine and Grandma Nettie's old feather bed in our new Homewood house. I liked opening my eyes to blue walls. And this room's windows wore blinds, up before we moved here. Yesterday Mother installed rods for new curtains. As yet, they lay folded atop our chest-of-drawers.

What did *not* look strange: that chest-of-drawers. Stuffed with mine and Grandma's doo-dads, it looked as at-home here as in our Bug Swamp bedroom. So did Grandma Nettie's mahogany wardrobe wearing mirrors on both doors. Ready to view anyone entering, that wardrobe occupied a third of our room's back wall.

Now, *this* looked strange: Grandma, sleepin' away just like she'd lived here forever. Till the day we moved Grandma fought leaving the farmhouse she'd shared with Grandpa Hamp and their children.

Feeling kindly toward my sleepin' granny, I won't mention that her mouth stood ajar. She breathed in and out. Nary a pause. Thank the Good Lord no flies buzzed nearby.

I eased out of bed. Excitement trembled my fingers so, I fought with my spiffy ballerina skirt's waist button. Deep pink, glowing the color of Mother's Bug Swamp climbing roses, my new skirt flared wide. Last week Mother felt like shopping, and boy, had I let her. Besides the skirt, she bought me the prettiest silk blouse I could have done without; but, it felt so soft, and these days I do love pink. Any shade.

Believe you me. Never for a second did I question God's memory; but this was a threshold of my life. I had to remind Him. *Lord,* I prayed, *lead me through this day. Please.* That was Grandma's and my "pinkie fingers" prayer before sleep last night.

A shake of my head dislodged three pin-curls. Removing other bobby pins and running fingers through ever-sought ringlets, I thought, *thank goodness it's not a year ago.* That 1945 morning, walking up Conway High's brick steps scared me so, my teeth rattled.

Of course last year everyone welcomed anything new over bad old World War II. Since December 7, 1941, the morning Japanese planes rained bombs onto Pearl Harbor, our family, the Bug Swamp Community, our country, every right thinking nation in this universe concentrated on defeating our misguided enemies. Then, spring of 'forty-five, *hooray!* War in Europe ended. Later in the year Japan surrendered. No more did we wake up each day wondering, "Who killed who?" on last night's battle field. We woke up happy. Our world had found peace. Yet, in early fall, smack dab in the middle of Horry County, I faced new battles.

Conway High School, one of a few secondary schools in our county, sat twelve miles distant from my Bug Swamp farmhouse. A neighbor I'd known forever, Mr. Mack Booth, drove our big, yellow bus. His assigned route proved so convoluted, our jarring, rambling ride lasted over an hour, and that wasn't my latest, life's scariest venture. I hadn't realized schools came in this size. Why *three* Good Hope Baptist Church sanctuaries would be hard-pressed to seat Conway High's many pupils, not to mention its multitude of teachers. As a floundering eighth grader at this humongous school, I felt like a tiny green frog in an ocean-size mud puddle.

Not so, the year before. Fall of 1944, I'd felt plenty big. At Eldorado # II Frank Sarvis kept me from being a seventh grade class of one, and thanks to a great teacher, Mrs. Mildred Bedsol, that spring I passed my Conway High School entrance exam with flying colors.

Probably my first eighth grade school day will haunt me forever. Never have I felt so "out of pocket." Amidst throngs of students, I followed my assigned homeroom teacher from a vast gymnasium echoing every sound, down a hall with no end, up a flight of stairs, finally trailing nice Mrs. Eunice Thomas into her classroom. There she distributed our schedules. In no time flat, a shrill bell jarred us. Disrupting her spiel, we students popped out of our seats. Barely noting the instructor's "Have a good day," we sped from the room. Up and down hallways, eyeballing each other we shook our heads, we rubbed shoulders, desperate to locate our next period class rooms. Like me, most confused, anxious students came from one to four-room-size schools, far-flung across our large county of Horry.

I managed to plough through last year's first school day, also the rest of the year; but, on this Monday morning, September, 1946, Conway High's ninth grade teachers had best prepare themselves for thirteen year-old *Miss Billie Faye Hamilton.*

Well, who besides me would stroke my ego? Compared to last year, today should be a piece of cake. Entering ninth grade thrilled *teen-age-me* to the soles of my open-toed sandals, for now, I lived at Homewood, almost to Conway, where everything worth seeing, hearing, or knowing about happened.

How could Grandma just lie there and sleep through all my excitement? And Jack. Like me, today my "baby" brother would start a new grade, his, the fourth. He should have left an hour ago. Mother's plan: Jack was to ride to school with Aunt Dalma, Grandma's sister-in-law, our new neighbor, and our Homewood landlady. Probably Jack's door slam, leaving, woke me.

Certainly Mother hadn't. Never once had she said, "Wake up, Billie. It's a school day," and my mom always woke me on school days. Hmm. Maybe Mother considered "teen-ager" me more responsible.

"Boi-oing." In the living room Grandpa Hamp's mantel clock, in its new site on our old center table, alerted me to the present. Half past seven. Thirty minutes before bus time.

Mother hadn't forgotten me. I found my breakfast stowed in our house's fancy *enamel* stove's warming closet. Too heavy and bulky to move, Grandma's old iron range still knuckled down in its Bug Swamp kitchen. That bothered me nary a whit. I heard Mother, moving around upstairs, probably trying to straighten and clean-up their bedroom before Daddy came home. Today Jack and I, and our dad faced new experiences. Actually Daddy's began last night. At midnight our tobacco farming dad started his new job at Dargan's Lumber Company.

How convenient. The house's last tenants left a full-length mirror on our dining room door. Warm ham biscuit in hand, I studied my image. Not too bad for a first school day. At least my hair looked fluffy. Since last summer I've shampooed twice weekly. Cousin Frances Marion suggested, as a final rinse, I use watery lemon juice. Nobody has said so, but for a month now I know I've looked blonder.

Leaving, I tip-toed past Grandma's closed door. Sounded like she was trying to shake sand out of our sheets. Didn't she know? This Homewood yard was grassy, not covered in grainy, Bug Swamp sand.

I could have said, "Bye, Grandma," but I didn't. She and Mother might talk too much. Make me late. I opened the door; closed it softly; scooted outside. They'd know I'd left.

What a happy day! The sun was shining so bright, it must be for me, and Homewood air smelled just like our Bug Swamp privet hedge. Inside, Grandma was humming, or rather "do-ta-do, do-ta- . . . the apple tree, with anyone else but me."

Outside my new bedroom window, I stood underneath branches of an apple tree I didn't know who planted. Looking up, I spied something familiar. The sky. And birds. They flew "ever which-a-way." Did they think it was spring?

I nibbled my biscuit. Clean curls tickled my neck. *Wow,* I shivered, *this* is *what growing up feels like.* A branch or two above, a bird twittered, "Billie, Billie, Billie." I pursed my lips. I whistled, "Birdie, Birdie, Birdie."

Mother's face appeared in the upstairs window. Her finger pointed toward the road.

Waving, I dashed out of the yard to the highway. No way would I miss my new bus ride to school.

That afternoon, returning home, I pushed opened the door. I fell onto the couch, notebook and new books still glued to my hands.

Mother's eyes sparkled. "How was it?"

"Like last year," I took a deep breath, "just harder to get around. My classrooms are far apart, and I'm glad I like English, for I don't know about this teacher. But I think I'm gonna like Latin, 'Amo, amas, amant.' And can you believe it? There are two adult war veterans in that class." I sat up and stacked my books beside me. "Then, just before lunch, in study hall Miss Payne, her name's Margaret, but she is a pain. She's on your neck if you whisper a word. I don't know how she hears ya. That library is a hundred feet long. Maybe they set up microphones somewhere.

"They have 'em in the office. We had chapel this morning, sent out to every room in the building.

"Oh. I almost forgot. I have Miss Quattlebaum for fifth period history. Miss Laura Jeanette." I failed to add that a cute, brown-eyed boy sat behind me.

"And I made it into Fulton's, or rather Mr. Booth's science class. Barely." Mr. Booth was a cousin of sorts, and very popular. A veteran, last year he married Grandma's niece, Cousin Elise. She was Conway High's typing/short hand teacher; also, Mother's and my church-singing buddy.

I pursed my lips just so. "Hau nau, brawn kau!"

Mother said, "What are you saying?"

"'How now, brown cow.' That's what Miss Epps drilled into us in our drama class today. She's teaching us to pronounce our diphthongs."

"Whatever," Mother said. "What about recess?"

I perked up. "That was fun. A big old junior or senior, he plays the piano like he's got twenty fingers. His name is Raymond Something or Other. And boy, can a lot of those town girls and boys dance. They shagged, or whatever you call it; they boogey-woogied all over that gym floor."

Grandma came in from the kitchen. "I heard you say you had chapel. Did somebody sing? Did they pray?"

"Yeah, Grandma. A duet sang *Amazing Grace*, and everybody in our home room stood up. We recited *The Pledge of Allegiance*. Then we prayed *The Lord's Prayer*."

Grandma nodded. "As you should have; but, I don't know about all that dancing."

"Our teachers don't mind. It must be okay."

Grandma shook her head and made that sarcastic, upside-down "u" she makes with her mouth. "Depends on a body's version of okay."

Tired after my first school day, it seemed like a million years since Friday. That's when we moved, lock, stock, and barrel, from Bug Swamp to Homewood.

I still rubbed shoulders with my Bug Swamp buddies: Joe, Bertha Mae, Mary Joyce, Bobbie, Betty Jane, her older sister, Edna Mae, Peggy Jo, Hazel, Josephine, others. Actually, today in study hall, Edna Mae taught me how to write my name in shorthand.

"Where's Jack?" I asked. "How was his first day?"

"Fine. He's in the same room as Jesse. They're over at the Millers, playing. I heard complaint, not one from your baby brother."

Why Mother still thought of Jack as a baby, I had no idea. 'Course I was just as guilty. I still called him "my baby brother." Jack was all of nine years old; or, I wouldn't be thirteen, would I?

I slumped onto the couch. Before I knew it my eyes closed shut.

Daddy! I suddenly realized he was probably upstairs, trying to sleep. And I had talked so long and loud.

Right on cue, down the stairs traipsed my dad, poking out elbows and popping his suspenders. I ran to his side. "Daddy! How was your new job?"

"Fine," he said. "I can manage pickin' up and puttin' down boards."

Jack bounced in from Jesse's. Mother said, "Hey, Son, your teacher assign any homework?"

"Just to write down my name, Daddy's name, and our address. I finished that at Jesse's."

"Then come on, everybody!" Mother smiled when Daddy kissed her cheek. "Let's eat supper. Rassie needs a little family time before he takes off for his midnight shift."

Already seated, Grandma presented her cheek to her son. Giving his mama a quick kiss, Daddy pulled up his chair. We positioned hands into prayer peaks. Daddy prayed, "Thank the Good Lord for supper."

Grandma frowned. "Rassie, is that what you say to the Lord after the big day He's granted us?"

"Thank the Lord for our big day, and for Dot's fried chicken and butterbeans. Amen. Now, let's eat."

Grandma sighed. "Whatever will I do with my boy?"

Jack laughed. "Daddy's not a boy, Grandma. Daddy's a man!"

After supper I grabbed my notebook. At school today I'd promised my new friend, Naomi Hardwick, that I'd give her a copy of my schedule. And I needed to jot down a few other tidbits.

I caught Grandma looking over my shoulder. Naomi would have to wait. I shut my notebook. "Grandma, let's you and me hit the hay. I'm so tired."

Grandma frowned. "You need to see Hal?"

Grandma's brother, Uncle Hal, was our family doctor. "I'm not sick, Grandma. I feel like too much is happening too fast. I miss 'you and me' time. I miss your stories."

"Well, tonight's no time for tale-tellin'. We both need our rest. After school tomorrow, if you hanker for a story, we'll get together over a big old pan of potatoes."

I sighed, breathing out most all my fears and woes. Thank the Lord for Grandma.

Chapter 2

My Grandma

I reminded myself: once, Grandma was a girl. I could hardly imagine her young like me. She talked a lot, but never much about her early days. I had heard about the time her pa, my Great-Grandpa Hezekiah Holmes, sent his young daughter next door to borrow a "bull tongue," whatever that was. Earlier, her dad told her "bull" was a dirty word. Nettie should call that animal a "booing-beast."

Grandma knocked on their neighbor's door. When someone answered her knock, she lit into saying, "Papa wants to borrow your 'bull tongue.'" But when she got to the word "bull," she said, "Papa wants to borrow your . . . 'booing-beast' tongue."

The neighbors laughed. Color stung Grandma's cheeks. Practically in tears, she ran the mile home. When Grandpa Hezekiah heard what Nettie had asked to borrow, he about bent over double, laughing.

I wanted to hear more about Grandma and Grandpa Hamp, what both were like as young people. Her friend, store keeper Mr. Arthur Dorman, once told me that Grandma, he called her Net, was the prettiest little blonde girl he ever saw.

My grandma: young, blonde, pretty? That seemed totally unreal; a grandma I couldn't imagine.

In the next couple of weeks, Grandma Nettie remedied that. Over potatoes and onions I heard her version of how she and Grandpa fell in love. After we finished our vegetables, Grandma kept on talking. She told me about her youth, about living, for a couple of years, in far-away

Almo, Georgia; how she felt, leaving behind everything and everybody she knew. I guess our Homewood move brought these old times to mind. Probably moving away from a place she felt was home, now and forever, amen, had a lot to do with her palavering about "back then."

As early as I can remember, Grandma taught me her version of God. She tickled my fancy with tales of mocking birds and goblins, gators and bears. She told me about her own grandmother, Peggy Holmes Allen, *the best, the sweetest woman ever to grace this earth!* My softly wrinkled Grandma Nettie, sporting a gold capped "dog"tooth, and a scar in one corner of her mouth, so old she couldn't sing in church these days, once, she had a grandma!

Years before I was born, Grandma had a husband. I know him, my grandpa, because she relished sharing memories of her love. In our Bug Swamp parlor, Grandma would sink into her peach Damask chair in the "jam" of the chimney, stare into the past, and commence some tale about her hard-working, handsome hubby. Grandma was close to my age when the following took place. Peeling Irish potatoes, I learned what possibly led Grandma into marrying Grandpa Hamp.

Hampie and Nettie

In the early eighteen nineties, like other girls in her Bug Swamp community, Rosahnel Cincinetti Holmes needed no reminding that a good-looking young man lived about a mile down the road, probably the son of the neighbor she'd visited, borrowing that "booing beast" tongue. A few other boys lived nearby, for instance, Lex Stevens. A school mate, a neighbor, and a pleasant young fellow, he'd been a friend since babyhood; but, just last Sunday the good-looking boy a mile down the road, that fellow turned around in his pew and smiled. Big. At Nettie.

Turning fourteen in April brought Nettie brand new thoughts. Girls married at her age. Maybe it was time she learned what this courtin' business was about. Her brother, Dave, went a'courtin'. When he started gettin' all gussied up, Nettie had said, "Where you goin'?" Dave said, "A'courtin'. I'm goin' to see Lucy." Now they were married.

One morning Nettie lay propped up in bed, wondering what she'd dreamed last night. Whatever, it left her with a good feeling. Maybe she'd dreamed that the fellow foremost in her mind these days liked her too. Maybe, like Dave, he'd come a'courtin.'

What if he did? Would he hold her hand? Then what? She'd talk to her sister. Freddie was a whole nine years older than Nettie; but, she never had cared much for courtin'.

Sometimes when Freddie wasn't around, people called her "Old Maid." Not surprising. Nettie's sister was already twenty-three. No marriage in sight.

These days Freddie cooked the family breakfast. Already dressed, she checked out her teeth in the mirror, then brushed her hair. Now was the time. Nettie should talk to her sister.

Uh-uh. Freddie would laugh.

With little help from her, Nettie's mouth popped open. *It* said, "Freddie, what do boys and girls do, a'courtin'?"

No surprise. When she finished laughing, Freddie said, "Forget courtin', Net. I'll tell you about something better. See that there peach tree?" She pointed outside their window. "Every morning, as soon as your eyes pop open, look at that tree. When you spy its first bloom, pick it. Eat it."

"Eat what? The peach blossom?"

"Yep. Then don't be surprised when somebody ups and gives you a great, big smack on the lips."

Snickering on her way to start breakfast, Freddie threw out over her shoulder, "That's the fellow you'll marry!"

Nettie had never heard of such. Still, Freddie's challenge added one more rung up the fourteen year-old's curiosity ladder. Early each morning, Nettie pulled back her window curtain. Ashamed she was such a silly, the girl could hardly wait for that tree to bloom. Finally, on a limb closest to the window, one peach bud spread open pink petals. Looking left, then right, Nettie snuck outside. She picked and chewed to smithereens that tender blossom. Yuck! A peach would have tasted sweeter.

Later, doing her chores, Nettie stepped up to the well curb. Just as the girl let down her bucket and filled it to brimming, a handkerchief whipped across her eyes. Firm hands turned Nettie's blindfolded face, and "Somebody kissed me 'smack on the lips.'" Grandma couldn't believe it happened, just like Freddie said. Wonder if Freddie was in on this!

The handkerchief, as well as the kiss, belonged to that rapscallion, Hampie Hamilton. And they must have done some courtin', for before long, so did Nettie!

Over a hundred and twenty years ago at this telling, during the last decade of the eighteen hundreds, Rosahnel Cincinetti Holmes became the bride of Hampton Lafayette Hamilton. They were wed by the Reverend W. S. McCaskill, minister of Good Hope Baptist Church, a large, bell-towered wood structure replacing Bug Swamp Baptist's original 1874, log-built sanctuary.

Little time passed before Grandpa Hamp, anxious to provide well for his new bride, whisked her away from everything familiar. Accompanying another young couple, Sam Booth and his wife, Nan, Mr. and Mrs. Hamp Hamilton boarded a train for Georgia. At their pine forest destination, both men acquired jobs "pulling boxes." These Bug Swampians were to spend two years working in Georgia's turpentine business before returning home.

The next Friday, tired and aggravated, I came home from school. Miss Quattelbaum had given us a pop quiz and I hadn't studied. Grandma saw I was upset. She said, "What'll lift your spirits, Little Bushy?"

I said, "Grandma, tell me more about living in Georgia. You weren't but a year or two older than I am right now."

Grandma rubbed her hands together, then patted them. She said, "First, get you a drink of water; then lie down on the couch. This tellin' will take a while."

With both of us comfortable and the house quiet, Grandma told me all about their trip to Georgia, how lonely, how interesting, how much fun, and how weird the place and people could get. Actually, the weirdest was the young lady, Nan Booth, accompanying Grandma, Grandpa, and Nan's husband, Sam, to a town drawing unemployed people from all over the Southland. I'll relay Grandma's story in my words:

Nan Booth's Leg

In 1894, my future grandparents, Hamp and Nettie Hamilton, her heart astir with a mixture of feelings, accompanied Bug Swamp friends, the Booths, to Almo, a village located near Valdosta, Georgia. That train trip awed Grandma. Through cinder-laden smoke, she viewed paddle-boats on rivers widening to the sea. Strange looking people walked streets in Charleston and Savannah, and the new bride ate thick sandwiches brought aboard the train by people speaking with accents as thick as their sandwiches.

"Whew!" Beyond Savannah, marshland smelled to high heaven, while Hampie's bride's bottom grew plumb numb, sitting so long in that hard, jarring seat.

At long last the couples reached their destination, and the young husbands went to work for Mr. Bryan, owner of the turpentine business. Assigned a job, "pulling boxes," Grandpa soon advanced to the lofty position of circuit rider. Traveling through the woods on horseback, he kept tabs on "box-pullers."

Grandma and Nan busied themselves sewing patchwork quilts. The girls traipsed through piney woods. They reminisced about their distant families.

"Nan," Grandma pointed skyward, Georgia trees standing tall before her eyes, "that self-same sun shines on Papa and Mama that shines on us. It helps me to remember that."

"As long as I have Sam, I'm fine right here in Georgia," Nan declared.

Grandma knew. She loved Hampie as much as Nan loved Sam. Still, newly-wed and away from home on her first long journey, Hezekiah and Madora's young daughter wished she could shake off this mighty lonesome feeling.

One morning after Grandpa left for the woods, too early, knocks jolted their cabin door. Grandma, intent on catching another forty winks, sighed. She plodded to her door. There stood Nan, just a'complaining. "Net," she fretted, "my leg's so sore I can't hardly stand on it!"

Grandma's dad's uncle, Dr. Henry Holmes, had taught his great-niece how to heal with herbs and such. Eons ago, noting what he called "a cancer" in one corner of Grandma's mouth, Uncle Henry covered it with "a poultice." That concoction removed Grandma's sore, plus more. Where normally her smile tipped up, now gaped a huge hole, which, thankfully, soon shrank, leaving Grandma wearing a permanent, miniature "kiss."

Grandma pulled out from under her bed the stash of herbs she'd brought to Georgia. Mixing a formula for infections, (Nan called it "a putrid smelling mess!") Grandma applied the poultice to the girl's leg, already exhibiting a knot of aggravated flesh midway the outside of its right calf, skin around the risin' dry-puckered, fiery red.

A few days passed. Nan's leg worsened and her spirits sank to the bottom of her laced-up shoe soles. "What'll I do, Net?" She wailed. "Whatever will I do with this dad-burn leg?"

One evening Grandpa Hamp brought a fellow worker home for coffee. Elijah loomed in Grandma's doorway, a giant man, an ebony, smiling Goliath. He folded himself onto their doorstep and the three sipped cups of what Grandpa described to Elijah as "coffee strong enough to pull boxes." Grandma finished hers.

"Twirl your cup three times above your saucer, Missy. Then place it upside down for the dregs to drain," Elijah told Grandma.

Puzzled, Grandma followed his instructions.

Elijah took her saucer and studied dreg patterns. His face turned plumb serious. "I hate to tell you this," he said, "but looks like somebody in your family's so sick, they's turnin' 'em in sheets."

Relating the story, Grandma would shudder. "Elijah's saying such made a possum walk over my grave!'"

A day later she received a letter from her dad. He wrote, "Nettie, your Grandma Peggy is so weak, we use sheets to turn her in bed."

Young Grandma sank to her knees. She prayed, "Dear Lord, please help my grandma, and help me get over being lonesome for family."

Grandma felt shame for that thought. Hampie, *he* was her family.

Grandma said, "While I was prayin', the hair fanned out and waved all over my body. I grieved for Grandma Peggy, but Elijah's seein' her in my coffee dregs, that *pure-in-tee* stunned me. How could Elijah know that? Was it some kind of gift from God?" Anyhow, when Nan said, "Whatever will I do about this leg?" Grandma's first thought was *Elijah!*

"Nan," she said, "Elijah might can help your leg!"

"You think so?" Nan was ready to try anything or anybody.

Saturday morning Elijah met with Nan, and afterwards, the girl set about preparing for her "cure."

"This is strange, Net." Nan hobbled around supported by a cushioned stick under her armpit.

"Can I help?" Grandma asked.

"No." Nan looked doubtful. "Elijah says I have to do it all, and once the spell, he called it that, once the spell starts, I can't speak till it's over!"

Grandma didn't like that word, "Spell." Still, she couldn't help gigglin'. "Not talkin' will be your hard part."

Nan poured two quarts of water into a wash pot; then pitched in a measure of sulfur they'd bought from Mr. Bryan's company store.

"Nan," Grandma said, "before you go any further, I think we should talk to the Lord. Make sure we're not trustin' in who we shouldn't!"

Nan shook off Grandma's hand. Grandma said, "I'm gonna pray whether you do or don't." She sank onto the step. Closing her eyes, she pleaded: *If it be thy will, Lord, cure Nan's sore leg. Be with her every step she takes today. Bless us all. Bless Elijah. I pray he is your child, dear Father.*

Looking grim but determined, last of all Nan dropped into the pot a silver dollar Grandpa Hamp lent her. Then she struck a match to kindling beneath the pot.

Fire blazed and water boiled. Hard. Grandpa's coin rattled. It clanked. Like a blind bird trying to escape its nest, that silver dollar zoomed far beyond the lip of the wash pot, only to slam back inside.

That coin looks like somethin's after it! Silent, bug-eyed, Grandma sat on the steps beside Nan. Smelling like rotten eggs, sulfur rode Almo, Georgia air, while that silver coin cavorted "hither and yon."

After about half the water disappeared, Nan scooped the rest into a basin. She bathed her leg in warm, yellowish water, her silence totally un-Nan-like.

Next, she picked up the pan of water and crooked her finger at Grandma. Dragging one foot, hugging the pan, and leaning on her cane, Nan led Grandma through a pine thicket to where underbrush thickened and the ground turned spongy.

Grandma remembered Elijah's directions to Nan. He said, "No matter what you hear in them woods, don't look back!"

A tree limb cracked. Not moving her head, eyes wide, looking left to right, Grandma searched the woods before her, hoping to translate rustling bushes into scampering squirrels, raccoons, maybe 'possums. Startled by swooping turtle doves, Nan stopped, so suddenly, Grandma smacked into her friend's backside. Almost, Nan broke her silence, catching herself in the *nick* of time.

The two transplanted Bug Swamp girls scrambled down shallow ravines. They trod fairy paths carpeted in curly, green moss. On reaching a stream Nan laid down her cane and poured yellow-streaked water into the current. She and Grandma watched the oily mixture swirl in rainbow hues: lavender; orange; blue; gold. Awestruck, they gazed as branch water, intermingling with many-colored tints, flowed out of sight.

"Well, that's that. I've done all Elijah said to do." Tongue loosened, Nan clearly felt disappointment. She pulled up her skirt and stuck out her leg. That risin' poked way out. Still as huge as a pigeon's egg, it gleamed. *Lord, help her now,* Grandma prayed.

The more Nan thought about Elijah giving her false hope, the madder she grew. "Look at my leg, Net!" Upset, angry, Nan strode off through the woods, swinging her pan and popping her frock tail, her cane, unused, tucked beneath an arm.

Grandma whispered, *Thank you, Jesus.* She yelled, "Nan, if your leg's so sore, how come you're walkin' so fast?"

Nan halted. She grinned. "Dad-burn-it, Net, the pain's gone!" Nan never was too lady-like.

Thank the Good Lord, Nan's pain never returned, and, gradually, that pesky sore went away.

That day, back at Grandma's cabin Nan said, "Net, hand me the lye soap." Using zeal coupled with determination, Nan scrubbed Hampie's borrowed acrobatic silver dollar "to a fare-thee-well." Greenish scum sloughed off the coin. Lying on the kitchen counter that dollar glowed: a round, metal spook.

Grandma refused to touch what had acted like a Sovereign of Satan. Nan wrapped it in a piece of brown paper and left it on the wash shelf.

"There's your dollar, Hampie, beside the basin," Grandma told Grandpa, coming home from his Saturday afternoon checker game.

Grandpa unwrapped the coin. "What's this?" He twirled the object between thumb and forefinger. "Is this the dollar I lent Nan?"

"One and the same," Grandma said.

Grandpa scratched his head. "What do you know? I lend Nan a silver dollar. It comes back a gold piece!"

"Fool's gold," Grandma sniffed. "I don't like what happened today. I need to see Elijah."

Hampie's ebony friend with the quick smile and pleasant manner agreed to stop by that evening. The last time he'd visited and they drank coffee, Elijah had read dregs in Grandma's emptied cup, like she'd heard of some people reading tea leaves.

Tonight instead of sitting on their front steps, Hampie invited Elijah inside, and they pulled up chairs around the table. The aroma of Grandma's just-baked teacakes put both men in a pleasant mood. Handing him his cup of coffee, she said, "Elijah, when you were here before and we had coffee, you looked at dregs inside my emptied coffee cup. How did you know my grandma was bein' turned in sheets? From back home Papa sent me a letter. Grandma Peggy, Mama's mama, the family was having to turn her in sheets."

Elijah looked puzzled. "I told you what I saw in your cup. The dregs looked like people turnin' a person in sheets."

"Who taught you that, Elijah? I'm scared of anything resemblin' witchcraft."

"My mama showed me how to read tea and coffee dregs. Nobody I know ever called that witchcraft."

Grandma tried a different approach. "Do you believe in the Lord, Elijah?"

"I sure as the Lord do, Missy. With all my heart I believe in The Good Lord."

Grandma was young, not quite fifteen; but Nettie Holmes had been raised to read her Bible and pray, every day. She took Elijah's hand. She said, "Elijah, pray with me?"

Grandma said Hampie heard her, and ran toward the shed bedroom before she collared him. Grandma prayed, *Dear Lord, Elijah and I are asking you to listen to us. We're your servants, Lord. We want to say and do Your will. Help us, we pray. Help us both to know Your will, and then to do Your will. Teach us right from wrong. Good from bad. We ask these blessings in the name of Your Son and our Savior, Jesus Christ.*

"Elijah, it's your turn to pray. Pray for yourself. Pray for me."

"Yessum," Elijah said. *Lord, You heard the missy. Come here this very minute. You're always welcome, Lord. Teach us. We'll listen. We want to do what's right, Lord. Always.*

Together Grandma and Elijah said, *Amen.*

Back to Bug Swamp

The sick woman Elijah "saw" turned in sheets was Peggy Holmes Allen. In 1894, paying her Grandma Peggy a final visit before boarding a train for Georgia, my future grandma had hugged her beloved grandparent and said, "I'll see you soon." In the buggy, just before rounding a curve, Grandma looked back. Standing behind her picket fence and looking sad, Grandma Peggy waved till bushes hid Hampie and Nettie from sight. That was my grandma's last view of her grandma, on this earth anyway.

In 1896, young Hampie and Nettie returned to Horry County, Grandpa wearing a bulging money belt. Grandma, herself bulging, neared the birth of their first child, Aunt Sally.

After speaking to Grandma's family members, those home at the moment, Grandpa Hamp rushed down the church road to his mom's house, anxious to reunite with Olive McNabb Hamilton and his brothers and sisters.

Meanwhile, Grandma Madora grabbed her daughter's hand and led her down the hall. "Nettie! Come see your baby brother and sister." Twins, Bertie and Gertie were born while Nettie was wandering around through tall Georgia pines with Nan, Sam Booth, and Hampie.

What little angels! Bert lay closest to his big sister. Nettie picked up that doll who immediately reached for his sister's cheek.

Not wanting the sweet little girl to feel ignored, Nettie returned Baby Bert to his nesting place, causing him to let out a loud "Waah!" She picked up Baby Gertie, who immediately let out a similar "Waah!"

Awe struck Nettie, head-on. Inside this daughter, this wife who still felt like a child, huddled Nettie's own baby. How had her mother managed so many children? These two made eleven. When Nettie left home, little Hal was a mere babe. Where was Hal?

She spied him through the window. Leaving the twins long enough to dart onto the porch, Nettie called, "Hal!" Squatted down and picking up apples with their sister, Freddie, Hal looked over his shoulder at Nettie.

Nettie greeted her oldest sibling. "Hi, Sis! How are you! How are you, Little Man? Hi Sweetie Pie," she hugged the young boy Freddie lifted onto the porch. Nettie's heart said this growing, blue-eyed boy was no stranger. And it was time Sister Freddie got married; and picked up apples with her own little boy!

In a blink Nettie's mind turned from babies to dinner, for good cookin' smells drifted out through the window. Grandma's mouth watered. She could hardly wait to bite into her mama's fried chicken and crusty biscuits.

"Dinner, Chillern," Mama's voice rang out.

At the table, someone important was missing. "Where's Papa?" That's when the door opened and in walked Hezekiah Holmes. Seated at the table, he spied a "new" face. He said, "Freddie, introduce your friend."

Grandma laughed. "Papa! It's me! Nettie!" She ran over and clasped her dad in a heartfelt hug. Behind her the kitchen door opened. "Let me help you, Mama." Nettie reached for that yummy platter of chicken. "Oh, Mama! Hal's grown so much; and the twins. They're adorable."

Her dad asked, "Nettie! Where's Hamp?"

Freddie said, "Hamp dashed over to see his family. He'll be back shortly."

Chapter 3

The House that Hamp Built

In 1889, five years before Grandpa Hamp married Grandma, Great-Grandpa William Hampton Hamilton died. He left to his young son a hundred acres of land, the same as he left to each of Grandpa's three sisters and four brothers.

Wonder why that would never happen in Grandma Nettie's Holmes family? Great-Grandpa Hezekiah told everybody only sons inherited land, that girls married their livelihoods. Hmm.

Returning from Georgia, the second oldest of his siblings, Grandpa Hamp gradually broke into the business of raising sheep, hogs, and cows. As the years passed, he took on the growing of cotton, corn, then wheat, peanuts, and sugar cane, plus other crops of that era, even tobacco, on his hundred acre farm.

Early on Grandpa set about building their (our) low-country, cypress house, resplendent, Grandma thought, with three fireplaces, two porches, three bedrooms, and windows with real shutters the family could open and close. Later Grandpa would install windows with panes he bought at Adrian. Meticulously carving cypress plank strips into graceful swirls, Grandpa decorated Grandma's upper porch facade, stretched across the entire front of the house. Six columns supported this porch. For these, hip-high upward, he whittled square pillars into rounded shapes. Below hip-high, he sanded pillars into squares.

With the help of his brothers, Boss, Will, Jim, and Ott, Grandpa dug clay from his Bay Swamp back field, blended the clay with water, and molded the mixture into bricks. These he sun-dried before fashioning into fireplaces and chimneys. Foundations he sanded from sturdy tree boles.

In addition to Grandma's required exterior wood shutters, Grandpa constructed his home's interior and exterior doors. With little money for furniture, he built Grandma a dining table and benches, complete with end chairs. In 1896, Aunt Sally, Grandma's baby girl, was born in that house, followed during the next fifteen years by Aunt Molly, Aunt Laura, Daddy, and Uncle Charles. They all spent their early years enjoying the fruits of Grandpa Hamp's carpentry.

At my birth in 'thirty-three, our family still used Grandpa's dining table, a little taller than average. I clearly remember walking beneath the table. It never touched my head. 'Course I was a short little thing.

Our Home (Grandma's, Daddy's, Mother's, Jack's, and Mine)

Low country house builders gave their constructions long legs. In daylight my brother, Jack, and I lived beneath Grandpa's, *our* house, as much as inside it. Jack pushed his brick semblance of a car, creating trails leading everywhere. I investigated doodle bug hills, and erected frog houses. (I'd pack damp dirt over my foot, then remove my foot to leave a cavern.)

Growing up, I was aware, and certainly Mother was, that our family lived with Grandma, not vice-versa. Of course never did my sainted grandmother stress this. Mother simply yearned for a home where she could choose spots to plant her own trees and flowers, and she liked annuals. Shade trees protected so much of Grandma's yard, few sun-loving plants would thrive there.

In the mid-thirties Horry County shifted the passing road several feet away. This freed a garden-size square of soil embracing full sun. Daddy tilled the plot, and at last, Mother planted her own flowers: zinnias, daisies, petunias, violets, pansies, lilies, and marigolds. As a focal point, she played up a hill of giant Bear Grass. In its center grew large, waxy-white, saucer-shaped flowers. Out from this ornament Daddy placed arbors where Mother's pride, masses of red, yellow, and white climbing roses, hugged naturally growing thin pines, as well as rope-strung arbors.

My Turn

July 8, 1933, eighteen months after Mother and Daddy married, I squalled my way into the parlor of Grandpa Hamp's hand-built cypress house. Present that Saturday were Papa and Mama Todd, Grandma Nettie, Daddy, and of course, Grandma's brother, Uncle Hal, the doctor delivering me. With little folderol, he presented the seven pound blanket-full to Daddy, who passed me to Grandma, around whom all congregated. All, that is, except my tired, but happy mother, and probably Uncle Hal.

I can imagine their comments. Mama Todd: "Ooh! She's a sweet little thing! Look at all that black hair!" It turned blonde, later. Mama's idea of mortal beauty was black hair overshadowing blue eyes, probably a throwback to her Irish heritage.

No doubt Daddy's mind jumped into high gear, composing suitable lyrics and tune to *my* song. Early-on, he serenaded me quite often with this ditty:

> *My youngyunt girrers, des the same,*
> *My youngyunt girrers, des the same oh des the same,*
> *My youngyunt girrers, des the same oh des the same.*

Later, when Baby Jack Edsel popped in, his song was:

> *My little man as sho as you're born, this evenin' this mornin',*
> *My little man as sho as you're born, this evenin' this mornin'.*
> *My little man as sho as you're born,*
> *You've got a pretty little white dress on,*
> *This evenin', this mornin', right now.*

While Daddy was good at singing his feelings, I see Papa Todd smiling, as though he and I shared a secret. Many times we did.

And Grandma Nettie. I can't imagine the workings of her mind, for I was her eighth grand-baby. However, Grandma liked everyone. She definitely loved me, or, to escape my many "who's, where's, when's, why's, and how's," she would have flown our coop to live with Aunt Sally, or Aunt Molly, or Aunt Laura. And I would have died without her. Living with Grandma, whether at home during The Great Depression, while Allies battled Nazis before or after our country joined the fray, or now, at Homewood, our haven for a while, I preferred her stories to anything on the radio, or at the movies.

Don't get me wrong. I liked movies and radio plays, all except *Inner Sanctum*. That was scary. At least one I heard I've never forgotten. While I tried to stop up my ears, Mother and Daddy stayed glued to the set. An eerie being floated outside a relative's door, moaning, "Let me i-i-i-n. I'm out here on the law-aw-aw-awn-n-n."

Signs of the Times

My birth year, 1933, comprised an era of events. Of less direct consequence to me than my birth, Adolph Hitler became chancellor of Germany. In East Chester, New York, police made use of their first radio system. Germany began mandatory sterilization of those with hereditary illnesses. Wiley Post flew the first ever, solo flight around the world. Work began on California's Oakland Bay Bridge. In Germany two-hundred Jewish merchants were arrested in Nuremberg and paraded through the streets. U.S. congress passed our first minimum wage law: thirty-three cents per hour. (Hmm. Thirty-three. The same number as the year of my birth.) In Bug Swamp, Horry County, South Carolina, Mother dressed her baby girl in a batiste dress she hand-embroidered and paraded me up the aisle between Good Hope Baptist Church's polished mahogany pews, sharing me with her world.

Not totally oblivious of events transpiring around and about, like most friends and neighbors in their tobacco farming community, my parents concentrated on people, places, and things they could see, hear, and touch. Hard work and constant church-going occupied their time, and while The Great Depression flattened everyone's pocketbook, pigs in a pen, chickens in and out of their coop, and seasonally growing vegetables lessened our grocery costs. Grandpa Hamp's legacy, our house and farm, made credit possible due to a mortgage Mother tortured herself over. Still, until World War II erupted, God, our church, and Mr. Burroughs's credit provided almost everything for which our family felt any great need.

Daddy would have added, "Except for your mama's peace of mind."

Chapter 4

A Christmas Airplane

Fall of 1946, happily content in our Homewood house, already I appreciated memories. I felt glad to be thirteen, and that our country's nemesis, The Great Depression, had virtually passed; plus, World War II had ceased its torment. Our minds relived enough of war's destruction, we felt truly blessed by its absence.

Not so the first holiday following our joining the war. December, 1941, while in Europe sirens blared away and bombs shattered cities, our family celebrated a Christmas I'll remember as long as I live. Why? That's when a part of me grew up a mite faster than I deemed necessary.

After December 7, 1941, World War II struggled its darnedest to preempt Christmas. Sadness floated like a blackout curtain amidst our celebration of the Christ Child's birth. However, the nearer Christmas Day, the merrier grew our rejoicing. Santa Claus *would* come on the eve of Jesus' birthday, and while I'd heard of bad children who received a lump of coal or a switch for Christmas, I knew no one that sinful. Certainly I wasn't.

For a while we thought we'd miss seeing Daddy's baby brother, Uncle Charles, and his wife, Aunt Rock this holiday. Visiting us Thanksgiving, they'd said Aunt Rock's brother, B. P., and his wife, Naomi, planned to spend Christmas with their family in Waresboro.

That brought us sadness. Uncle Charles and Aunt Rock's visits were our best presents. Drawn almost double by fiendish rheumatoid arthritis, Uncle Charles' sense of humor belied his condition. He drove a car, taught agriculture, ran a cannery in summer, and exuded a wealth of good will. His Bug Swamp friends always gathered around our home during "Charlie" visits.

At the last minute our Georgia relatives said they were coming. Somebody in B. P.'s family was sick, and they were staying home. Poor B. P. Lucky us.

The day they arrived Grandma awoke early. Blue eyes a'sparkle behind rimless glasses, she turned to me. "Little Bushy, Waresboro's about three hundred miles away. If they started out before daybreak, they can be here by noon!" Most roads were more easily traveled than our Bug Swamp thoroughfares.

On December twenty-third, our guests drove into the yard, parking beneath the cedar tree. Before they could open car doors, we rushed outside.

My brother, Jack, could hardly wait for this, his fourth Christmas morning. I don't remember what I wanted, or even what I received from Santa. Jack wanted an airplane. These days every time a plane flew overhead, we ran outside and scanned the sky. To think that a man sat in a cockpit, steering a machine light enough to fly through air mystified my young brother. He could visualize himself, years in the future, flying just such a plane.

After visiting with Uncle Charles and Aunt Rock during a supper of backbone and rice like only Grandma could cook, Mother sucked in her breath. "Folks, you know what tomorrow is? Christmas Eve, and no way have I finished shopping." She eyed Daddy. "Sure hope Santa's still hanging around Conway."

The next morning Cousins Rob and Brooke came over to visit Cousin Charlie. Later the family loaded into two cars, and we motored the few miles to Maple Swamp to visit Aunt Sally and Uncle Homer. (Aunt Sally was the baby curled up inside Grandma in the mid-nineties, when she and Grandpa Hamp returned to Bug Swamp from Georgia.)

Aunt Sally's house looked much nicer than ours. It wore a coat of white paint. She greeted us at her front door. Entering, I gasped. Their tree was beyond beautiful! Leona, Geneva, and Frances Marion, all must have out-done themselves helping Aunt Sally decorate. If already I hadn't known Christmas was upon us, I knew it now.

Whoa! I smelled bacon. That meant I'd get to eat my aunt's yummy grits. Nobody ever, before or since, has cooked grits tasting as velvety, as mouth-watering as Aunt Sally's. Her secret? After I grew up she told me. She boiled those grits in artesian water.

Grandma chose to visit with Aunt Sally and Frances Marion while the rest of us went Christmas shopping. I wanted to stay, but I couldn't resist shopping.

Wonder what book Frances bought me this year. That's what we gave each other every Christmas. Before I wrapped hers, I read it. We bought each other books we wanted to read.

In Conway, Jack and I wandered through red and green tinseled stores with Daddy while Mother bought presents. Later we four met at Horry Drug Company where a wonderful lady with a sweet smile, Mrs. Walsh, set chocolate-nut-pineapple sundaes in front of Daddy and me. She dished up strawberry ice cream for Mother and Jack. After reaching our sweetness saturation points, Jack and I accompanied Mother while Daddy shopped. Finally, Daddy met us in front of Burroughs's. "Home! Home!" he said. "I'm worn to a frazzle!"

Amidst interesting paper bags we wedged ourselves into the car; however, I worried not a whit about their contents. Mother bought gifts for the *rest* of the family. *Santa* had *mine and Jack's* presents at the North Pole, just waiting for dusk. That's when he'd gear up his reindeer.

About a mile out of town, Jack popped up with, "Mama, what if Santa doesn't know I want a 'airpane'?" Jack couldn't pronounce certain sounds.

"You wrote him a letter, didn't you?" Mother said.

"Yes, but . . ."

Mother stiffened. "Rass?" Her eyes completed her question.

Daddy raised his eyebrows, widened his eyes. He shook his head. Slowly.

"Oh, my!" Mother's voice quavered and she looked toward heaven.

At Homewood Daddy turned in at Cherry's store. He left us in the car while he went inside, but soon returned, shaking his head.

Mother repeated, "Oh my!"

Daddy whirled the car out onto the highway, back towards town.

I asked, "Where are we going?"

"Umm," Daddy grunted.

I wondered, *what is going on?*

By this time daylight was a memory. Mother's hand crept to her throat.

We drove around the block, parked, and Daddy ran to Mack's Five and Dime. He rattled the door. No one came. He tried the other toy store on the block. We knew Burroughs's was closed because earlier they'd locked the door behind us.

Jack said, "I want to go home."

Daddy sounded tired. "Me too, little man." He drove slowly homeward.

Within a mile we met Uncle Charles and Aunt Rock. Daddy pulled over to the roadside. He and Mother stepped over to the other car, and the grownups exchanged quiet words. Afterwards, we continued home and Uncle Charles drove on toward Conway.

Mother cleared her throat. Jack was about to fall asleep. "Jackie Boy," she said, "what would you do if Santa didn't bring that plane?"

"He will, Mama," Jack yawned widely, "he'll 'bwing' my 'airpane.' I know he will."

Picking up Grandma at Aunt Sally's and arriving home a little late for Christmas Eve, we "set our hats" in individual chairs. In our family that's what we did instead of hang stockings. I chose an arm chair, carefully placing in it the straw bonnet I'd worn all summer. That hat would hold a lot. Into my chair's twin, Jack "set" his wide-brimmed straw hat, the hat Mother said if he kept jammin' it atop his head, my brother's ears would turn into cup-handles. Mother, Daddy, and Grandma, picking chairs, also left hats for Santa to fill. I went to bed with Grandma. Mother tucked Jack into his bed beside hers and Daddy's.

Shortly, Uncle Charles and Aunt Rock bustled in, rustling paper and depositing packages. Aunt Rock spoke in a whisper, loud enough I heard over Grandma's snuffles. "We've got it, Dot!"

"How?" Mother asked.

Uncle Charles said, "All the stores looked closed, but I went around to the back of Edwards'. A woman answered my knock, and I told her my sad tale about a little boy whose heart was set on an 'airpane.' Here's their last one!"

Certainty bombs went off in my head. So. That's why Daddy broke speed limits back to town.

Next morning, anxious to see what Santa brought, Jack's feet flew across the floor. He drew in a happy breath. "Look, Mama! He did 'bwing' it! Santa 'bwought' me my 'airpane'!"

"God bless him," Aunt Rock's warm voice shook.

Little did they guess, as I pored through fruit, nuts, and candy to whatever "Santa" was *supposed* to have left me, what that search for a Christmas "airpane" brought me; a truth I wasn't happy to possess. However, before the next year ended, I got over my disappointment. After all, a girl has to grow up sometime.

Mary Jane

To me, Uncle Charles and Aunt Rock personified Christmas. They were as much a part of that holiday as Christmas trees, gifts, and decorations. More so. However, the second year of World War II, Christmas of 'forty-three, my treasured Uncle and Aunt parked beneath our cedar tree with cargo more precious than trees, decorations, even gifts. They brought with them their six month old treasure: bright eyed, sweet faced Mary Jane, Grandma Nettie's eleventh grandchild.

Grandma's arthritis may have been troubling her; but, she grabbed that baby girl as soon as her son opened their car door. Making it to the porch, we had barely said, "Hey," and kissed a soft cheek, before Grandma's granddaughter number one, Leona, drove into the yard.

Leona bounced out of her car. "Hey you all," she raced up front porch steps and hugged our guests. She squatted down to Mary Jane's eye-level. "You're so beautiful." Breathing in a deep sigh, she looked toward heaven. "Someday I want a girl just like you."

Grandma frowned. "There you go, 'Leoma,' puttin' the cart before the horse."

As soon as all that greeting folderol took care of itself, Grandma said, "Everybody, come on in. Let's us set a spell and palaver."

Grandma carried the baby to her peach colored chair. She held Mary Jane up to the light.

"Palmer, Rock, this is the prettiest child! I'm so proud I've got me one more grandbaby." She looked at me. "How many does this make, Little Bushy?"

"Mary Jane's your eleventh grandchild, Grandma, your eighth granddaughter. You and I figured that out last week."

"So we did." Grandma passed Mary Jane to Leona. "You know, Leoma," she said, "this baby's special." Grandma routinely addressed Leona as *Leoma*. "Mary Jane came to us on the twenty-third anniversary of Hampie's passing. She was born and Hampie died on the longest day of the year." Grandma's face wore the sad look it mirrored each time she dwelt on this subject. Grandma let few days pass without paying homage to June twenty-first.

Mary Jane reached for Leona's nose.

Daddy said, "Did you have a good trip, Charlie?"

"Pretty good. The best part was gettin' here, wouldn't you say so, Rock?"

Aunt Rock said, "Without a doubt."

Grandma sighed. "Have any of you really thought on this? Last June twenty-first, twenty-three years ago, Hampie and I were workin' in the field. He couldn't wait for six o'clock. That's when Sally and Homer were to bring you to see us, Leoma."

"And they did. They did bring you. Trouble was, Hampie was nowhere around. He was already gone to where good Christian men go when they die." She looked at her family, suddenly aware she'd thrown a damper into the conversation. "Do shut my mouth. Everybody! Who's ready for Christmas?"

"Not me," said Mother, taking Mary Jane.

Usually, as soon as Leona entered our door she told us a joke. By now she'd gone too long, jokeless. She stood up, rubbed her hands together, and just like Grandma, turned down the corners of her mouth. "Well," she smacked her lips, "there were these two girls. I'll call 'em Geneva and Frances Marion. (Leona's younger sisters) One day Genny and her boyfriend had some kind of disagreement. She'd had as much as she could take. Lying on Mama's new rug, she rested bare feet on Mama's even newer couch." Leona turned to Grandma. "Geneva looked plumb pitiful. Then mad. First she kicked that couch. Then she drug feet bottoms against that sofa's print. Like they itched. She said, 'Right now I feel like nobody loves me. Everybody hates me.'

"Frankie and I were playing a new game. Frankie jumped my man. Pleased with herself, she snickered. She said, 'You're wrong, Genny. Not everybody *knows* you.'"

Everyone laughed but Grandma. She said, "Geneva wiped her feet on Sally's brand new couch?"

Leona cleared her throat and rubbed her hands together. "How about this one?"

Again she eyed Grandma. "There were these two old women sittin' on the porch, their spit cans at their feet. One said, 'I do wish my old man would quit bitin' his fingernails. I'm afraid he'll bite 'em to the quick.'

"'My old man used to do the very same,' the neighbor woman said. 'He don't now.'

"'Why not?' asked the first old lady.

"Her neighbor giggled. 'I hid his teeth.'"

Everybody laughed. "Ha, ha, ha!" Even I thought that joke funny. I thought Mother might split her sides. Grandma just shook her head. She said, "Poor man. He'd have a hard time chomping down on an ear of corn without them teeth. He'd have to eat gruel. I feel sorry for him."

"Grandma," Leona tsk-tsk-tsked. "Here's one more joke. Maybe you'll like this one:

"There was this Sunday School teacher. After the class's closing prayer, she said, 'Don't go yet. I'm giving you an assignment for next week. Go home. Read the seventeenth chapter of Mark. Next Sunday morning be prepared to discuss what Mark says about liars.'

"A week later, after students sat down and answered roll call with a Bible verse, the teacher said, 'Everyone who read your assignment, raise your hand.'

"About half the class raised their hands. The teacher smiled. She said, 'You with your hands down, go outside. Play any game you want till the church bell rings. The rest of you, stay put. You're the ones to pay heed to this lesson. There is no seventeenth chapter of Mark.'"

Grandma clapped her hands. "That was one good joke. I knew there was no seventeenth chapter in Mark. I learned to read from them New Testament books." She looked around at each of us. "Don't that Leoma beat all? I do love her jokes."

Leona walked over to Grandma. She kissed her cheek. "Thanks, Grandma. I've got to go now. I didn't even tell Mama I was coming."

"Come again soon and bring everybody else," Grandma said.

"Yeah," said Uncle Charles. I'm going nowhere tomorrow. I'm gonna rest up from my trip."

That Christmas was our last Mother celebrated with her brother, Mace, before Papa and Mama Todd's youngest took off for Fort McClellan, Alabama. There our armed forces would ready him for battling soldiers he knew little about.

Thank goodness Daddy didn't leave us. Like Uncle Charles with his rheumatoid arthritis, and our next-door cousin, Leo, suffering deafness, doctors declared Daddy's status, Four-F. His appendix, rupturing at eight, resulted in life-long hernias. Besides, Daddy was too old for armed services. Grandma Nettie said so.

During Mace's August, pre-shipping-out furlough, Louise gave birth to their son, Roger Dale, and not until the war ended, did Mother's brother see his boy again. Like I told Grandma. War was for the birds! (An expression I used about anything I hated.)

Overseas and at Home

Just when Uncle Mace left for overseas, turmoil in Europe was coming to a head. Earlier, newscasters told us about scads of our troops landing at Normandy. Mace came in on a later boat, joining General Patton's third army. That winter, something called The Battle of the Bulge took off into full swing. Newsmen were always reporting how, thanks to our planes, bombs were raining down on Germany, just like, thanks to Germany's planes, bombs had been raining down on England. All the time France, Belgium, Holland, Poland, Canada, Norway, Australia, New Zealand, Yugoslavia, Greece, even Russia, our allies, were helping us do all we could to wipe out our enemies. What a mess a few mad men could make of this world.

1944's Christmas was the last Uncle Charles' family shared with us for two years. Christmas of 1945, stuffed to the gills with her second baby girl, Aunt Rock gave birth shortly after that holiday.

Actually, our Georgia family visited us the following July. On this trip Mary Jane shared our adoration with a beautiful, dark haired, baby girl, not quite as old as Mary Jane the first time we saw her. Grandma's newest grandchild, Sarah Anne, was named after her mother. Aunt Rock's real name was Sarah.

Grandma so monopolized this baby, even I had a hard time touching my new cousin. "Wash your hands, Little Bushy," she'd say. "You'll give this baby germs. We don't want her comin' to Grandma's house and leavin' with a sickness. Nor Mary Jane. Then, Palmer would be takin' home not one, but two sick babies."

Grandma was our only family member who called Uncle Charles by his second name, Palmer.

Fourth of July weekend found our family at Myrtle Beach. Aunt Sally, Uncle Homer, Frances Marion, Mother, Grandma, Daddy, Jack, and I, Uncle Charles and his family drove three cars, seventeen miles from Bug Swamp, to reach the beach. We dropped Grandma off at Hotel Kelly, Adrian's Mr. Kelly Thompkin's Myrtle Beach establishment.

That day Grandma sat on their hotel porch with Mr. Kelly's wife, Miz Lizzie, while everybody that wanted to, went swimming. Jack already wore shorts, Mother said could double as a swim suit. She brought him other clothes for afterwards. I wore last years' faded, stretch suit. Ugly, but I didn't care. Mother didn't own a bathing suit; so, she rented one. Nobody else but Frances Marion wanted to swim.

Aunt Sally, holding, or carrying Mary Jane, and Aunt Rock holding Sarah Anne, along with our three men, chose to walk up and down the strand. 'Course, if Daddy, or Uncle Homer, or Uncle Charles had cared to take a plunge into the briny, they could have come in overalls. I saw some men jumping waves in just such.

I followed Mother into the bath house. Like Mother, entering and leaving the dressing room, I stepped into a container full of some watery germ killer.

Frances Marion wore a yellow swim suit under shorts and blouse. She, Jack, and I raced out to the strand. We chased each other. "Wait, Frances," I yelled, when she went out farther than I felt safe. Mother yelled, "Jack!" every time he took a step. Me, I loved standing in close to water's edge, with foamy waves rolling in, then out, washing away sand from all around my feet. That left me standing on my own little island. In the distance I saw big fish jumping. Daddy said these were dolphins. He said dolphins were smart and liked people. I wished they'd swim in closer. Jack wanted to swim to them. Mother made sure he didn't.

Aunt Sally's baby girl was at least two years older than I, maybe three. Still, we were friends. She and I played Old Maids. Grandma didn't allow cards in our house, but she said nary a word about Frances Marion's cards. Trouble was, Frankie always beat me at whatever we played. When I spent nights at Aunt Sally's, my cousin and I slept in Geneva's old room, next to her parents' bedroom. After Uncle Homer ordered, "Girls, lights out," we'd whisper. Just about every night I spent there, Frances would say, "Billie Faye, who's your boyfriend?"

I'd say, "I don't have one. Do you?" She wouldn't say, but she talked a lot about some boy with the initials, H.B.B. I remember, but I won't say his name.

At the beach we picked up a star fish or two, some clam shells, and Jack found a couple of conchs, one with a live something or other inside. The other was empty; so we took turns holding that one to our ears, listening to the ocean's roar. Of course we heard the ocean better without the conch shell. Jack nearly tripped over some kind of fish washed ashore. That thing had long teeth. Meanwhile, Frances Marion found a hard, black doo-dad, Daddy said was probably whale waste.

Uncle Charles said, "Rass, that's debatable." Daddy said, "Debating's your territory, Charlie."

After swimming and jumping on-coming waves, Mother, Frances, and I got dressed in the bath house before Mother returned her suit. She whisked Jack into and out of that woman's bath house, under Jack's protest. He had to be quiet. People would look. Then, we picked up Grandma from Hotel Kelly, and packed into cars, motored over the new Inland Waterway to see Aunt Laura and Uncle Murph.

Grandma told me stories about all of her children, Aunt Laura's the saddest. Grandma's youngest daughter gave birth to two boys, but neither lived. Present at both births, Grandma told me, "It's my opinion, if Laura had had better doctorin', her babies might be with her today."

We drove into Aunt Laura's yard, and she ran to our car. Eyes teary, she hugged everybody within reach. She said, "You don't know how glad I am to see all of you. Come into this house!"

Actually, back then we saw less of Aunt Laura than of Aunt Molly's or Aunt Sally's families. Uncle Murph didn't have a car, and they lived farther away than the others. However, a year or two later Grandma's youngest daughter and her mate moved to Howell Siding, a couple of miles from our Bug Swamp door. Then, we visited them often.

Shepherding us into her dining room, Aunt Laura said, "Anybody who wants to, wash up. We should eat before dark. That's when fireworks start."

After all that playing in the ocean, I was starved. Most of the adults ate at the table, but Mother took her food onto the front porch with Frances Marion, Jack, and me. From here we had a perfect view of the new canal, stretched out about forty feet beyond us. This canal was wide enough to float huge boats, and it still wore edges of sandy clay from recent excavations. Mother said this *Inland Waterway* was supposed to reach all the way to Florida. Three boats passed while we ate Aunt Laura's fried fish, hush puppies, and cole slaw. Delicious.

Soon came loud popping. Mother called out, "Everybody, fireworks started."

They had to be deaf if they hadn't heard. I couldn't bear all those loud booms, like huge guns going off, but I liked the pretty colors spangling the sky. They looked like stars exploding. What to do: Fingers jammed into both ears, feet dangling, I sat on the porch's edge, eyes glued to the sky.

None too soon, Aunt Laura brought out a big, round, chocolate cake. Before she could cut it, Sara Anne started crying. She wouldn't stop. Grandma said, "We need to go. We'll stop by Hotel Grace and see if Hal's home. He'll know if this baby's sick."

Aunt Laura sighed. "You can't leave me with all this cake." She wrapped over two-thirds of it in wax paper. Slipping the sweet stash into a paper bag, she placed the bag into Uncle Charles hands, then kissed his cheek. "Little brother, I'm sorry you have to run off like this. I know you can't help it. Just don't you come home another Christmas without seeing me." Aunt Laura looked closer to tears than before.

I hugged her. "I'll come see you, Aunt Laura." We left. Frances Marion and her mom and dad stayed a while longer.

Thank goodness Uncle Charles baby girl wasn't sick. By the time Sarah Anne reached home, she was snoozing away.

Next morning I woke up after the chickens. What was all that noise? Laughing. Splashing. Still wearing my nightie I ran onto our back porch. In the middle of our sandy yard, plopped into a washtub full of water, neither Jack nor Mary Jane wore anything but underwear. They slapped the water, spattering each other and anybody within reach. On the porch steps with Mother and Grandma, Aunt Rock was spooning apple sauce into Sarah Anne's hungry little bird-mouth. I thought to myself, *Jack should be ashamed, in a washtub full of water, bathing with a little three year-old girl.* Really, I felt jealous. Growing up sometimes got in the way of fun.

Soon Uncle Charles and his girls left for home. I told Mother, "I enjoyed their visit, but I'm about ready to stay put for a while."

Grandma said, "You're ready! Girl, at your age, you don't know what ready is!"

That fall I entered eighth grade high school. My thought: *if the Good Lord will just help me through this grade, from then on it'll be clear sailing.* So much for thoughts!

Chapter 5

Home at Homewood

Back in 'forty-one, I learned the brutal truth about Santa Claus. Five years later, now a grown up thirteen year-old ninth grader, living at Homewood, had I ever been so young that adult knowledge saddened me? Right now Jack was nine, a year older than I when "Santa" brought him his "airpane." I bet he'd wised up by eight. Maybe not. Shortly, events as ethereal as Santa Claus would baffle me as greatly as I had felt disappointment on my eighth Christmas morning.

About two months after we moved into our new house, I lay snug in Grandma's feather bed. Beside her, I slept so soundly I didn't even hear her snuffles. As if from some far away region I became aware of Mother's voice. She sounded strained. "Billie Faye!" she called from upstairs. "Are you deaf? Answer me! Is that you, walking up and down these stairs?"

I mumbled, "No Ma'am, I'm asleep."

Lights popped on upstairs. They stayed on for the night's remainder.

Frying bacon the next morning, Mother talked to herself. "Never in my life! Somebody walked those steps up and down. Kept me awake all night long!"

"Who, Mother?" I asked. "I didn't get out of bed. And Grandma didn't leave the room."

Daddy called down, "That bacon smells good, Dot. Tell Ma about your visitor."

"Not my visitor. 'Tip-tip-tip,' all night long!"

"What kind of varmints do we have traipsing up and down them stairs?" Grandma mused.

"I'm wondering," Mother said.

Now, if that had been that, our family probably would have forgotten all about our "dead" in the night visitor. However, "she" returned, night after night. I say "she" because Grandma told Mrs. Miller about the visitation, and Mrs. Miller told her of a Mrs. Cox whose husband murdered her on our stairs.

Why were we hearing this now, and not before we moved?!

Mrs. Miller said that's how, five years ago, our landlady, Aunt Dalma, bought the house for so little money. Wonder if Great Auntie knew she'd thrown in an added attraction for our rental fee?

After we learned of the murder, according to my parents those "tip-tip-tips" failed to stop at the top of the stairs. They continued on into Mother's and Daddy's room, halting only at the foot of their bed, and then, not until Daddy demanded, "Whoa!"

Saturday, Grandma and Mother were sorting through a dish pan of collard greens. They called this "lookin' the collards." I sat opposite them reading "As You Like It" for Miss Epp's drama class. December eleventh, this next Wednesday evening I was to play a court lady in the school production.

Eyeing a ruffled green leaf, Grandma's lips turned down and she shook her head. "Why, Dottie?" she said to Mother. "Why would a man kill his own wife?"

"He was drunk," Mother said. "Alcohol can make you do things unthinkable. Lucy said her screams woke the neighbors."

I dropped Shakespeare. "I don't want to live here. Anymore. Not in a house where somebody was killed on our stairs."

"Well, we can't just pull up stakes and leave. The Lanes are in our house. Where would we go?"

Sunday morning Mother dragged herself into the kitchen. "That poor old haint'll be the death of me yet. All night long, the higher she climbed the steps, the noisier she got. This time she groaned, loud enough to wake a sleeping bear." Mother looked at Grandma and frowned. "You didn't hear a thing."

"Nary a thing," said Grandma. "I don't think she's around; but, say she is, and I don't," Grandma eyed me, "this won't hurt."

My sleeping buddy trudged to the foot of the stairs, Mother and I following. "Hon," she addressed the vacant stairs, "don't you know there's a better place for you than here? The Good Lord's a'waitin' at the top of a far nicer stairway. Why don't you turn loose this place? Nothing's here for you anymore. We live here now."

I wish I could say that was the end of our problem, but I can't. Footsteps, or some "tip-tip-tip" noise persisted throughout the nigh-onto-two years our family lived in Aunt Dalma's house. On nights Mother sprinkled powder on the steps, or spread out crackly paper, our visitor stayed away. Let one night pass when Mother neglected her skullduggery, and poor invisible whoever, Grandma said "Probably mice!" was at it again.

Never did I witness any middle of the night spectral visits. I slept too soundly. Maybe that was why I worried so little about a poor old haint supposedly hanging around earth. I asked Grandma if she was scared of our visitor. She said, "Little Bushy, I can't get too worked up over something I can't see, nor have I heard her, or it, whatever. I just know we're all in the hands of the Good Lord, our Father Almighty, and as long as He's in charge, I won't worry a whit. I'm just sorry anybody ever had to die like poor Mrs. Cox."

While I never heard those "tip-tip-tips" up our stairs, once, on a Saturday morning my brother and I heard heavy breathing neither of us could account for. We checked under the house; upstairs where Daddy slept. Then, one evening while Mother, Grandma, and I sat around the dining room table talking about death, and where, how, or if ghosts fit into God's plan, the outside door to the living room opened; then closed. The three of us looked up, expecting someone to enter. No one did. Later Daddy said, "It was the wind, you sillies!"

Dramatic Moments

I had loved Good Hope Elementary School's stage. It boasted a substantial roll-up curtain. On it someone had painted sand, surf, sea, sky, and horizon, so real I felt I was at the beach. Almost. Similarly Conway's community auditorium, shared by Conway High and Elementary School, dazzled me with its deep stage, its professional apron, foot and spot lights, as well as a rope-pulled, heavy, wine velvet curtain. I couldn't wait to stand on that stage with lights blinding my eyes, spouting somebody else's words. Or singing songs. Doing anything.

Conway enjoyed its Artists Series. Professionals from New York and elsewhere performed on this stage. Recently my parents brought me here to watch the solo performance of a beautiful actress. She emoted the part of Theodosia Burr Alston, daughter of Vice President of the United States, Aaron Burr, and wife of South Carolina farmer-politician, Joseph Alston. This young woman lived with her husband on a plantation overlooking the Waccamaw River. The apple of her father's eye, Theodosia found her loyalty divided between her able husband and a father whose reputation had become tarnished. In a duel, Burr killed his political adversary, Alexander Hamilton. Wow! He had my last name!

Theodosia's dad had just returned from France to New Jersey. She must go to his side; but her husband said, "Don't leave me, Theo. It's been no time since we buried our baby."

Joseph spoke the truth. Still, knowing her dad and his needs, no way could Theodosia Burr Alston deny them. During the night she turned a sorrowful face to the home she shared with her husband, climbed into a rowboat, (nothing larger would fit on-stage) and was never seen nor heard from again.

How dramatic. I thought I'd die!

The playbill added a bit about Theodosia, sailing from Georgetown on a ship called The Patriot, a vessel heading for Yankee land and lost on open sea. (My present day research indicated Mrs. Alston could have been captured by pirates.)

For me this play held significance. Where the Alston's dwelling stood in Theodocia's day, in our day my family held picnics. Lucky for us, a Yankee business man bought the Alston estate for his sculptress wife, Anna Huntington. Together they created Brookgreen Gardens, a magical place abounding with birds, deer, alligators, and other coastal wildlife, as well as local tourists like our family. Besides live animals, Anna peopled gardens with her masterpieces as well as with those of other famous sculptors. Paths wound around hedges and shrubs, their intricate labyrinths leading to bluish reflecting pools. Centered in at least one of those pools and spouting water was a little bronze boy doing exactly what Mother told Brother Jack he must never do in public.

I needed go no further for entrancement than the garden's entrance. On either side of a gateway, massive sculpted stallions, rearing up on hind legs, pawed the air.

Captivated by the professional actress's portrayal of Theodosia Burr, what a thrill! On this Wednesday evening I'd become a Shakespearean court lady and perform on this self-same stage.

Watch Yourself, Jack!

Actually all my life Mother had me "saying speeches" for people. About six or seven, I'd don a "Grandma dress," powder my hair white, poke my tongue into my lower lip, and faking a dip of snuff, act out the *Betsy Baker* skit for any company visiting. Aunt Dalma put that "bee" in Mother's bonnet.

"You know Betsy Baker? Well she's my daughter. She took it into her head to get married, and get married she did. Etc., etc."

In grammar school I performed in school plays, and all my life I sang, at home, at school, at church, wherever. My brother, Jack, and I were blessed to be born into a family of singers. Mother sang alto. Daddy, shy and retiring in most social settings, contributed a deep, velvety bass to our family quartet. I sang soprano. Jack, the darling of the family, at an early age and barely out of diapers, that boy sang harmony. Sitting in Mother's lap, Jack sang before he could talk. He hummed Mother's alto. I can imagine Jack, *before* birth, singing in Good Hope's church choir.

On Sunday mornings Grandma Nettie's brother, Uncle Bert Holmes, his shirt collar buttoned tightly around his musical throat, reached for the tuning fork, always in his shirt pocket. He pinged it against a pew. "Do-mi-sol," he sang, seeking proper pitch for the hymn or gospel song selected.

Sometimes Uncle Bert chose the songs sung. Mostly, congregation members made that decision.

"Anybody have a song you like for this morning?"

Probably Mr. Collin Hucks raised his hand, for he was desperately trying to wean Good Hope singers from their new-found gospel songs, back to traditional hymns. "Hymn book. Page one hundred ninety-nine!"

"Everybody! Pick up your Broadman Hymnals and turn to page one ninety-nine, 'How Firm a Foundation.'"

In the thirties, Good Hope Baptist Church had no nursery for babies. Mother held Jack in her arms from the first days of his birth until her toddler, curly headed and fidgety, grew large enough to sit beside her. Attached to Mother, matching counter tones came as naturally to Jack's baby self as singing melody to "Just As I Am, "Over In Glory," "The Old Time Religion," or a song I considered boring because its tune lacked sharps, flats, syncopation, not that I knew that word, or flights into alto, bass, or tenor solo passages. That song was titled "Somebody Loves Me."

Our mother would have made an ideal "stage" mom, for she organized Uncle Bert's daughter, Patricia, Jack, and me into a trio. At this time I was eight, Patricia, six, and Jack, four. Mostly we performed at Good Hope Baptist, but sometimes we sang at a convention of churches meeting every fifth Sunday at alternate Horry County houses of worship.

If our trio had a name, I don't remember it. Yet, Mother saw that we practiced. She pulled up a chair, sat down, and lined us up, keeping time with her head and mouthing each word of our song. At first all three of us sang melody. Afterwards, Mother fine-tuned us. "Patricia, you sing the lead. Jack, take the high part. Billie Faye, you alto."

Patricia sang soprano, and Jack tenored whatever harmony suited his purpose, *always* blending. My job was to sing the harmony part Jack didn't, in alto range, of course.

Since I was oldest, and tallest, I stood between Jack, to my left, and Patricia, to my right. Early on, stage fright never truly gripped either of us. We were doing what seemed natural.

Sunday morning church was the high light of our week. Men and women, boys and girls who wore "ever'-day" clothes to hoe, or poison, or harvest crops, to sweep yards, or tote slop to hungry hogs, we cleaned up shiny and proper in our Sunday best. Farmers, dressed for church at Good Hope Baptist, would have looked quite proper on Wall Street with their suits and ties. Well, maybe.

Members visited with each other between Sunday school and church. "Hey, Rob! You didn't find enough work to keep you busy this week? I got a ditch bank you can shrub!"

"Gertie, how's your eczema? Have you talked to Clyde Dorman about her itch poultice? It worked for Mama."

"Maybe we ought to pray for this rain to be over with. I'm sick and tired of standin' around, watchin' my 'baccer wilt in the field!"

Buzzing voices gradually died down. Uncle Bert drew everyone's attention with his tuning fork and by singing the first line of "What a Friend We Have in Jesus."

First song sung, lines wrinkling his tall forehead, Mr. Joe, superintendent of Sunday School, made the morning announcements:

"Uh, I just want to tell you, uh, all, uh, this morning, uh, that, uh, I, uh, am so, uh, grateful, uh, to the Good Lord, uh, for allowing me, uh, to come to his house, uh, this morning, uh, to worship. Uh . . ."

Uncle Bert popped up. "Time for one more song. Open your Stamps Baxter song book to page seventy-eight. 'Ping! Do mi sol . . .'"

> *I'm glad Jesus came, glory to his name,*
> *Oh what a friend is he.*
> *He so freely gave his own life to save*
> *From bonds of sin set free.*

Since Good Hope had no full-time pastor, Uncle Bert, song leader, also took charge of the service. "Folks, it's time for our morning prayer. Mr. Fed, will you lead us?"

"Let us pray."

All over the church came the sounds of feet shuffling, people rising from their pews and falling to their knees.

"Oh Lord, Ruler over earth and heaven, this morning we beseech You to send Your spirit down here 'mongst these, Thy poor servants here today. We kneel before You, not just on these pore old knees, but with our hearts as well. Show us mercy, Lord. We honor You, oh God, the only way we know how. Bless all our members, at home, or abroad, 'grieved or infirmed. Turn the hearts of any sinners 'mongst us to see Thy face, oh Lord, our strength and our redeemer. We pray in the name of our Blessed Savior, Jesus Christ. Amen."

"Thank you, Mr. Fed."

People rose from their knees, sat down, and leaned forward.

"Folks, today we're in for a treat. Our youngest trio has a message for you, in song."

Throughout the service Mother made sure her charges sat prim and proper in the front pew. Now she urged us forward. A refectory table sat before the minister's lectern. Our trio lined up before the table.

In that era, since our church lacked musical instruments other than voices, I hummed the pitch. Softly, of course. "Umm,"

> *Somebody loves me, answers my prayer.*
> *I love somebody, I know he cares.*
> *Somebody tells me not to repine.*
> *That somebody is Jesus, I know he's mine.*

Into the second verse, I became aware that Jack failed to face the congregation, and Mother stressed, "Face the front!"

Jack faced me. That's when he spied the table behind us. Lowering one shoulder, he stuck it beneath the table top and lifted the table an inch or two, all the time singing his high, sweet harmony. *"I love somebody, I know he cares . . ."*

I grabbed Jack's arm to stop his weight lifting before a Bible, offering plates, and other religious paraphernalia slid off the table.

Jack jerked away from my grasp. *"Somebody tells me not to repine. . ."*

Mad at his sister, Jack sank his teeth into my upper arm, and still singing around a mouthful of flesh, bit hard. *"That somebody is Jesus. I know He's mine."*

I checked out Patricia to see if she had noticed. She looked worried. I hurt and my face flamed. Jack was hopping mad, or maybe he was just hopping. However, we sang that last verse all the way through without missing a word, a beat, or a note. However, some of Jack's singing sounded definitely muffled.

Afterwards, Uncle Bert shook his head. "Let me see that arm." He checked out Jack's teeth marks.

I don't remember Mother's reaction. It couldn't have been good.

Court Ladies

With everything leading up to our move, and then, actually moving into our new home, Jack, Patricia, and I hadn't sung together lately. That was okay. Miss Epps, our drama teacher, had assigned me a part in Shakespeare's "As You Like It." I was to act the part of a court lady this next Wednesday evening.

Grandma heard which night Miss Epps had scheduled our performance. She grumbled, "Little Bushy, Wednesday's prayer meetin' night." I didn't remind her that we'd skipped prayer meetings our whole three months at Homewood.

We court ladies numbered five. "Look at you all," I said, performance night.

"Have you looked in a mirror?" My cousin, Frances Marion, snickered.

Grease paint plastered our faces, mascara and liner fringed and ringed our eyes, while lipstick coated our lips in paint as red and glossy as rubies. Miss Epps had arranged our hair in artful styles, she said, "befitting" Elizabethan court ladies.

Backstage in Mrs. Leethard Bryan's seventh grade classroom, awaiting our stage cue, the five of us fidgeted in front of a long mirror someone lent for the performance. We turned this way and that, tugging at a bit of lace here, a stray strap there.

Tonight I wore an evening gown belonging to Uncle Dave and Aunt Lucy's beautiful, dark-haired daughter, Dora Lee. The dress, with its black lace over yellow satin, was almost as lovely as its owner. I hoped it would pass as Elizabethan.

Our stage appearance loomed near. Excitement mounted. Miss Snider, the play's assistant director, poked her head through the doorway. Making a circle with index-finger and thumb, she said, "Looks good, Girls. We have a full house with chairs in the aisles!"

I trusted that Daddy got up from his "day's" sleep in time for my family to find good seats. Uncle Homer and Aunt Sally, Frances's parents, were coming too.

Never would I have told a living soul, but I yearned to play the part of Rosalind. Miss Epps cast only upper classmen in starring roles.

Miss Snider opened the classroom door. "Come on Girls." She shepherded us down the hall, all the time waving her hands like twin sparrows, undecided which way to fly. "Let's go. You're on in five minutes." She shooed us ahead, down the hall, and onto stage wings. "Oh," she whispered. "Break a leg!"

Frances Marion rolled her eyes at me, but I had too much to think about to roll mine back. I gave Cousin Dora Lee's gown one last tug at the waist, patted hair that felt like it might tumble down any second, and hoped Miss Snider had been right about those red dots at the inner corners of our eyes looking natural from the audience. The mirror said we looked like someone's hand, holding lipstick, took a wrong turn. Twice! Grandma would howl, laughing, if she saw me up close. So would I, if I had time.

The play's second act nearing its end, Raymond Thigpen, playing Duke Frederick's court jester, emoted some of Shakespeare's better known lines:

"All the world's a stage,
And all the men and women merely players:
They have their exits and their entrances; ....."

Oh boy! My entrance was lines away. As soon as the curtain closed and opened again, I would stand exactly where, at this moment, Raymond bent over the duke.

I peeked through a crack in the curtain. Spellbound, people in the audience leaned forward in their seats, as though words coming out of plain old Raymond Thigpen's mouth poured out pure gold. Goose flesh rose on my arms, my scalp, sending shivers all over my body. Acting created magic; nothing less. It turned ordinary people into kings and queens. Or in my case, tonight it would turn a Bug Swamp, tobacco farm girl into an Elizabethan court lady! Shivering, I hugged myself, and like Miss Epps taught us, I drew in long, deep breaths.

Too soon the play ended. Along with the rest of the cast, Frances Marion, the other court ladies, and I took our curtain calls.

At the final close of the curtain, Miss Snider, her blue eyes holding something I hadn't seen there before, took hold of my hand and Frances's, pulling us into the bright lights of the hallway. "Girls, there's something I must tell you." She ushered us into the classroom where we had dressed for the play. She left the other court ladies to do what they pleased.

My thought: *did Frances and I commit some dreadful dramatic crime on stage?* Tentatively, we sat at desks, since that seemed indicated.

Miss Snider looked at us, away from us to the blackboard; she tightened her mouth; then, as though forced, looked at us again. In sober tones she said, "Frances, Billie, I have something to tell you."

My mind screamed, "*What?*"

"Mr. Bert Holmes, your uncle, I'm so sorry. He died tonight."

Frances stared at me. I stared back. My thoughts turned crazy. I heard what Miss Snider said; but, my mind seized on one thought, Frances Marion's red dots. They stood out in her eyes like wrong-colored, misplaced pupils.

"Uncle Bert, dead?" The question came from Frances.

"Just before the play, he was dressing to come. That's when he had a heart attack."

"Does Grandma know?" My voice sounded like somebody else's.

Twin to Aunt Gertie, dying back in 'thirty-nine, Uncle Bert was Grandma's baby brother, and in hers and my eyes, special. With his ever-present tuning fork in hand, he led our church in congregational singing. Many Sunday afternoons our home belonged to Uncle Bert, Aunt Dalma, and their daughter, Patricia. I considered them close family. Aunt Dalma contributed to our Sunday dinners, sometimes beef stew, a roast, possibly her lemon glazed cupcakes, my favorite. Whatever we ate, we had fun around the dinner table. And afternoons, we, as well as neighbors who came visiting, sang hymns and gospel songs.

Crushed. That's how I imagined Grandma.

"Your families are at your uncle's house. I promised I'd take you there after the play," Miss Snider told us.

Silently we changed from costumes to our own clothes, and still wearing grease paint, numbly followed Miss Snider out to her car. Frances sat in front. I climbed into the back seat, my mind a'swarm with wild thoughts.

Uncle Bert couldn't be dead! That man was totally alive! Too lively, Grandma said. On Sundays he didn't have to drive out to Bug Swamp. He could have attended a fancy church in town, but he chose to go where he was needed. Every Sunday morning found Grandma's baby brother pinging his tuning fork on Good Hope's front pew, singing out the pitch of his beloved gospel songs.

Uncle Bert hadn't eaten with us lately. We didn't live near church any more. Now, they visited with Cousin Gen, or Rob and Maude Hamilton; but, the last Sunday before we moved to Homewood, Uncle Bert sat at the head of our table. After finishing his dinner, he picked up his plate and said, "See, Dalma, this food's so good, Nettie won't have to wash my dish."

"That scoundrel," Grandma called him, "licked his plate, Aunt Dalma scolding, 'Bert Holmes, what'll I do with you? You're the most uncouth man east of the Mississippi!'"

Even Patricia, said, "Daddy! Yuck!"

Lights from closely spaced houses on either side of the street flashed past. Miss Snider searched for words. "You girls can take comfort. At least your uncle didn't suffer."

That was something. We passed Uncle Bert's older brother's house. Uncle Mack was probably with Aunt Ira and the rest of their family at Uncle Bert's … correction: now Aunt Dalma's home.

About two hundred yards past the road to our Homewood house, Miss Snider turned slowly into Uncle Bert's driveway. Cars overflowed the yard. Lights streaming from oversized windows colored tops of hedges and grass pale gold.

"I'll see you girls tomorrow." Miss Snider never left her car. "Tell your family they have my deepest sympathy." She backed out of the yard and sped back toward town.

Frances and I looked at each other, both feeling lost. Some sweet, wild fragrance hung in the air, and if I hadn't known better, I would have thought it the scent of moonlight. Light from our overhead moon, and windows cast long, eerie shadows beyond the birdbath.

I should never drink from that bird bath. Uncle Bert said so, although in the middle was a convenient spigot. For the longest time Frances and I lingered.

Uncle Bert's home contrasted strongly to his sister's Bug Swamp cypress house. My cousin and I climbed steps to the high ceilinged porch. On tile our feet made hollow, clicking sounds.

Frances rang the bell. Mother opened the door. Hugging us, she said, "You girls finally got here."

"Where's Grandma?" I wanted to see her, but death left me unsettled. *What should I say? How should I act?*

"Grandma's lying down. Your daddy's with her. We left Jack with Randall at Papa's house."

I glanced around the living room. Neither Grandma's sister, Aunt Freddie, nor Aunt Dalma was in evidence. Maybe Patricia was with her mom in her parents' back bedroom. Beyond the parlor, at the dining table sat Uncle Mack and Aunt Ira with people I didn't recognize. Frances Marion walked over to the fireplace where Aunt Sally and Uncle Homer sat shoulder to shoulder in the wine Victorian love seat I liked so much.

Weird that I could think about liking a love seat with my own uncle lying inside a coffin at Goldfinch's funeral home. Dead.

Other relatives glanced my way, some nodding. Nobody talked aloud. I trailed after Mother into the bedroom, separated from the parlor by curtained French doors.

Sources of Light

In Aunt Dalma's front guest room, Grandma Nettie, her back to me, lay on a four-poster bed. I leaned over and kissed her cheek. I said, "Grandma, I'm so sorry about Uncle Bert."

I wasn't surprised to find her in bed. When anyone died that Grandma Nettie loved, on hearing about the death, she turned boneless, or should I say muscle-less. Whichever, she usually collapsed.

Daddy looked uncomfortable in his straight-backed chair. His eyelids were red. I asked him, "How did you get Grandma here?"

"Your Uncle Homer lied. He told Ma, Uncle Bert was looking for the source of a recent leak, that her brother climbed onto his roof, slipped off, and fell onto some stiff bushes."

Mother said, "That got her here, but when Aunt Freddie met us at the door, right off, your grandma knew there was more to it." Mother nodded. "Yep, the usual happened. Grandma sank to the floor. Your dad and Homer picked her up and laid her there." Mother indicated the bed.

I had spent a night or two at Uncle Bert's. This room was where I slept. Suspended in the east window, a set of glass shelves held crystal animals. Mornings, when the sun beamed its light, radiance filled these creatures with fire. Tonight they sat cool and remote. *Probably like Uncle Bert at Goldfinch's.*

Earlier tonight I'd anticipated my senior school year. What senior year? By then, I may not exist. Why make plans? Why have goals? Old Shakespeare had the right idea. Just like I waited in the wings tonight to hear my stage cue, Death ever lurked, waiting to pounce when least expected.

I stared at Grandma. Her soft face held more creases than usual. I wondered: *How does she stand it? She's lost her father, her mother, her husband.* I counted on my fingers. *Two brothers, three sisters, and now,*

Uncle Bert. She probably has as many dead loved ones to go to, as she has live ones down here, to stay with.

Grandma turned her head. Light on the bedside table turned her gold-capped tooth into a miniature star. She touched my "grease painty" face.

I'd forgotten I was at a wake looking like a clown.

She said, "How'd the play go, Little Bushy?"

"It went fine. Fine." I swallowed a sizable lump, and squeezed Grandma's always velvety hand.

"I'll be there for your next performance."

"Tomorrow night?"

"If the Lord's willin', Sugar."

"But will He be? Will He be willing?" Afraid I'd cry, I looked toward the window. On the center glass shelf, a crystal swan flamed, afire suddenly with a leaping radiance. I'd seen this happen before, but only at sunrise.

The source of this brilliance had to be the bedside lamp, and flames leaping inside the swan could be seen only from a certain vantage point.

Grandma advised me time and again. "Little Bushy, truth is right there in front of you, if you're willin' to see it."

Maybe love, from the vantage point of Grandma's living family, could give her the comfort she needed.

Grandma's eyes held sadness, but besides sadness, something else. I saw love. Hope. Both, potent stuff.

Hope filled my heart. *Shakespeare, you were one smart old dude. The world really is a stage. And Death? He drags in at the last minute and has very few lines.*

I reached for Grandma's hand. "Grandma. Sit up. You can do it!"

She raised up from the pillow. Holding onto me, the grandma I knew and loved swung her legs over the side of the bed. Daddy rushed to help. He didn't want his "ma" trying out legs too weak to stand on.

Grandma looked up. "Rassie, I'm all right." She meant it.

Next night, hoping to see my family, I peeked through the curtains. "Frances!" I whispered loud enough, Miss Epps gave me a dirty look. Up the left aisle, sporting Uncle Homer on one side and Daddy on the other, Grandma Nettie beamed. Already seated in row four, Mother and Aunt Sally made room for their husbands. Grandma sat nearest the aisle. That's all I had time to note before "play time!"

"As You Like It" began in all of its Elizabethan glory. Finally, wine curtains fell on Act V. Rosalind, really Conway High's Merilyn Huggins, appeared onstage alone. In her epilogue Rosalind, not her male counterpart, Ganymede, spoke to the audience. In twenty or so lines, she told women, "for the love of men," she hoped they enjoyed the play. She charged the men that if they loved the performance, she would kiss as many as had bearable breath; at least that's what I got out of what Miss Epps called Rosalind's epilogue soliloquy. The audience must have liked Shakespeare's comedy, for applause rose "as high as the rafters."

Grandma. Wonder how she liked our production. Frances's eyes sparkled. She looked at me; I looked at her, both determined each would reach Grandma first.

Chapter 6

A Photo's French Connection

Uncle Bert died December 11, 1946. Grandma's brothers, Uncle Willie, and Uncle Bud, died earlier, Uncle Willie as a teenager, and Uncle Bud from bad medicine. Uncle Mac, Uncle Dave, and Uncle Hal, Grandma's remaining brothers, grew even more precious to her. On this Saturday morning, two weeks before Christmas, Grandma said, "Billie, help me drag this trunk into the dining room."

Like our family Bible, Grandma's old spare chest was so precious I was surprised she'd let me touch it. In 1894, she'd packed her trousseau, such as it was, into that trunk before marrying Grandpa Hamp and leaving for Almo, Georgia.

Last spring, before we moved to Homewood Aunt Sally gave her mama a new photo album. The occasion was Grandma Nettie's sixty-fifth birthday. I hold onto fond memories of that spring, for we were just approaching our World War II victory.

Grandma threw back the lid of her trunk. Every memento she held precious, small enough to fit, resided in that trunk, including family pictures. Lifting out a box overflowing with black and white photographs as well as older tintypes, she lovingly spread them out on our dining table.

Grandma and I were still pals. Our lives might have changed with this move to Homewood; but, I still came to her to calm my nerves. I well remembered the days we sat on our Bug Swamp porch and dipped together, Grandma's jaw packed with her Sweet Society snuff, and I, slurping Hershey's cocoa and sugar.

"Billie," Grandma said, "Can you help me with these pictures?"

"How should we group 'em?"

Sipping her second cup of coffee, Grandma clicked her tongue, her habit when thinking through a problem. "Tsk, tsk, let's keep families together."

I spread out relatives and friends on the kitchen table. "Who's in this picture with Uncle Murph?" The snapshot of Aunt Laura's husband beside a fellow soldier, both in World I uniforms, looked like the kind where you sit in a booth, put in money, and out slides a picture. Both young men appeared exhausted.

Grandma picked up the small photo and examined it with her magnifying glass. She said, "Nobody I know. I s'pose Murph met him in service. Wonder if he was there the night the Allies and Germans met in no-man's land?"

"Where?"

"In no-man's land. That's land between two opposing armies. Murph says that at Christmas, officers on both sides, ours and theirs, agreed to call a truce. No fightin' on Jesus' birthday. Christmas Eve, our fellows started off singin' 'Silent Night.' Across the way, when the Germans heard our men singin', they joined in, 'cept they sang in German. Can you imagine? Enemies. Singin' together! That broke the ice. First one soldier, then another crept toward the foe. In the middle of no-man's-land, they showed each other pictures of family, waitin' for 'em back home. Next day, 'Bang, bang.' Fighting back to normal. Or abnormal. That's what I say war is."

I pasted corners for Uncle Murph and his friend on a page by themselves. He and Aunt Laura had no children, but somewhere Grandma had several other pictures of her youngest daughter we would find later.

In one photograph, a scrawny young man cavorted on a beach. "Who is this, Grandma? Was this taken at Myrtle Beach?"

"Not unless there's a Myrtle Beach in France. That's your Uncle Hal during what people called 'The War to End All Wars.' Twenty-eight years ago my next to youngest brother was in the navy."

I saw little of Uncle Hal in this skinny boy. Grandma's doctor brother now weighed over two hundred pounds.

"Is that a Navy swimsuit, Grandma?" Uncle Hal wore a one-piece, form-fitting bathing outfit. I had never before seen a man wear a swimsuit with straps. "Men dressed in strange garb during World War I."

Grandma shook her head. "Now's what's strange. People at the beach today go half-naked!"

Because Uncle Hal lived a bachelor's life at Conway's Hotel Grace, Grandma worried that he didn't eat right. Used to, any time she saw his little black car race past, probably another house call, she started sifting flour. Rolling up sleeves, she plunged two clean hands into self-rising flour, pure lard, and milk. This mixture she worked into an oblong roll of dough from which she pinched small blobs. Dipping hands into dry flour, Grandma proceeded to roll and shape her tiny, trademark biscuits, crowding each into the round, greased, lard-stand lid she used as a pan. Last of all she patted each biscuit into a cookie-size disc.

Lately we hadn't seen much of Uncle Hal. Come to think of it, none of our friends came to see us. Did they think we'd fallen off the face of the earth? That's what I asked Grandma.

"Hal's comin' today."

"How you know?"

"He told Dalma and she told me. He'll be here in less than an hour. Why do you think I'm baking biscuits, the middle of Saturday morning?"

Just as Grandma's hot, flaky biscuits turned golden brown, Uncle Hal's little black car scooted into our side yard. His greyish hair as perky as bristles in Mother's scrub brush, Uncle Hal scooted up our back steps.

In Conway hospital, after a successfully performed operation, Grandma's second youngest brother always strode down the hospital corridor, whistling, his stock-in-trade. Today, instead of whistling, he entered our kitchen, singing. "Hey! Ba Ba Re Bob, Hey Hey, Ba Ba Re Bob ..."

From the kitchen, Grandma said, "Hal Holmes, what kind of song is that? I'm used to people singin' themselves into my kitchen, but this is a new one on me."

Uncle Hal gave his sister an Eskimo kiss. "You know Tex Beneke, don't you? And Glenn Miller?"

Grandma said, "I know Bill Monroe. I know Ernest Tubb."

Uncle Hal chucked me under the chin. "Net, I smelled your hot biscuits cooking as soon as I turned into this yard."

"Glad to see you, Hal. These days we're close enough you can drop in any old time."

"This isn't my first visit here."

"You've come when we weren't home?"

"No. About five years ago I was called to see Mrs. Cox. She was sporting a beat-up face. Looked like somebody used her for a punching bag. I wasn't too surprised to hear she was killed."

"We heard her husband did it. On our stairs."

"That's what the sheriff thought. He started looking for Sam Cox; but, the man had fled the place. Never been seen around here since."

Grandma looked at me, then at Hal. "Rass and Dot think Mrs. Cox has gone nowhere."

Uncle Hal looked puzzled. "What do you mean?"

"I mean Rassie and Dottie say they hear her on the stairs. About every night. She tiptoes up them steps like she's seekin' help."

"She? Pssh! They're hearing mice. Or rats. Net, I'm surprised at you. You know there're no ghosts."

"I'm not the one to talk to. Tell my chillern. Now sit down, Hal. Eat this biscuit while it's hot. You want syrup or jam?"

"Neither. Give me a heapin' spoon of sugar."

Grandma settled her brother at the end of the kitchen table. She served him four hot biscuits, small ones, along with a mound of sugar. Also a cup of black coffee.

I watched as Uncle Hal poured coffee into the sugar. It melted and spread, covering the plate's blue and white oriental bridge. Breaking a biscuit, he sopped up the sweet, amber mess. "Want some?" He asked me.

I must have been staring. I don't know why. Certainly I'd seen Daddy eat biscuit and coffee-sugar.

"Fix Billie some, Net." Probably Grandma's next-to-youngest brother wanted me occupied with something besides watching him eat.

I dipped my biscuit into the sugar mixture. Uncle Hal studied me, waiting. I frowned. "I'd rather have syrup."

Grandma nodded. "Me too."

"All this time I thought you two were kin to me." Uncle Hal stood up and stretched. "Thanks, Net. That was good." He spied his picture at the end of the table. He held it up to sunlight streaming through the open back door. "Who is this skinny cuss? I sure don't know him anymore."

"You've changed some since World War I." Grandma took Uncle Hal's "unlikeness," and tossed it back onto the pile. "So have we all."

Turning to go, Uncle Hal changed his mind. Again he reached for his photograph, this time cupping it in both hands like he held something breakable. And his face changed from the jolly one I knew. He said, "Seeing this picture brings back memories I'd just as soon forget. I didn't know how close I'd come to combat that very night. And never meet a German."

Grandma looked puzzled.

"Our higher-ups decided some of us needed a break." He indicated his beach picture. "My buddy, Curt and I, climbed up the cliff to a village and rented a couple of rooms in an inn. We changed into dry clothes, determined to sample some authentic French cooking. That's what the inn advertised."

Leaving forgotten, Uncle Hal reclaimed his chair. He idly tap-tapped the picture on the table. "Net, I've never told you this before."

I rested my chin in my hands. *Telling stories must run in Grandma's family.* Uncle Hal's voice sounded interesting. It moved through valleys and over hills. His eyes narrowed when he wanted to make a point, and he rocked his straight chair so far back, I worried he'd slip to the floor.

"This inn was run by a family. I don't remember their name, but I'd recognize either's face today if I accidentally ran into one in Timbuktu. Back then I trusted people. At least I thought Frenchmen were supposed to be our friends."

He flipped the picture across the red-checked table cloth. It landed face down. Touching his index finger to his tongue, Uncle Hal slowly chased around a few stray grains of sugar left on his plate, blue eyes the same color as Grandma's looking like he was chasing memories.

"There were four people in that fine little family. Pops, Pere, whatever the French equivalent of Papa, he spoke a little pidgin English. Of course neither Curt nor I spoke a word of French, except *oui* if it served our purpose. By this time night was upon us. Pushing open the front door of this place, we were greeted by Pops. Seeing us, he smiled so wide you could count his back teeth. He slapped our backs, looking happy to lay hands on a few U.S. dollars.

"I decided we'd come to a good place. If her husband's girth was any indication, Mrs. Pops must be one fine cook. And they had a daughter. Despite two ugly parents, this girl was little bitty, dark, and pretty as a Georgia peach.

"Well, we started upstairs with our bags. That's when a son that could have won a top-notch wrestling match, picked up my duffel bag in one hand and my damp, scrawny body in the other. He really did!"

Grandma laughed behind her hand. "He couldn't do that today!"

"What's that Net?"

"I said don't talk so fast, Hal. I can't follow you. I'm about deaf."

"Sorry," Uncle Hal gathered his thoughts. "Where was I? Oh. Yeah. We went upstairs. Curt and I planned to share a room to save money, but Samson stowed my gear in one and Curt's across the hall. My room overlooked the street, so narrow, you could about touch the upstairs porch on the other side.

"I was tired, so right after a supper of some kind of meat slathered in a cheesy sauce, but very good, I went to bed. Curt took off for a corner hangout." Uncle Hal grinned at Grandma. "I was Mama's good boy."

"About ten Curt returned. He pounded on my door. I could have slugged him. He woke me from a sound sleep, dreaming I was home in my own bed. Curt acted scared, and smelled like rotgut. Aroused like that, I didn't know what to think.

"Curt plopped onto my bed. He shook so the springs rattled. He said, 'Listen to me!'

"I said, 'Stop it, Curt. You're drunk. Listen to yourself.'

"He said, 'Hal. Hear me out.'

"I said, 'Man, what's got you so riled up?'"

"Curt grabbed my finger pointing in his face. His expression dried up any protest from me. He said, 'I sat at the bar with a French fellow. He spoke English. He asked me where I was staying. When I pointed to this inn, he told me to get out of here; not stay for a minute, that I was in real danger.'

"I knew my buddy was about three sheets to the wind. Still, he insisted the fellow spoke the truth. I thought ... I hoped it was all pure malarkey. Curt said the man told him if we did stay, not to blow out the lamp, that the inn keeper would probably kill us as soon as he thought we were asleep, that absolutely he was a mean, greedy man who killed strangers for a lot or a little. He'd done it before.

"We decided to put out the lights and see for ourselves. Across the hall Curt piled pillows beneath his covers to look like a man asleep. I made a roll beneath covers on my bed. Then, we crowded together under my room's second bed. We lay there, waited, and watched."

Grandma picked up her coffee cup and bammed it down harder than I thought necessary. "Hal," she said, "little pitchers have big ears!"

She meant me, of course, and I wasn't "a little pitcher!" I was thirteen years old!

"It's all right, Net."

"Grandma! Let him finish. I want to hear this!"

Uncle Hal took up where he left off. "I figured we'd hid under the bed long enough. The floor was hard, and we were acting like characters in a bad book. Finally I said, 'Man, this is crazy. I'm going to bed.'

"What stopped me, I heard tip-toeing up the stairs. Somebody stumbled. Somebody else said, 'Shh!'

"A key turned in the lock.

"Remember? I said my room looked out over the street? Lights out there lit my room bright enough, through the bedspread's fringe, I could see the face of the innkeeper's son. Samson. The bi-i-i-g fellow. Strong. Face squished up like a bull dog's.

"He had this hefty club." Uncle Hal looked at me. "Sort of like the ones giants sport in fairy tales. He lifted that club over his head and brought it down. 'Pow!' Right where my head should have been.

"Without checking *me* out, thank goodness, or the mess he thought was me, he turned toward the bed Curt and I huddled under. I just knew that over-grown jackass could hear my teeth rattle! His smelly feet stopped a bare inch from my nose. What next? When he bent over to pick up a coin someone had dropped, I could have counted the hairs on his knuckles. He snatched my duffle bag, closed the door, and left. Probably went across the hall to Curt's room, to smash in his head.

"I said, 'Lord, it's time to answer Mama's prayers!' Curt and I opened the window as softly as we could, dropped onto the street, me in my skivvies, and we ran like the very devil was after us, straight back to our ship."

Grandma broke the spell. Frowning, she said, "Hal, you left your bag?"

Sometimes I had trouble understanding Grandma's mind.

Uncle Hal slid his chair from the table. He said, "Girls, I've been here way too long." He blew Grandma a kiss. "Gotta rush back to the hospital."

I said, "I enjoyed your story, Uncle Hal. I'm glad that old Frenchman didn't smash in your head!"

"Oh," Grandma said, "Who's sick this week?"

Uncle Hal said, "Nobody you know; but, yesterday Gladys Dorman called and said come see them, that they'd just boiled a mess of peanuts. Come on out to the car and I'll give you some. I've enough to feed an army."

People were always giving Uncle Hal vegetables, watermelons, anything, for he doctored most for practically nothing and never would take a penny for our family's services. Of course Daddy took him a mess of cooked chittlin's every hog killin' time. Uncle Hal expected that.

His little black two-seater disappeared in a whoosh of dust, and Grandma and I went back to work on the picture album. We put the skinny-turned-chubby storyteller on the page with his mother and dad, Great-Grandma Madora and Great-Grandpa Hezekiah. (Holmes)

That night Daddy ate his fill of boiled peanuts, then sat down and leafed through our handiwork. I had written the names of each person in white ink beneath his or her picture. He came across Uncle Hal's.

"That was taken in France the day before Hal was nearly killed," Grandma said.

"Humph." Daddy's answer.

Actually, Daddy thought a lot of Uncle Hal; but, because of an episode with fourth grade math, (Uncle Hal was his teacher.) Daddy always walked on tenterhooks around his uncle. In case of sickness meriting a doctor, Daddy's blood pressure crested, and his heart hammered ratta-tat-tats into Uncle Hal's stethoscope. He always assumed that Daddy, like Grandpa Hamp before Daddy, and Great-Grandpa William Hamilton before Grandpa, suffered high blood pressure and a heart ailment.

~~~

Many years later, in my Athens easy chair I prop up my feet, Grandma Nettie's photo album in my lap. For most of the people in this album, life has ended, on this earth anyway. My beloved grandma died at seventy-three of severe arthritis. In 1959, at a business dinner, surrounded by doctors, Uncle Hal choked on a morsel of steak and keeled over dead. Possibly the medical community had yet to gain familiarity with the Heimlich maneuver, or Uncle Hal's pride kept him from making a scene.

Daddy's high blood pressure and heart problems passed away with Uncle Hal. In fact, Daddy lived to be eighty-three, dying of squamous cell cancer metastasized to his liver from we're not sure where. That renegade cancer slaved quite a while to destroy a powerful heart Uncle Hal's stethoscope said was defective.

Grandma's rectangular, red photograph album, with its black pages covered in mostly black and white pictures, now belongs to me. Several pages in back still wait to be filled. Say, maybe … I click my tongue, "Tsk," thinking. "Kayla," I call out to my granddaughter, painting her fingernails. "Would you like to help me paste pictures in our photo album?"

Chapter 7

My First Job

Here I was, a thirteen year-old girl with little to do since moving from our farm. Dag-nab-it, I wanted to work this Christmas vacation.

I'd wanted to work at twelve, last year, and I did, for a short, short while.

That fateful Saturday morning I went to town with Daddy. "Park on Main Street, not in Burroughs's parking lot," I begged.

Daddy had no trouble whatsoever, parking diagonally. I sat in the car for a few minutes. Then, in spite of not having any pal to accompany me, I hiked around the block twice, knowing many faces of people passing, having watched them on that, and other Saturdays, making their "'round the block," so-journs.

Finally I dredged up nerve enough to enter Eagle's Dime store. After idling a mite, I made myself ask to see the manager. Just before I bolted, a young man approached me. "Are you Miss Hamilton?" asked the man.

"Yes." I wished I wasn't.

"Looking for a job?"

"Yes Sir, just through Christmas."

"Can you start right now?"

"Yes Sir. I guess so, Sir."

This Mr. Bradley ushered me to the back of the store, opened a door, and showed me upstairs to a balcony overlooking downstairs sales counters. "Meet Mrs. Bradley," he said. "Just do what she tells you. Pay is twenty-five cents an hour." The man looked at me askance. "How old are you?"

Grandma always told me not to lie. I eyed my toes. "I'm twelve, but I'm in the eighth-grade."

Mr. Bradley shook his head. "That's mighty young." He seemed undecided.

Mrs. Bradley smiled, and her smile was almost as pretty as Cousin Bertha Mae's. "She'll do fine, Henry. I just need some gifts wrapped." Mr. Bradley disappeared before I could say "scat!"

Mrs. Bradley took me to a long table where about a half dozen items awaited wrapping. She said, "Here's some scotch tape and there's the gift wrap." She handed me a pair of scissors. "Tissue paper and cards are beneath the table."

Wow! I was in business! I reached for the first gift, a box of chocolate covered cherries. A piece of cake! I pulled out a foot and a half of red paper dotted with green holly. Wrapped and tied with narrow, green ribbon, my first package looked fairly nice. I breathed out the breath I hadn't known I held.

That's when Mrs. Bradley walked through the doorway carrying a two and a half foot long object with one end pointed. She placed it upright on the table. A clock.

"Wrap this carefully. It's very expensive and we need it to look special."

That statement rattled me. Wrapping a bed sheet I wasn't worried about, I put that aside and eyed the clock. I breathed fast enough to have walked two more blocks. Delaying, I picked up two pairs of socks, found an appropriate box, and wrapped those. I wrapped two more gifts, still not daring to start on the clock.

Mrs. Bradley returned. "You haven't wrapped the clock? Purchasers are coming for it in five minutes."

Oh my. Five minutes. Picking up some tissue paper, I enshrouded the clock, for I had no box the right shape or size. Hoping it was the right size, I cut out a pretty metallic gold wrapper, then picked up the clock.

In my haste to place it just right on the paper, I hadn't realized the clock's base was so heavy. It slipped over the table's edge, and before I knew what had happened, "POW!" That costly timepiece lay on the floor. I picked it up and heard tinkling beneath its tissue paper. I was afraid to look.

My worst fears realized, I thought to myself, *I can wrap up this clock and no one will ever know its face is shattered. Or, I can tell Mrs. Bradley what happened and take the consequences.* For a minute I stood stock still. That was long enough to hear every card class teacher, ever class room teacher, Mother, Daddy, and especially Grandma say, "Girl, don't try to cover up mistakes. Admit 'em and take your punishment."

Not that I'd always followed their instructions. Once, in first grade, Aunt Dalma told me to take a message to our principal, Mr. Nichols. She said, "Billie, tell him that Charles Graham has to stay after school. Again he cut in line today, after over and over, I warned him not to."

Well, I knocked on Mr. Nichol's door, and who should open it? Charles Graham. Behind him Mr. Nichols came to the door. He said, "Yes?"

I said, "Mrs. Holmes sends you a message."

Charles caught my eye. He shook his head. Barely.

Mr. Nichols repeated. "Yes?"

I said, "Mrs. Holmes says … Mrs. Holmes says that Charles can go home as soon as the bell rings." Why had I told that lie? I only knew that next day Aunt Dalma kept me after school, and driving me home, told Mother and Grandma all about my lie. After memorizing The Ten Commandments, and a new Bible verse each day of the next week, I decided I'd better remember to tell the truth.

Mrs. Bradley opened the door. I tried not to cry. "Mrs. Bradley, I'm so sorry. The clock slipped out of my hands. It broke." I hung my head.

Silence followed my confession. Finally, she said, "I'll get Mr. Bradley."

Never in my twelve years of living had I known more fear. Of what, I didn't know exactly. I only knew I'd broken something expensive, something valuable.

Mr. and Mrs. Bradley returned. She said nothing. He just stood there, looking at me. My heart pounded loud enough they should have heard it.

A tall man, Mr. Bradley squatted before me. I heard his knees pop. He took my hand. He said, "I hired you, knowing you're twelve. Tell you what. I don't pay you for the wrapping you've done today, and you come back when you're older."

I blinked my eyes. Had I heard correctly? I said, "I know the clock was expensive. I'm sorry I dropped it."

He stood up and patted my shoulder. "I have six more like this one. We'll wrap one of those." He smiled, then said, "Have a nice Christmas."

I said, "You too!" Thanking both of my new friends, I ran downstairs and back to our car before Daddy ever returned from the livery stables. I didn't tell him about my job or my dismissal. I was too close to the emotion of it. After we went to bed that night, I did tell Grandma. I didn't know what her reaction would be.

She said, "Little Bushy, I'm proud of you for askin' for a job, and I'm especially glad you told the truth after droppin' the clock."

"If I had lied about it, I couldn't have faced you, Grandma."

"God's the one you have to face when you do wrong, Child. He's the one sittin' up in heaven, a'wantin' every person on earth He's created to do what He would if He was human instead of our Creator."

"What would He have done today?"

"The same as you. The very same."

"He wouldn't have had to think long and hard about it."

"That's because He is God. Little Bushy, you're trying to mix me up."

"No I'm not, Grandma. I'm just tired I guess."

"Well then, go to sleep."

"Goodnight, Grandma. I love you."

"I love you too, Little Bushy."

All that happened last year. This Christmas, I still needed a job. Mr. Bradley had said to come back when I was older. Well, I was no longer twelve. I was thirteen.

On Saturday, the day after Uncle Bert's funeral, I went back to Eagle's Five and Dime. A mite more confident than last year, I spoke to a nearby clerk. "I'd like to speak to Mr. Bradley, please."

I spied Mr. Bradley in a side aisle, a box of stuffed animals at his feet. I tried to smile, although I felt it looked fake. Trying to be grown-up, I stretched out my hand. "Hello, Mr. Bradley. Remember me? I'm Billie Faye Hamilton."

At first the man looked puzzled. Then he broke out with a huge grin. "Hi there, Miss Hamilton. I remember you. How long ago was that?"

"Last year, Mr. Bradley. You said come back when I was older. Well, I'm older. Do I get to work this year?"

He said, "Follow me," and we made a repeat performance of last year. We walked to the back, took stairs up to the balcony, and greeted Mrs. Bradley, knee deep in gifts for wrapping.

She spied me. "Who? On yeah. I remember you. Have you come to help me this year?"

"Yes Ma'am, and I've been practicing. I've used newspapers, wrapping everything from toys to clocks," I said, coloring, remembering the one I'd dropped.

She waved her husband aside, telling me, "Let's get busy. We've got two hours to wrap all of these doo-dads."

I'm happy to say, in two hours I'd wrapped everything she placed before me, without breaking a single item.

"Can you come back Monday after school? I'll take you onto the floor."

Could I?

So many good things happened the first year I lived at Homewood: first, playing an Elizabethan court lady; then, my first real job at Eagle's Dime Store where I earned twenty-five whole dollars working ten, ten-hour days. I finished up during the mad rush on Christmas Eve.

Before working I had five dollars, thanks to chores I'd done for Grandma. Abrams Department Store offered lay-away. Using my original money as down-payment, I picked out gifts for all my family. At lunchtime each Monday I made a payment. By mid-day Christmas Eve, I had paid for Daddy a necktie, Mother a scarf, Jack a spinning top, and Grandma a white satin scarf. I wrapped all of my gifts at Eagle's Five and Ten and brought them home in a plain paper bag. No one was the wiser. I didn't earn enough money to buy Uncle Charles and Aunt Rock presents. They understood. I did blow up balloons for Mary Jane and Sarah Anne.

At school, I joined the glee club, for now, afternoons, I could get home much more easily. Later, our group accompanied Mr. McDaniel, our director, on a field trip to Florence, South Carolina. He wanted to show us the music store he owned, or possibly worked at, before teaching band and chorus at Conway High.

While heartbreaking, in the eyes of God I did another good thing. I went to Uncle Bert's funeral. I attended his heavenly bon voyage.

A bad thing: one afternoon, arms loaded with a stack of books, as usual I stood at the front of the bus because I got off first. Mean old J. C. Bennet crept up behind me and draped a snake, a real, live snake around my neck. I sank to the floor of the bus. I screamed and screamed. Oblivious to anything but fear, I don't know when J.C. retrieved his snake, what kind it was, or if he was ever punished. I just knew I'd like to be the person horse-whipping him!

Another thing: Daddy called it good, Mother called it bad. Two months after Christmas, in February Daddy got laid off from work at Dargan's Lumber Company. Mother sat at the kitchen table smoothing out his last paycheck. Daddy said, "What's your problem? Mr. Bennet, (mean old J.C.'s dad) says Stilley's Lumber Supply needs help, and they hire women. Want a job?"

Both of my parents applied, and both got jobs. That left Grandma, Jack, and me, wide eyed and staring. We did have more money coming in. We just had no one with time to spend it.

Back at Bug Swamp, still home in my sub-conscious, my family believed chickens should dictate our farm family's bedtime routine. Nowadays was comparable. My parents went to bed early to report to work by seven a.m. Some days I felt like we had no family time together. Grandma felt the same. Poor Jack. He had Grandma and me, but that wasn't like having Mother and Daddy around when we needed them.

Afternoons, Jack got home from school before I did. Lucy picked up him and Jesse. About every afternoon Jack and Grandma visited with the Millers. Some days found old Mrs. Miller and Jesse at our house. I'd much rather have seen Mother here, treadling her sewing machine, stitching up aprons or some such.

In early spring our school year was going full blast. While school no longer dismissed in April, this was the time of year when teachers buckled down, cramming into students' heads information necessary to advance to the next grade. I needed to study. Jack needed attention.

"Billie Faye, where's my spool toy? I can't find it anywhere."

"Billie Faye, let's play checkers."

Grandma would sit in for me on that one. Some days she spent so much time with my little brother, I'd get jealous. Shades of my past. I decided that it was time Grandma and I shared our work with Jack. I'd grab the broom, sweep the kitchen floor, then say, "Jack, it's your turn. Sweep off the back porch. Steps too." If he did? Fine. When he didn't, and that was often, I'd complain to Grandma, "Jack's being lazy. I swept the kitchen and he's supposed to sweep the porch."

Finally Jack grew fed up with his bossy sister. He threw down the broom and yelled at me. He said, "If you want grass pulled from around that old flow, pull it yourself." I'd promoted him from porch sweeper to grass plucker.

I complained to Grandma Nettie. I said, "I hate to say this, Grandma, but Jack's growing lazier and lazier. He needs responsibility."

Grandma said, "I well remember certain things back home. Sweeping the floor, you could pause five minutes between broom strokes."

She was right. I remembered. Time had stood still while I imagined myself the actress I'd be someday, or maybe a glamorous singer clad in slinky silk, draped across a piano in a smoky lounge, belting out throaty torch songs before a throng of adoring fans. (I went to the movies.) Jack was nearly the same age now I was then. Of course he was a boy, and he'd rather go see westerns than read books, which was what kept me in trouble with Grandma and Mother when I was his age.

Been there, done that. I'd just have to stop being such a pesky big sister. He was a sweet *old baby brother*. Dad gum it!

Chapter 8

One Love Each

Lonely after Uncle Bert's death, Aunt Dalma asked me to spend the night with her and Patricia.

"I just can't," I told Mother. "That house is too empty without Uncle Bert." For several nights I made excuses. I told Aunt Dalma I had chores. I had to work on a home economics project with Mother. Jack needed me to help him with health homework. Finally, I ran out of excuses.

After a tasty supper of steak Aunt Dalma thought she should cut up for me, she, Patricia, and I drove to Wednesday night services at First Baptist Church in Conway. A visiting preacher, Reverend Chet Smith, (Not his real name; the man was famous.) spoke about love at first sight. A handsome fellow, dark, on the slight side, and walking with a limp, the preacher's eyes glowed with sincerity. He said, "I believe this with every fiber of my being. When God created you, and you, and you," the reverend pointed to various members of the congregation, "he also fashioned your counterpart, a mate to love you, to nurture you, to comfort you, to share your life. And he planted within your heart an instant desire for your intended."

It seems that one day the preacher saw a woman on a train depot platform. Already seated on the train, he felt an absurd impulse to dash off the train and meet her. Not following this impulse, he dreamed of her constantly.

A year later Reverend Smith spied the same young woman riding a horse through a meadow. She pulled over beneath the tree where he sat reading his Bible. The horse grazed, the preacher read on, or at least he held the Bible in front of him. In reality, his heart, faster than any horse, bolted into his throat. He studied the girl, lithe, dark, her mouth ripe for a kiss. He never said a word. She galloped out of his life.

A third time he met her at a tea honoring a newly elected senator. The door opened and the politician entered. On his arm arrived the lady of the preacher's dreams. *At last,* he declared to himself, rushing to grasp the girl's hand lest she get away a third time. She shook his eager hand politely and her eyes met his as the senator said, "Reverend Smith, allow me to introduce my wife."

In his sleep that night the girl reappeared. Her dark eyes reproached him. Like the dream she was, her lips moved, silently mouthing the words, "You had your chances."

Rev. Smith never married.

I could not get that sermon out of my mind. What if I let my "right person" get away? Would I be doomed to live a single life? Would I turn into a dried up old prune face like a Good Hope church member I knew?

Already thirteen, I could count on one hand the boys I had liked. Could Roy be my special one? Or Billy Smith? (Not his right name!) Roy didn't talk much; so, a girl could imagine all sorts of things he might say. Billy's face looked as pretty as any girl's. And he talked nonstop. I probably liked him because two thirds of the females in the student body did. In elementary school I liked Alec Jones, and when I was four, Billy Harris, my cousin, for goodness sake. Certainly God never intended anyone to have that many mates!

Hey! Why should I worry? I could leave all this to the boy. Let him find me! That problem solved, at least for the moment, I settled down to sleep in the same room Grandma had slept the night Uncle Bert died.

Next morning I checked out the crystal animals in their window shelves. Just as they swam in eastern sunlight, Aunt Dalma called out, "Breakfast."

Into my dramatic phase, I decided my aunt's kitchen personified yellow sunshine lined with clouds of airy white curtains, starched and ironed!

Bacon sizzled on the stove. Patricia was ready for school. No longer a child, she was a pretty young girl. Aunt Dalma placed three pancakes before me.

Patricia held up a finger. "I want one."

Aunt Dalma shook her head. "This girl has no appetite."

"Mama," Patricia said, "I can't hold everything."

"See?" Aunt Dalma's voice sounded teary.

What could I say? I hated to see her sad. That's why I'd put off coming.

She turned bacon. "Billie, the preacher's sermon. How'd you like it?"

Around a mouthful, I said, "I enjoyed the speaker. But I don't agree with him."

"Why not?"

"If God intends just one person for each of us, how come so many men and women get married twice, some people three times? Or more?"

"You know," Aunt Dalma said. "I don't agree with him either."

And she must not have, for two years later she married one of Conway's bank presidents.

She was still my Aunt Dalma.

*(Five years later at Winthrop College, this same minister, **Rev. Smith**, spoke during our Winthrop Christian Emphasis Week. He told us college girls the same story, "One Love Each," he had related to Conway First Baptist's congregation. Was that message truly meant for me?)*

~~~

Spirits, Dead or Alive

After spending the night with Aunt Dalma, eating steak for supper, going to church, and hearing the preacher tell about love at first sight, then eating pancakes and bacon for breakfast, next morning, I was dropped off at my house by Aunt Dalma. I waved to her and Patricia and ran inside. I'd soon board the bus for school.

The first words out of Grandma's mouth: "Where's my scarf?"

"Oops," I slapped a hand over my mouth. "I gave it to Aunt Dalma. She liked it with her suit. She said this color suited me more." I pulled out of my bag a silky pink scarf.

Grandma's voice carried a rare edge. "Billie Faye, I like my white satin one. You gave it to me. Remember?"

"I'm sorry, Grandma. I'll tell her you want to swap back."

"Never mind. If Dalma wants it, she can have it."

Daddy sat at the breakfast table. He lowered his paper. He said, "Ma, you sound just like somebody else I know."

I never did learn the person he was talking about.

Grandma laughed. "I do, don't I? Why is it that a body sees everybody's faults but his own? Never mind my satin scarf, Little Bushy. This one's just as pretty and will go well with my navy blue dress. And Dalma's right. Pink does look better on you." I felt sad that I'd traded Grandma's scarf. I didn't know she'd liked it so much.

Settling down to a routine, life grew almost as normal as if we'd never left Bug Swamp; but, there was still Mother's "visitor" to deal with. Our guest "tip-tip-tipped" up those stairs whenever she chose. Mother said so anyway. I never heard those night noises. In my mind they represented just one more facet of the house's ambience: its low ceilings, its creaks and cracks, as well as other weird, unexplainable commotions. After a while we seldom thought about or discussed our uninvited, stair-tapping guest.

One night, like most, my homework lay strung out on the dining table. Grandma sat in the corner sewing on buttons, and Mother was hemming my new dress. "Dottie, do you ever think of the hereafter?" Grandma bit off a thread. "I mean can you imagine what it's like up there?"

"Doesn't the Bible say the streets are paved with gold and the walls are lined with jasper?"

"And it says we each have a mansion. Won't that be something! Nettie Hamilton, livin' in a mansion! I bet all the people we love, no longer with us, at least the ones that love the Lord, I bet they're up there right now, walkin' on golden streets and not stubbing a toe. Just think of a place where all our wants shall be supplied!'"

"Do you really believe that, all our wants?" Mother re-threaded her needle. "We don't always want what's good for us."

"When we get to heaven we will. We'll be transformed there, not like the puny people we are here."

Mother pushed back dark curls. "I wonder, who do you reckon came for Uncle Bert when he died? I bet your parents were there, and Aunt Gertie." She was Uncle Bert's twin sister, and mother to Elise, Genevieve., H. B., and her youngest, Little Oliver.

"God may have sent his angels. There's so much we don't know about the hereafter."

"Wonder if the dead ever come back to us? Really? We're supposed to be happy in heaven; but, I know, when I die I'll want to know what Billie Faye and Jackie Boy are up to, and my other grandchildren. If a body's supposed to be happy in heaven, wouldn't a trip down here to check on her earthly family serve that purpose?"

Mother said, "There's so much goodness in heaven, we'll probably know what we need to; whatever the Lord sees fit; but, I wonder. Do you reckon Uncle Bert might have met some new friends where he is?"

"Nobody's new or old in heaven, Dottie. A day's like a thousand years and a thousand years is like a day. No time there. No new. No old."

"Hmm. I wish I knew if any of our loved ones are listening to this conversation."

"They might be. Like I said. If the Lord sees fit."

Then like one other time we'd talked about our dead loved ones, the front door opened. I stopped writing in the middle of the word, hap-py, and looked toward the door. Both Mother and Grandma looked up from their work, expecting someone to enter.

Just as easily as the door opened, it swung almost shut.

"Well, I never!" Grandma said.

It opened again. Daddy stood there with a bag of groceries. "You never what? Come help me with these groceries. Were you expecting somebody else?"

Mother ran to help. Soon Mother and Daddy sat down at the table.

"We were just a'talkin'," Grandma said, "about heaven. We can sit here and talk forever and ever; but till we get to heaven, we won't know what happens there. All I need is to know the Lord will be with us and in charge. Where He is, everything'll be fine."

I said, "Grandma, everything will be 'heavenly!'"

She swatted my bottom like she has since I could remember. "Smarty pants," she said.

Mother said, "Makes me want to open my Bible. There's so much I'd like to understand."

"Then, open it! Read it!" Grandma was ready, anytime, for us to read our Bible.

My ninth grade school year went flying past like the rockets we heard scientists were working on. Next year, a tenth grader, I'd begin my third year in high school; but, I wouldn't know what to call myself. If the state hadn't tacked on grade twelve, I'd be a junior. I guess I'd just be a junior twice. More likely a "two-times" sophomore. Shucks! Even figuring out what class I was dealt in numbers.

Whatever, three years from June of 'forty-seven, I would graduate from high school. Then what?

Mother said, "College."

Soon Mother and Daddy took Jack and went for a visit to Papa and Mama Todd's. Aunt Leatha was feeling puny, and that worried her mama. Grandma said she didn't feel like going and wanted me home with her.

I looked up from my book. "Grandma, don't you ever tire of piddling?" I had just finished reading a story in my literature book, all about a man in the Arctic, desperate to strike a match. The man writing that story had the same first name as my baby brother. The man's last name was the same as the capitol of Great Britain I studied about in geography.

There sat Grandma, as desperate as the man in the Arctic, except she was trying to match up small squares of red, blue, green, multi-colored plaid, with some flowered material. I said, "I can't believe you, Grandma. There you are, still a'quiltin'. We already have so many, you left two thirds of 'em stacked up at home."

Grandma said, "Little Bushy, you've been here, goin' onto a year, and you still talk about our farmhouse as home. I like that."

"I can't help it, Grandma. I lived there all my life. Now, about another quilt ..."

"During cold weather one can't have too many coverlets. Besides, waste not, want not. What would I do with all your mama's scraps if I didn't make quilts? Take this needle and sew these pieces together."

Grandma couldn't fool me. She'd brought most of those scraps from home. Mother didn't have time to sew like before.

I sewed. The harvest table bench Grandpa made long before I was born needed padding if I sat there for long. I moved to a softer chair, deciding, if I had to work, I might as well be entertained. I tied a knot and bit off the thread. "Grandma, while we're doing this, you could tell me about Bill Darbey and the weird stuff he did."

"I've told you that before. You could tell it to me."

"Not like you tell it, Grannikens." Sometimes it helped to sweet talk my grandma.

"Let me see your square."

I held up the red and green flowered pieces I sewed together.

"They're about straight."

I picked up a third royal blue square with a bit of red and green in its plaid. I pinned it to the second square, mumbling, "I wish I knew all you know, Grandma."

"Take those pins out of your mouth, girl. You could swallow one!"

While I deposited my mouthful into a pin cushion, Grandma pursed her already pursed lips. "Dear me, Little Bushy, if you keep on pumpin' me dry every day, you'll know *more* than I do."

"I've been thinking, Grandma. I'm almost in the tenth grade. I've got just a few years left before leaving home. I hope to store away all you'll tell me."

"Here's what," said Grandma, "your mama and daddy'll be back soon. It's Friday. Remember how we used to take turns, tellin' stories on Friday nights?"

With Mother and Daddy at work constantly, and Jack and I busy with school work, it had been a month of Sundays since we'd had any regular story-tellin'. I said, "Yes! Tonight let's surprise Mother and Daddy. Jack, too."

What's Next?

Kind of late, my parents ambled in. Jack had played so hard with Randall, he looked like a sleep walker.

I opened my mouth to say, "Story time!"

Before I could *out* with a word, Grandma put her finger, "shush," to her lips. I guess she saw trouble in Mother's face. She reached for my hand and squeezed. "Let's us all go to bed early. Listen, you all, when have we had us a good old-fashioned story-tellin' night? Let's plan to share stories this comin' Friday evening."

Daddy said, "I'd like that."

Shucks. I guess I could wait.

Next morning Mother still looked sad. I crept up behind her and put my arms around her waist. I said, "Something's wrong, Mother."

"Yep," she said. "I might as well out with it. Leath is sick. She's really sick. When she smiles and her lips tighten, her gums bleed. I've never seen that in anybody. Her doctor says she needs help from doctors at Duke Hospital. Ones here have done all they know."

I did not like hearing this.

Chapter 9

My Dear Aunt, Leatha

Ivey Leatha Todd Mishoe

Sunday, after church our family stopped by Papa Todd's, just to speak, for I needed to get home and finish a term paper due Monday.

We parked near the back steps. Daddy almost didn't get out of the car, for back at Homewood Mother had left an old hen on simmer. She needed to add and cook rice before we were ready to eat.

Mother, Jack, and I ran up the back steps into Mama's kitchen. She said, "Hm. I didn't know you all were coming."

"We're not here to eat. We just came by to see you. I've got to get home and finish our dinner. I guess Leath is in bed."

"Yeah," Papa Todd said, he and Randall coming onto the back porch through the house's front passage way. "Go see Leath. That'll perk her up."

By now he and Daddy sat down on the kitchen steps, probably talking about Papa's tobacco, and how happy, or sad, Daddy was that he hadn't had that responsibility this year. Grandma sat in the car, and Mama Todd went out and spoke to her before returning to her Sunday dinner.

Since Leatha's sickness she used Mama's front bedroom, Mace's at one time. Across the hall from the parlor, that room was more convenient for visitors.

Leatha lay propped up on pillows. I stooped over and kissed her cheek. "Hey, Leath," I wished I could say something perky.

She looked at me with eyes made bluer by their weakness. She said, "I sure Lord wish I could get out of this bed. I am sick and tired of being sick and tired."

Mother said, "At least you're well enough to tell us how you feel."

"Yep." She sighed. "Dottie, they're doin' it. Papa and Jeff are taking me to Duke Hospital this week." She noted Mother's expression. "Don't look like that! Sooner or later it was bound to happen. I wish I was already gone and back."

Mother sat in a chair by the bed. I just stood, not knowing what to say. All I wanted was to see Leath well and happy. If a trip to Duke would bring that about, she should go. Maybe. Definitely. Whatever was best.

Mother just sat for a minute. Then she whispered something to Leatha. Leath looked at me and I saw in her eyes a hint of my old auntie. She said, "Who's the boy?"

I said, "What boy?" What had Mother told Leath? Never had I said a word about that boy in history class, the one named Billy, like my name, but spelled with a "y." I blushed, mumbling something nobody understood.

Leath said, "Dottie, look at Billie Faye. Girl, I see it all over you. Guilty as charged."

Leatha liked nothing better than to tease, whether it was Mother or Mace, sometimes Daddy, although she knew he didn't take well to anybody's leg-pullin'.

Leatha use to say my mother was "stuck-up," that she was vain, whatever that meant. When little, I thought "stuck-up" meant stuck up in a tree somewhere, for just before that, Mother had accused Leath of being a tom-boy, liking nothing better than to climb trees. Maybe dancing, although Mama and Papa Todd frowned on their children jiggling their bodies for the world to see. I wished Leath could hop out of that bed and dance a jig, right here in Mama's front bedroom.

I always thought Mace and Leatha were closer to each other than either was to Mother, out of the nest and gone before nineteen. Mace called Leath, "Buddy," and buddies were pals, weren't they? He always called Mother, "Dottie," and while he teased her like he did everybody else, he didn't joke around with Mother the same as he did with Leath.

That's when Randall and Jack popped in. Leatha said, "Hey, Jack. You're growing like a weed." Jack smiled as big as he liked to feel.

Randall said, "What about me?"

Like Mama Todd, Mother opened her arms wide. She said, "Come here, Big Boy. Smell my nose."

That's when Mama Todd ducked her head into the doorway. "If anybody's wondering where Mace and Louise are, they took Roger Dale to see Louise's parents; and Rass, he's ready to go."

Outside, probably twiddling her thumbs, Grandma still sat in the car's front seat, with Daddy behind the wheel. Tired of waiting, he had sent Jack inside for Mother and me. Now, he blew the horn. "Beep-beep!"

"We've got to go, Leath," Mother passed her hand over Leatha's ample curls. "That old hen simmering on my stove will have cooked to death if we don't get down the road."

Leath looked like her eyes might shut before we got out the door. "Tell that boy your aunt says 'Hey!'" she threw at me.

I said, "There's no boy!" But there was. He just didn't know it.

I was glad we stopped and saw my aunt before they packed her off to Duke. Over the years Papa had managed to save a sizable sum of money. Thank goodness for those savings. It took every last penny of it to treat my dear, plucky aunt.

Doctors at Duke Hospital did help her improve. They diagnosed her illness as Leukemia, and after a series of blood transfusions, sent her home. Off and on she returned to Conway Hospital. With instructions from Duke's doctors, local physicians continued Leatha's prescribed treatment. Luckily Daddy possessed the same rare blood type, AB Negative, as my aunt. When Leatha needed a transfusion and the hospital had none of that type on hand, they tapped Daddy as donor.

At this progression of Leatha's illness, my mind snapped these pictures. Between hospital visits, my aunt crept around looking frail but determined. Always small, now she looked slight. One day we drove across hard-packed sand crawling with tree roots, and like many times, parked near Mama Todd's back yard, kitchen steps. On Papa's back porch, hugging her knees, Leatha sat atop Mama's long freezer. She wore a dress made of some soft, flowered fabric. I'd watched Mother sew this dress with its long waist and gathered skirt. She sewed me a twin to Leatha's. That was my last vision of my aunt before she took to her bed.

"Look who the cat dragged in," she said to Mother. Even in sickness Leatha tossed out dry tidbits. I loved her humor.

Since we moved away, I didn't see my aunt as often. I missed her, for before Jack and Randall came along, I was her favorite child. Leath said so.

The year I was three Daddy planted a new cash crop, green lima beans, my favorite vegetable. Still is. On this day Papa and Mama Todd, Leatha and Mace came to pick beans and fill baskets. Afterwards, Daddy would take the beans to market.

One would think on bean-pickin' days our menu would have screamed, "Beans!" It didn't. That day Grandma cooked collards. At mid-day dinner, Leatha sat at the end of Grandpa Hamp's kitchen table, and I sat in her lap. I know we had collards for dinner, because Leatha kept stuffing them in my mouth. She didn't give me time to nibble a bite of cornbread. Finally, I grabbed her chin. I looked into her eyes. I said, "Eashie! Hang the bread on the thumb, and hang the collards on the bread."

Sitting in my aunt's lap and being spoon-fed collards, I have a vivid memory of that day; but, if I had no memory of it, people's harping on how I told Leath to feed me, made that account definitely mine.

About a month after our Sunday visit to Papa Todd's, the day our chicken had simmered on the stove at Homewood, a young man, later marrying Cousin Bertha Mae, appeared at my library study hall door. I waited until Miss Payne's back was turned before slipping out of her library. This young man, James Earl, drove us to the hospital to see my aunt. I knew Leatha's room number, for I heard Mother tell Daddy. Without visiting the front desk, James Earl and I slipped up two flights of stairs. I pushed open Leath's door.

Propped up on two pillows, my aunt said, "Billie Faye! What are you doing here? It's the middle of a school day! I'm gonna tell your mama."

I said, "Please don't, Leath. I needed to see you."

She kept my secret, but I told. Mother said, "Billie Faye Hamilton, don't you ever cut school again!"

I said, "I won't." But I lied. Once, for lunch, I snuck out with my school chorus girlfriend, Helen, the sheriff's daughter. We ate at her grandma's house.

Mother did a good job, pretending my aunt would survive her illness. While they were together, Mother played like nothing was amiss. I wondered how these two sisters interacted, alone.

Seventeen months after Leatha's Leukemia diagnosis, the Good Lord took her home. That day I sat with Mama Todd in her kitchen, surrounded by relatives, by friends, by sadness. We all knew my aunt's days on this earth were sorely numbered. Suddenly, from his mother's bedside, Randall burst through the dining room doorway. "Mama!" He sounded desperate. Sailing into her lap, the eight year old cried, "I want to be your little boy!"

That's what he became. Later, I heard adult Randall say, "Papa and Mama always thought they took care of me. I thought I looked after them."

That last year, due to his mother's illness, Randall missed a lot of school. Near death, Leatha talked to her boy. She said, "Son, make school a top priority. Study hard. Learn something that will take you good places in life."

Randall took to heart his mother's advice. He finished Conway High School, Clemson College, earned a Master of Divinity degree at Wake Forest University, and a few years later received a PHD from Harvard, at the same interim earning another master's degree from MIT. Later he studied at Karl Jung University in Switzerland. Leatha would have been proud. I should have said, "Randall's mama *is* proud of her baby boy."

Chapter 10

Aunt Molly and Her Family

Always when Uncle Charles visited, I loved riding in the rumble seat of his sleek, black car. Bouncing down Bug Swamp's sandy roads at thirty to thirty-five miles per hour, I leaned back, enjoying. The wind blew my face. It played havoc with my hair, much more liberating than being pulled down the road by a couple of mules. At a fast clip, if a-mind to, I could have out-walked either Old Mary, long dead, or Old Pet, still in our Bug Swamp barn stall.

Lucky for me when Uncle Charles visited, his aim was to see his whole family, and that included us, plus his sisters, Sally, Molly, and Laura.

Grandma's second daughter married a man who took to himself a best friend, Jim Barleycorn. That acquaintance accounted for the fact that sometimes their family lived in a near mansion, at other times a near hovel. Where or which mattered not a whit to me. I loved going there, for I loved Aunt Molly, her children, *and* Uncle Hartford, a fine carpenter-craftsman when he kept ample distance from his no-good friend.

Uncle Charles' little black car, in spite of its few visits, when pointed away from Aunt Sally's, headed straight for Aunt Molly's house. With wind in my face, we scooted down Horry County roads toward Loris. Always Aunt Molly lived somewhere in the town's vicinity, usually near Allsbrook, a wide place in the county road; if not there, she lived nigh Cane Branch Baptist Church.

On this trip we decided that Uncle Hartford had worked more religiously than usual, for his family resided in a large, brick bungalow. The driveway to their yard led us through a stand of tall pines. Aunt Molly, seeing Uncle Charles' "Georgia" car, flew off of their screen porch. She embraced her younger brother. "I'm so glad to see all of you. Come in. Come in!"

Grandma, Aunt Rock, and I climbed out of the car. I ran off to find Georgie and Billie Ruth. The grownups could do their own visiting.

I found my two girl cousins sitting before the living room fireplace, playing Jack Straws. Knowing nothing of this game, I joined them. The art of tossing long straws onto the floor, then picking them up without touching any other straws attracted me nary a whit.

Georgia and I were the same age. She took me to the room she shared with Billie Ruth, showing me her latest doll. Then, the three of us scooted outside for a game of hopscotch before dark.

On certain Sundays, after church our family traveled the ten or so miles to visit Aunt Molly's family. Occasionally we'd show up to where we'd visited last, and they would have moved. Again. Aunt Molly's dearest wish was a home of their own. Uncle Hartford built houses for a living. Why couldn't he build one for his family? Sometimes Aunt Molly thought her dream would remain just that.

When Grandma's love-struck, middle daughter married her young man, he took Molly Ruth Hamilton home to a farm, left him by his father. The Great Depression, coupled with Uncle Hartford's drinking habits, whisked away that livelihood. In spite of her husband's carpentry skills, Aunt Molly never knew true security; not until something happened that scared the drunken "bejeebies" out of her mate.

Uncle Hartford received his paycheck on Fridays. On this Friday night, like some others during his and Aunt Molly's marriage, no Hartford; all day Saturday into Saturday night, no husband returned home to family. By then Aunt Molly's imagination, coupled with raw nerves, ran amok. She sought to act natural. Her five children would worry: their father, knocked in the head by thieves and murderers and buried somewhere; Hartford, thrown out of the car in an automobile accident where he was either maimed or killed; Aunt Molly's "better" half, helplessly drunk, sprawled somewhere in a ditch.

The last scenario proved correct. Sunday morning a bedraggled Uncle Hartford, reeking of stale alcohol tinged with puke, his forehead cut and covered with dried blood, body bruised, damp hair plastered to his head, the source of Aunt Molly's confounding worry trudged up their front steps.

On perpetual watch, Aunt Molly flung open the door.

Her husband bowed his head, crying real tears. "Sugar," he said, "I wouldn't blame you if you never speak to me again. But, as sure as I am standing here, I've drunk my last drop of liquor. As God and my dead mama are my judges!"

Tight lipped, but relieved, Aunt Molly bit her tongue, determined to let him finish.

"I don't have a penny to show for last week's work. I lost it; don't remember where. What I do remember is coming-to in a ditch, way over there toward the other side of the church. I woke up to what I thought was the church congregation, singing.

"Come to think of it, I reckon it was angels that woke me. And Mama Georgie was there. My mama, long ago dead. She looked at me with such soulful eyes. She said, 'Son, what have you done to yourself? You've got to promise me: this is the last time you'll be such a fool. I did not raise a drunk.' That's what she told me.

"I said, 'Mama, I'm sorry! As the Good Lord is my judge, I promise you. I'll never drink alcohol again.'

"And Molly, I'm promising you: I'll never, as long as I live, spend another dime on liquor. Hear me?" He raised his head and looked at Aunt Molly. She saw truth shining through his bloodshot gaze. For their remaining years on this earth together, Uncle Hartford kept true to his vow.

Leton, husband of Uncle Hartford's eldest daughter, earlier built Lena Bell and himself a house on land given him by his father. Their home sat in a field adjacent to Cane Branch Baptist Church Cemetery. Cashing in on an opportunity to live near his daughter, as well as a chance to build Aunt Molly her promised home, Uncle Hartford bought from Leton an ample house-lot, an acre or two beyond Lena Bell's.

Immediately Aunt Molly's now determined husband laid out a foundation. Pounding nails into board after board, using spare time from work as well as scraps and leftovers from other building jobs, he added to his home project. As soon as Uncle Hartford sealed the framework, Aunt Molly said, "Let's move in. It'll be easier for you to work."

One Sunday, about the time Jason Hardee, a World War II casualty, was shipped back home and buried in the next door cemetery, our family made a sojourn to see Aunt Molly.

First, we turned into the yard of the unpainted gray bungalow with its tree bole front steps. That's where we'd visited last. Daddy coasted to a stop, and Grandma peered through the car window.

"Chillern," she said, "I do believe Molly's moved again."

In the back seat between Jack and me, Mother shifted the warm pot of Kentucky Wonders to her other knee. "Lena Bell can tell us where."

I was glad they moved. I never liked that dark old house.

In probably less than a mile, Daddy turned off the main road onto a rather long driveway. Lena Bell and Leton's bungalow sat in a tree-shaded yard carved out of a huge field. In their yard Jack Hardee and his nephew, Lonzie, were tossing a ball.

Daddy braked. My brother, Jack, popped out of the car and joined the boys. Mother gazed out her window. She said, "I do believe that's a new house in the field. I never noticed it before."

As we climbed out of the car, Lena Bell pushed open the porch door. She wiped floury hands on her apron.

"Come in," she said. "I'd go out there, but my bread's about to burn."

Jack and Lonzie ran up and gave us all hugs. "Grandma grabbed Jack Hardee's hand. "Who lives in that new house?" She asked him.

"We do," Jack said. And that's how we learned Aunt Molly had her own home.

Lena Bell returned. She said, "Do come inside. I can't visit out here. I'm too busy cooking."

Grandma said, "Not right now. I want to see Molly."

Into the car we piled and drove a tad further to their new house.

By this time Aunt Molly saw us. Mother climbed out with her pot of beans, and Daddy carried them into the house.

"Look out, Rassie," Aunt Molly called. "The front room's not floored, yet."

But the kitchen and bedrooms had floors, and Aunt Molly was as proud as if she owned a new mansion.

That day Jack Hardee and Jack Hamilton ate chicken and dumplins' with Lonzie at Lena Bell's. The rest of us, except Mother, ate beef stew, rice, and Kentucky Wonders with Aunt Molly. Mother never ate beef. Afterwards, Georgia and I visited the cemetery where we saw Jason Hardee's new grave. His picture in uniform adorned his tombstone. Also, we found Joanne's grave. Joanne was Lena Bell's three year old, sweet baby girl, dying in 'forty-two.

I believe that was the afternoon Hamp, Aunt Molly's older son, and his girlfriend, Lucille, drove over in a cool automobile and introduced us to Lucille's cousin, Otha Russ, a cute young man in a Navy suit. We all piled into Hamp's car and rode through the countryside. Later, Billie married Otha. They parented three sons.

Before, and after Aunt Molly's own home, we spent various Sunday afternoons with their family. After sharing dinner, our Jackie Boy, and Aunt Molly's Jack, born the same year, enjoyed goofing around. I tagged along with my girl cousins. Some days we visited neighboring friends in the area. On an earlier Sunday visit we walked along the railroad tracks near the huge Allsbrook house, the sprawled-out one with its mile of porches. On a nearby railroad track out of Loris, a store remained open on Sundays, rare in that era. Goodies in that store looked so tempting, we made up reasons to revisit it. Holding out empty palms to one grownup or another, we were able to buy long, white candy cigarettes boasting pink, artificial fire tips. Sneaking around, we found another adult with change, returned to the store and bought tiny green and red, liquid-filled wax bottles. Biting into the bottles, we swallowed the bit of drink and chewed the flavored wax like chewing gum.

Occasionally, if I were lucky, Aunt Molly let Billie and Georgie return home with me to Bug Swamp. All week long, what a frolic.

Once, I had gathered together every evening gown anyone in the area would lend me. I needed a couple of them for a school play. Billie, Georgia, and I each donned long dresses. Smearing our faces with pancake makeup, and on our front porch, lounging in chairs, we waved at the few cars passing. Chatting, we pursed our lips, faking the lingo of actresses, princesses, or whatever highborn ladies our imaginations could conjure up.

Grandma never did say what she thought of three granddaughters, sitting on her "pizer," made up to look like loose women, and waving wildly at passing cars' occupants. At prayer time that night she did pray, "Lord, please look after my poor, misguided granddaughters."

To vary our escapades, down the road in a house built by our Great-Grandfather, Rev. Bill (William H.) Hamilton, we visited Cud'n Bertha Mae. Sometimes we meandered a little further down the road to visit Cud'n Bobbie. Even further down the road we visited Uncle Boss's daughters our age, Betty Jane and Edna Mae. And, I mustn't forget Mary Joyce. She was Grandpa Hamp's sister, Aunt Tennessee Harris's granddaughter. Always too soon, my Cane Branch cousins returned home, leaving me lonely.

Family Tragedies

March, 1948, during our Homewood stay, Leukemia ripped my Aunt Leatha from her family. After seventeen months of physical suffering and mental anguish, to our lasting sorrow, Papa and Mama's daughter, Randall's mommy, Jeff's wife, Mother's sister, and my Aunt Leatha who refused the title, "aunt," she died.

In the custom of that era, Goldfinch Funeral Home sent an ambulance for Leatha's body, embalmed her, and brought her home. Inside Papa's silver-roofed house where Leatha and Jeff spent romantic Sunday afternoons on the porch swing, Goldfinch set up Leath's casket against an inside wall near a window.

"While no one was looking, I stood over Leath's casket. I gazed at her face. I touched her cheek. Cold. I thought, *what is death? How can a body feel warm, think, carry on a conversation, then leave for once and for all! This time yesterday the aunt I'd loved all of my life, she was alive. Now, where was Leatha? Did she still love me? I still loved her.*

I'd heard Grandma say, "To be absent from the body is to be present with the Lord." I tried to imagine what that meant, being present with the Lord. I thought he was always present with us, if we asked him to be. A mighty deep subject.

In the hallway a stand held an official-looking book. Some people I didn't know were signing their names. I slipped out of the room. I needed to see Mother. Or Mama Todd. Somebody.

Earlier in 1948, not long before Leatha died, doctors informed Aunt Molly that she needed an inward-growing goiter removed. This operation was considered safe. Nothing for family to worry about.

During Aunt Molly's procedure, Grandma and I walked along the hospital's front garden pathway. Soon Daddy and Dr. Burroughs exited the hospital. "There's Joe," Grandma said. She always called Dr. Burroughs, "Joe," and he called her, "Joe." Some kind of joke between them. Daddy remained at the exit. Dr. Burroughs headed toward us. Grasping Grandma's elbow, the doctor steered her away from me. That quickly, Grandma crumpled to the ground. Daddy ran to her side.

"What's wrong? What's the matter?" I asked.

Daddy said, "Molly's dead. She died on the operating table. The anesthesia."

Aunt Molly left three children still living at home. Billie Ruth was seventeen, Georgia, my age, was fifteen, and Jack, eleven. Uncle Hartford never finished Aunt Molly's house, and after she died, he vowed he never would. Years later, Uncle Hartford's grandson, Lonzie, married. Lena Bell's son completed Aunt Molly's house, and lived there with his family, as well as with his grandfather. At a ripe old age, Uncle Hartford died there.

Back in 'forty-eight, Uncle Charles came home alone to attend Aunt Molly's funeral. He arrived in the afternoon and I rode with him to his sister's house. Like at Leatha's death, Aunt Molly's body lay in a casket in their now floored parlor, where friends and family paid last respects. I walked in with Uncle Charles. Beside her casket, gazing long at his sister, he bowed his head. Face covered with a handkerchief, Uncle Charles' body shook in silence.

Aunt Molly's children grew up, married, and left home, or, left home and married. So did I. Uncle Hartford made a butcher knife for my wedding gift. Many years later I still slice meat with that knife.

Billie Ruth re-married, this time a Mr. Fowler, producing more children in addition to her three Russ boys. Georgia married Ben, and their son is Joey. Today she's grandmother to Chelsea as well as Taylor.

Through the years, though times I spend with my cousins/friends are infrequent, when we manage visits, I feel the same love and affection I felt years ago. We share vital memories.

A Zillion Years Later

Re-reading this portion of my life, written several years ago, I need to insert something. Recently, I turned on the television to a Sunday night show called, Extreme Home Makeover. Animatedly waving his hands, Ty Pennington, the star of the show, shouted, "Hello-oo Suggs family!"

My Suggs family, although time had lengthened and shortened their number. Leton, Lena, and before them, three year-old Joanne, had died. Their second daughter, their third oldest child, Patsy, grew to adulthood, became a nurse, gave birth to a beautiful daughter; but ultimately, Patsy died of brain cancer. Prior to her demise her father died. Lena survived Patsy by scant years. Left were the couple's children: Lonzie, Jimmy, and their youngest son, Teddy.

It seems that Lena Bell's grandchild, Derrick, Teddy's son, a Loris, South Carolina police officer, lived in what had been his grandfather, Leton's home. Noting how Derrick was raising his wife's brothers and sisters, in addition to his own children, Derrick's cohorts contacted Extreme Home Makeover's show producers. They saw fit to build Lena and Leton's grandson, Aunt Molly's great-grandson, a palatial new home.

Wonder of wonders: on the big screen sat the house Leton built for his family. I witnessed a wrecking ball slam into a kitchen where I had enjoyed chicken and dumplings. That ball destroyed the home where my cousins lived out their dreams, and while Leton and Lena would have appreciated their grandson's blessing, I felt sad to see the home of their married years demolished. Yet, Grandma Nettie's great-great-grandson, on the big screen. Wow!

Chapter 11

A Present, a Middle, an End

Prepare yourself for more palavering

Moving to Homewood during my ninth grade school year created a new lifestyle for my family and me. First Daddy, then Mother took jobs away from home. Thank the Lord for Grandma, and for the Miller family next door. Aunt Dalma came over occasionally, but old Mrs. Miller, Lucy, and Jesse became our neighbors in every way. We visited. We rode with them to Homewood stores. We shared stories and lives. Lucy's sister from Charleston visited, and when Grandma turned her back, I couldn't believe some of the stuff coming out of Lucy's sister's mouth. That woman had lived!

Regretfully, after a month or two, one night her husband arrived and whisked her back to Charleston.

Thank the Good Lord for the sunshine of everyday life. With so many books to read, papers to write, and blessings to count, I had little time for boredom.

I still had a bee in my bonnet for acting. In tenth grade I played the part of an old woman living in a home whose front door boasted *The Purple Door Knob,* the play's title. A beautiful actress, played by eleventh grader, Vera Cherry, knocked on my, or rather the old lady's door. The play began with Vera emoting, "A boon! A boon! I crave a boon!" Of course she desired my purple door knob. I wish I could remember how the play ended. I'd have preferred *beautiful* Vera's role, a *beautiful* actress, to my part as a cranky, old, gray-haired lady, but "beggars can't be choosers." (That gray hair was achieved with a cloud of white baby powder.)

My next part was Beth in Louisa Mae Alcott's "Little Women." James Suggs, Aunt Dalma's nephew, acted the role of my father, returned home from the Civil War. When I died, James had to pick me up and carry me off stage. I don't know how he managed that feat. Afterward, I'm sure his back hurt.

Later, acting took a back seat to singing. I entered the talent contest at Conway High. During this period Horace Heidt's popular talent show was touring the country. A singer, Ralph Siegwald, from Charleston, South Carolina, won a segment of that contest and became part of the show team, his signature song, *The Lord's Prayer*.

I loved parroting Siegwald's song. At home I sang *The Lord's Prayer* so often, my brother ran around the house turning his pockets wrong side out. That's what Grandma said would shut up shivering owls. Anyhow, thank you, Brother Jack. I entered Conway High's talent contest, and thanks to my talented piano accompanist, Mrs. Rod McCown, and my fellow classmate, Sara Margaret Smith, I won first place. Yeah, Jack!

A couple of college years later, in Charlotte, I tried out for the still popular Horace Heidt show. I did *not* win that. However, I was present for a spiel performed by an up-and-coming young actor. Andy Griffith entertained our audience with his comic routine, "Whut it wuz, wuz football."

Remember Joe Hucks, my Bug Swamp school walking companion? At church, Katie Belle Hucks, our teacher, paired us. We sang duets. We acted in a play called "The Unbeliever." At high school we placed second in the same talent contest I won, and I was privileged to go to Joe's Junior/Senior dance, for we sang there.

I hasten to add that my good friend, cousin, and school companion, Mary Joyce Abercrombie, placed third in Conway High's talent contest. She sang "Buttons and Bows," from the show, "Oklahoma." Mary Joyce always was anyone's number one comedienne as well as a classy singer. Thus, Good Hope's four room school house's students made a clean sweep of the contest, winning first, second, and third places in our college-size high school's talent show.

In most instances, singing and a flat pocket book didn't jibe. Performing, I needed just the right garment. For Joe's Junior-Senior, I visited Uncle Hal and his wife, Aunt Aline. Uncle Hal didn't wed until past fifty; but, he made up for that by marrying a beautiful, sweet, nice lady from Marion, South Carolina. Uncle Hal commissioned her portrait by a talented artist, and it hung on their Third Avenue, living room wall, a block from our school. I prissed myself over to Uncle Hal's and asked Aunt Aline if she owned a dress I could borrow.

For a moment Uncle Hal's relatively new wife sat down and thought; then said, "Come with me." I followed her upstairs to the most lavish bedroom I had ever visited. Furnished in period furniture, the room's dominant feature was a lace-curtained, four-poster bed. From the top of their closet she pulled out a box containing the pink satin dress in her portrait. Thrilled, I slipped on this object of beauty. Shucks. Too long for my short self.

"I don't mind if you hem it. I'd give you the dress, but since it goes with the painting I can't," said Aunt Aline.

"Thank you!" I breathed. "I'm blessed you'll let me wear it." I never felt so lavishly clad.

The night of Joe's junior-senior, his sister, Jane, drove us to the dance. She made my corsage, perfect for Aunt Aline's rosy satin gown. Picked from Jane's back yard garden, Joe's sister's white irises looked almost like orchids. That night Joe and I sang, and threw in a few dance steps to "Shine on Harvest Moon."

A few years ago I picked up a copy of South Carolina's "Sandlapper" magazine. It featured a Conway home belonging to Uncle Hal's son and his family. Over their living room couch hung Aunt Aline's lovely portrait, and she still wore "my" dress.

No memory competes with 1950's senior class year at Conway High. A couple of talented girls, Betty Sue Jones, and possibly a later Winthrop College fellow student, Doris Jordan, I don't remember for sure, planned, organized, and produced a musical performed by numerous members of our student body, the title of the production, "This is the

Moment." An extremely proficient pianist, Mrs. Rod McCown, assisted by our classmate, Sara Margaret Smith, also our Conway High glee club pianist, directed and accompanied this production, as well as others before and afterwards at Conway High School. Again Joe and I sang and danced a few steps to our perennial duet, "Shine on Harvest Moon." At the end of the show, facing the audience in an arm-in-arm oval, all cast members sang, "This is the moment, this is the time, why don't we take it, and make it sublime…"

I'll never forget that "moment."

One of the first symbols of extravagance to pop up on the Myrtle Beach grand strand in 1930, was a grand hotel, so grand people called it 'The Million Dollar Hotel." Mr. John T. Woodside, builder, called it The Ocean Forest Hotel. In the ball room of this luxurious establishment, we Conway High seniors held our Senior Prom, as did other high schools nearby.

Mother surprised me. She said, "Billie, for this dance, how would you like your own evening gown?"

Beginning with Mother's friend, Zena, as a mere kid I'd borrowed her dress. Next, as a teacher in Good Hope's school play, I wore Joe Huck's oldest sister, Loula Graham's black ensemble. To become a court lady in *As You Like It*, I borrowed Dora Lee Holmes's black and yellow lace gown. I prevailed on the goodness of various friends for future fancy wear.

Trying on first a white, a pink, then a sky blue organdy and lace, strapless gown at Belk's Department Store, I adored the blue dress. If memory serves me correctly, Mother paid thirty-five whole dollars for that "thing of beauty," or was that sixty-five?

Our country's Great Depression cast its long shadow on Horry County High Schools' favorite dance site. However, everyone I knew still bragged that at our disposal was *our* "Million Dollar Hotel."

Later, after finishing secondary school and entering Winthrop College, I spent the summer following my sophomore year at Myrtle Beach. My school buddy, Naomi Hardwick, invited me to visit with her and her family that "working" summer. Naomi waited tables at Lloyd's Seafood Restaurant off Highway Seventeen. From Mr. and Mrs.

Macklin, Naomi procured me a job. I worked the same shift as Naomi's, breakfast and lunch.

My friend's brother, Jeff, also lived at home. One night he found himself short in the companion field, and invited me to a concert at our Ocean Forest Hotel. Wonder of wonders, the entertainer that night was Johnnie Ray. Quite talented, featured on *What's My Line,* music shows, and his own personal appearance shows, Johnnie Ray's unique rock and roll and blues created a precedence for new-style, up and coming singers.

That night, this popular Oregon musician of Native American heritage stood before the microphone. Flourishing a handkerchief, he wiped away what looked like real tears, singing *The Little White Cloud That Cri-ied.* He followed that rendition with *It All Depends on You, An Orchid for My Lady, Walkin' My Baby Back Home,* and *Just Walkin' in the Rain.* Certainly he thrilled me.

In the nineteen eighties, over fifty years past the Ocean Forest Hotel's opening, someone decided our fancy point of interest had served its purpose. Those scoundrels imploded our ball room site. Today, I leave and enter my Athens, Georgia, enclosed garage TV viewing room through one of Ocean Forest's room doors, complete with the metal number, "Room 173;" also a sink, a cabinet, a mirror, and a light fixture from that hotel turn my utility room into an emblem of the past, mine and Horry County's.

Psalm 122:1 *I was glad when they said unto me,*
Let us go into the house of the Lord.
<u>1948, Back to Bug Swamp</u>

After a couple of years at Homewood, Daddy said, "Let's us go home and grow tobacco!"

Surprise, surprise! Entering church, knowing I was again part of my "home" community felt good. If I so chose, after church I could walk home. When I was small, many times our family did just that.

That reminded me of long ago. Wednesday nights, strolling up the lane toward church, Daddy would lift me, his baby girl, astride his shoulders. He'd point his finger. "Look up there, Little Chu. See that man in the moon?"

No matter how hard I tried, I never saw Daddy's moon-man. The whole mile from home to church, I would squint upward. Gazing at our faithful, round, silver ball, I'd sway to the rhythm of Daddy's feet.

Good Hope Church had changed. Still in flux, our church was now pastored by a nice reverend from Loris. Some Sundays he ate dinner with us. At such times Preacher Clyde Prince never cared to eat chicken, nor chocolate pie. Poor man, his stomach ailment limited him to scrambled eggs and toast.

Sunday evenings we attended a special meeting called BTU, Baptist Training Union. At times those meetings turned into parties complete with refreshments. On Friday nights we held real, undisguised parties in our homes. We played games: "Laugh and Go Foot," "Gossip," "Spin the Bottle," and others. Yep. "Spin the Bottle" was a kissing game. These youth get-togethers were directed by my friend, Louise Hucks' sister, Katie Belle, a Good Hope Elementary school teacher and life-time resident of our community. Also she taught Sunday school and directed church plays I enjoyed.

A month or two after we returned to Bug Swamp, Jack Frost ushered in our first cold snap. Immediately Daddy's mind seized onto hog-killing. Like always, he drove to Uncle Dave's house and brought him over to do what Daddy could never do: kill a hog.

Friday evening, after all of that day's feverish activity, my stomach growled. And why in the world had Mother made such a production of house cleaning? She acted like the Queen of England or somebody special was coming. Still, that hadn't kept me from grabbing a plate and loading it with short ribs, liver, and rice, left over from our hog-killing, midday dinner.

Mother chided me. "Why eat now? I wanted all the dishes put away."

I kept stuffing my mouth. "I'm hungry, Mother." I was thoughtful enough to fold back Mother's pretty table cloth and set my plate atop her red-checked oil cloth.

That's when our front door opened. What sounded like a thousand feet paraded through our parlor. Katie Belle tapped my shoulder. "What are you eating, Billie Faye? Got enough to go around?" As before stated, Katie Belle was our friend, our Sunday School teacher, our BTU director, our Social Director, our Drama coach.

A half dozen friends stood within my line of vision and more stood behind. They all shouted, "Surprise! Surprise! Surprise!"

Mother said, "I couldn't tell you. Katie Belle said it was a surprise."

Our "mistress of everything worth doing" at Good Hope Church, Katie Belle said, "Billie Faye, this is your welcome home party. We're just glad you've moved back to Good Hope."

I pushed away from the table, happy, if embarrassed. "Me too, everybody. Thanks!"

That was to be my last complete year, living at Good Hope. May of nineteen fifty, I graduated from Conway High School, and that fall, moved to Winthrop College in Rock Hill, South Carolina. For the next four years Winthrop became my home, other than during summer vacations. Then, like Uncle Charles and other "wayward" Bug Swamp, now more properly, Good Hope citizenry, I visited home.

Part II

Luke 9:25

For what is a man advantaged, if he gain a whole world, and lose himself, or be cast away?

Winthrop College Days

Chapter 12

A New Life

D addy had never driven farther from home than Charleston. He told Mother, "See if you can get Lloyd to drive us." Lloyd Stevens was Joe Huck's twenty-ish adult uncle.

Jack said, "Billie Faye, wait a few more years to leave home and I'll drive you." That year Jack, thirteen, was beginning his freshman year at Conway High.

Soon we'd loaded up Daddy's car with everything necessary for my first jaunt to Winthrop College. "Tell Grandma I love her," I told Mother. She was staying at Aunt Sally's until Monday afternoon.

"You did tell your grandma 'bye,' didn't you?"

"Yes," I said, "I'm really gonna miss you, and Papa and Mama Todd." I needed to change the subject fast.

"Mother, you said you wanted a new coat this fall. I heard that Abrams is having a fall sale next week. Don't forget." I ran to the bedroom for one last look around.

My parents wanted to see where their daughter would live for the next four years. Located in Rock Hill, South Carolina, nestled in the piedmont region of our state, Winthrop College sat just twenty miles from Charlotte, North Carolina, but nearly two hundred miles from our Bug Swamp farm.

Last year I visited my new school. It registered over nine hundred students, little more, if any than the number attending Conway High. According to Winthrop mailings, "Powers that be" had assigned me to a freshman dorm, McLaurin Hall, which, for various reasons, became my home for three of my four years at Winthrop.

Rock Hill's city entrance looked like that of a thousand other towns. A street spiraling to the right of one leading into town led us past a square, brick hotel, onto Oakland Avenue. We drove past a couple of businesses, some city offices, then passed a movie theater to our left. By now we were amid residences. An expensive looking, near mansion sat on the left, and just beyond that, the Winthrop campus. My new home. Later I learned that the "near mansion" was really Winthrop's "President Edward's Mansion."

The second building and first dormitory visible from Oakland Avenue had a sign in front. The sign read, McLaurin Hall. I yelled, "Lloyd! Turn here." A security officer directed Lloyd to drive around to the right side of the dormitory. After parking, with arms full of last minute items remembered after packing, Mother and I slipped out of our car. Lloyd and Daddy held either end of my trunk. That left my suitcase forlornly waiting. Jack tried to help with that, but quit when the handle pulled off. At the end of a porch, up ancient steps sat a rope-pulley elevator. Jack wrapped his "Jack Armstrong" muscled arms around my suitcase, carried it to the porch with everything else I'd use for the next school year. "Jack Armstrong, an All American Boy," was a radio series my brother revered. We loaded my possessions onto the elevator, and proceeded up to the third floor, mid-hall, front dorm-room, indicated on my acceptance sheet. Inside this dorm-room, my roommate awaited.

What a nice, attractive girl! Jo Neil Tippens hailed from near McCormick, the South Carolina town where Worth Abercrombie, Mary Joyce's dad, originated.

Never could Jo Neil's father have held a more exciting position. He ran the movie projector for Jo Neil's hometown, Calhoun Fall's, local theater. Hearing this, Jack was ready to move there. He said, "I wonder if they show westerns, Saturdays."

My dormitory, old, red-brick, u-shaped, three stories high, sat up a lawn incline from the street we'd driven down. Oakland Avenue was as well-known as Winthrop itself. Actually, across Oakland sat the

Winthrop Teacher's Training School, making the street practically a part of the campus.

With Mother, exploring outside my new lodgings and facing McLaurin Hall, I noted that its left wing connected to an enclosed breezeway, leading to a side entrance of Winthrop's library. Mother said, "Billie Faye, how convenient."

I agreed. I liked my new home. Climbing several front steps to a rather spacious porch and passing through a double door, we met McLaurin's housemother, Mrs. Ethel Weaver. To the right of the entrance, sitting behind her desk in an open office, Mrs. Weaver greeted us with "Welcome to Winthrop!" She offered me a "sign-in" book. With our housemother's wavy white hair, kind, dark eyes, sweet smile, and friendly manner, she made leaving home and family slightly easier.

Several parlors accommodated visiting parents, friends, etc. One housed a piano and another a ping pong table. A friend I'd meet later, Joyce, from Marion, South Carolina, acted as at home with that piano as had Raymond Thigpen in our Conway gymnasium. Joyce liked to play, and I liked to sing. That suited me.

Mama and Papa Todd, Billie's maternal grandparents:
Cleva Felica Williams Todd and Talbert Decal Todd

Chapter 13

Lost? Or Saved?

Growing up in the Bug Swamp community, I always felt confused about my relationship with the Lord. From earliest memories He was the center of our lives: Grandma's, Mother's, Daddy's Jack's, mine. Sunday mornings and Sunday nights, like clockwork, Daddy took us to church. We attended Wednesday night prayer services. Most evenings we read the Bible aloud and each prayed sentence prayers. On Sunday mornings, even if Grandma found her waist money bag empty, when Uncle Oliver and Mr. Bud passed the offering plates, from some place each of us found a "widow's mite" to give to God. We went to Our Maker for all the answers to everyday living. Yet, for many years, of the three adults in our family, only one claimed the title, Christian. That's correct. Grandma Nettie.

My first Sunday at Winthrop I attended Rock Hill Baptist Church. To get there, tradition dictated that Winthrop students dress in Winthrop's navy blue and depart from campus via a walking "blue line." While our college put forth state values, apparently in that era state values equaled Christian traditions.

Meeting other Baptist students, I soon learned that most were church members. I wasn't. Many Christians I grew up with made conversion to Christianity mind boggling. I wanted to join Winthrop's Christian Association; but, since I'd never joined a church, I wasn't listed as Christian. I felt sadly lacking. What to do? Wouldn't joining a church other than Good Hope somehow dishonor Grandma?

God solved that. During spring vacation, my home church held its biannual revival services, and our pastor invited a neighboring Maple Baptist's pastor to lead our week-long service. Rev. Buddy Ward was brother to one of my old high school chums, Betty Ward. Not long after high school graduation Betty married Stanley Hardee, Jr., a member of Good Hope and ordained into the ministry by our church's own deacons. Also, Rev. Ward's wife, Margie Goldfinch Ward, played the piano and taught piano lessons. They approached me. They asked that each night I open services with the song, *I'd Rather Have Jesus.* No one seemed to have an inkling I wasn't a professed Christian church member.

The first evening I sang my song, Rev. Ward's sermon stated that to give one's life to our Lord was simple. One need only ask Jesus into his or her heart and strive to give Him total commitment. With open arms, a loving Lord awaited, ready, even eager to welcome His children.

I left my seat at the first note of *Just as I Am.* I spoke to Rev. Ward. "I want to tell the world that I'm asking Jesus into my heart."

In the Amen Corner Louise Hucks, Katie Belle's sister, sat with mutual friends. At Winthrop, she and I were classmates. Her problem was similar to mine. We commiserated about how many people in our home community made becoming Christian feel almost impossibly hard for plain old sinners like us. I remember certain grown men, revival after revival, answering altar calls. They'd kneel. They'd pray. They'd beg to be saved.

Too hard. Downcast, unsaved, at the last *Amen,* those husbands and fathers returned to their seats. Year after year they repeated their treks down the aisle.

Always I felt that if those nice men couldn't be saved, how could I? And now, Rev. Ward told us that our Good Lord was simply waiting to be asked, that He stood ready, eager to forgive our sins. I pushed in beside my friend. I whispered, "Louise, receiving Jesus is just as simple as the preacher says." Thus, that night both Louise and I asked and received into our hearts, officially, the Lord Jesus Christ as our personal Savior.

Good Hope was progressing, but still our church boasted no baptismal pool. Sunday morning all cars whose owners wished, lined up, and in procession drove to our family's fishing river, the Waccamaw. Cool in spring, we took wraps for warmth after baptism.

Our preacher wore what looked like a white robe over his suit. He waded almost to the river's midstream. While I stood waist deep in water, soft sand giving with each step taken, several people preceded me. I wondered, *how did Jesus feel, baptized by John the Baptist?* For some reason I felt perfect worthiness, and that wasn't like me. Of course I wasn't doing this using Billie Hamilton's strength. This baptism represented what I held in my heart, and that was a wish to live my life, as nearly as possible, like Jesus desired from a poor old sinner like me.

My turn. Our minister held out both hands. He supported and lowered me into the water. "I baptize you in the name of God the Father, God the Son, and God the Holy Spirit." He stood me to my feet.

I'd always heard that when a person accepted Jesus, he had some kind of unearthly experience. The night I chose our Lord, I felt gratitude. Relief. Finally, I'd acted on what engulfed my heart. This morning when the reverend stood me to my feet and water streamed from my body, I remembered how God descended like a dove at Christ's baptism. Suddenly, every goose pimple on my body vibrated. My hair stood on end. Shivers played havoc with my flesh, and not just from cold. That was my "supernatural" experience.

Back at Winthrop, life changed. Instead of plodding through each day, I asked Jesus to show me His way. Even my body felt lighter, and as yet, I still carried around that dreaded "freshman's ten pound-gain!"

Before I left home, already Grandma had eased Mother and Daddy into a better understanding of the Lord, and they discovered that their known world blossomed with their professions of faith. Before long, mentored by Fulton Booth, Elise's husband, and in 'fifty-three, by Robbie Crooks, Good Hope's first full time pastor, my baby brother, Jack, joined the rest of our family on our "Road to Glory." Grandma's words.

Always I had respected and honored Christ's existence, but now He wasn't just mine. I was His. I belonged to Jesus. I had given Him my heart.

Chapter 14

Aunt Minnie

May, 1952, home for summer vacation, I couldn't believe I had actually survived my sophomore year at Winthrop. Not a lot had changed on our tobacco farm. Mother and Daddy were still working like crazy to make it through another year of tobacco gathering. Jack, almost fifteen, was a tenth grader, and Grandma: she was just as sweet and kind and entertaining as ever; but, by now, arthritis was taking its toll. Grandma had trouble walking from living room to kitchen. That spring I had sung with my Winthrop choir in nearby Georgetown. A tall girl (We had no boys at Winthrop.) and a short "Billie Faye" sang Bastien and Bastienne, a two-role opera written by Mozart at the age of twelve. I was glad that hearing me sing in Mozart's opera thrilled Mother, but I so missed seeing Grandma Nettie beaming out her smile.

Actually, Grandma wasn't the sickest person in our family. Next door Aunt Minnie, widow of Grandpa Hamp's baby brother, Otto; Una, Myrtie, Leo, and Bertha Mae's mother; wife of Bertha Mae's dad, Leon Harrelson; *my* Aunt Minnie lay sick unto death. I pitied Aunt Minnie's three grandchildren: Linda, Aunt Minnie's smart, lively, only granddaughter, along with blonde, curly-headed Phil, about ten these days, and Joe, Myrty's brown eyed baby boy, slightly younger than Phil.

All my life Aunt Minnie made an impact on my existence. Visiting her often, with or without Grandma, I wondered how she kept Grandpa William Hamilton's hundred year-old farmhouse so immaculate. No matter what time of day, my next-door aunt welcomed us like she was a lady of leisure. Yet, not a smidgen of dust could be seen anywhere. Vases, pillows, anything atop mantels, tables, couches, chairs, they all knew where they belonged and stayed there! Sometimes I thought Grandma visited early in the morning, just to catch Aunt Minnie cleaning. And not only her house looked spotless. Back home Grandma would tell Mother, "Here it was, early Monday morning, and Minnie looked like she'd just stepped out of a band box!" Any week day Aunt Minnie powdered her face as becomingly as Grandma did hers Sunday mornings.

Probably Bertha Mae's mama's best feature, passed on to all three of her daughters, were her brown eyes. Just as attractive was her white hair swept back in shiny waves and twisted into a neat, back bun. Grandma envied Aunt Minnie that hair. She said about herself, "No matter what I do, my hair will never be white and shiny like Minnie's."

Aunt Minnie was a tease. We all knew that Leo liked a whole family of Blackwell girls. We never knew which one. All we heard was "them Blackwell girls across Bug Swamp Leo can't stay away from." One Sunday Bertha Mae and I were invited to Brookgreen Gardens on a picnic. Our dates expected us to furnish the food. Bertha and I made peanut butter and jelly sandwiches. Enough said about that. I believe Bertha Mae's date was James Earl, the fellow she later married in spite of those puny sandwiches.

Our fellows were late. Aunt Minnie, Leo, and Harrelson all sat around in porch chairs, marking time with Bertha and me. Aunt Minnie said, "Girls, where are those boys? They should be here already. They may never come! Poor Billie Faye. Poor Bertha Mae." Aunt Minnie sniffed like she was crying. She said, "James Earl, if you ever is a'comin' do come on!" She repeated that, probably six times.

Now, with Bertha Mae's mama desperately ill, I wished we could return to that summer Sunday. Today, all of Aunt Minnie's family, including the Hamiltons, the Stevens, the Goodyears, the Sarvises, the Lees, everyone kin to Aunt Minnie crowded nearby. I joined them, hoping I could find some way to help. At just the right, or wrong moment, I walked into their kitchen.

Certainly I had hung around our kitchen. I stirred custards for Mother's pies. I put on rice to boil. I made potato salad. But never, alone, had I cooked an entire meal, and by the looks of people in attendance, an army of hungry relatives roamed Aunt Minnie's house and yard. Her younger sister, Bertha Mae's Aunt Bertha Lee, saw me standing idle. "Come here," she beckoned. "I've already made tea. You warm up these vegetables." She indicated some peas and corn neighbors had brought. "What I really need you to do, fry this chicken, cook a pot of rice, warm the vegetables, bake biscuits, and set the table."

Wow! She left the kitchen and I stood stock still for a bare moment before taking out a pan full of cut up chicken, which I salted and peppered before looking for flour. Two or three people opened the door, but left when they saw just me.

Finally, I located pots and pans, grease, etc., and found myself elbow deep into cooking. I dredged chicken with flour before dropping each piece, popping and snapping, into hot grease. I boiled rice the required fourteen minutes Mother said rice took to soften. I warmed up the vegetables. Just when I felt overwhelmed for sure, Bobbie Hamilton, another cousin, popped in. "Bobbie," I said, "set the table. Put ice in the glasses."

She said, "For how many?"

"For as many as there are places at the table." At Aunt Minnie's a long table stretched almost the length of the kitchen. Probably it had been hand-built by Great-Grandpa, the Reverend Bill Hamilton, this house's originator, as well as the progenitor of all blood members of Bug Swamp's Hamilton family.

Oh, my land, I thought. I had forgotten to make biscuits. Not that I really knew how. I'd watched Grandma. I'd even practiced rolling out biscuits; but, no way did I trust myself.

On a pantry shelf I spied two loaves of bread. Grabbing the butter dish from the refrigerator, I buttered each slice, stuck them together, and placed the loaf in the oven. No biscuits for Aunt Bertha today.

Somehow or other, I cooked that meal. My first one ever, it must have been edible, 'cause I heard no complaints. Not that I listened for any. I got out of there as soon as enough diners arrived to fill places set.

Sad to say, Aunt Minnie died. After the funeral everyone left Bertha Mae, Leo, and Bertha Mae's dad, Harrelson, home alone. I told Mother, "I'm spending the night with Bertha Mae." We slept in Una and Myrtie's bedroom they'd left to their sister when those two married Randolph and Benny. Bertha and I spent a sad night, talking about how things use to be, and how old we were now. Poor old Leo sat on the back porch bench and Harrelson propped his feet on the bannister out front before each took to his bedroom.

Bertha Mae said, "Myrt and Une understand Mama's leaving us. But wonder how Phil and Joe feel, knowing their grandma's gone? And Linda. She was Mama's first grandbaby."

What could I say? "The boys will always know they had a loving grandma. She'll be their best memory. And Linda ...." That's when I stopped. I couldn't imagine how I'd have felt today, saying goodbye to Grandma Nettie. I never finished my sentence.

Later that summer I worked at Lloyd's Restaurant at Myrtle Beach and saw little of Bertha Mae. Not too long after that she married James Earl Johnson. On one of my trips home from Winthrop I went to see their first child, a beautiful little blonde whirlwind named Kathy. They started their family long before I felt grown-up.

Chapter 15

Love! And Death

In his poem, "Locksley Hall," Alfred, Lord Tennyson states, "In the spring a young man's fancy lightly turns to thoughts of love."

That said, I'll tell you how I met *my* love. March tenth, 1953, fate, really God, willed that I travel from Winthrop College to Clemson, South Carolina. "Billie, this year you'll go on both tours," Miss Katie Pfohl, our choir director, told me. The first week our choir performed daily in our state's low country. Those stops included Conway, Florence, Georgetown, Charleston, Kingstree, Marion, and Orangeburg. The second week of touring took us to Spartanburg, Greenville, Anderson, Easley, and *voila!* Clemson.

My roommate, Carolyn Tarrant, was daughter of a Clemson textile professor whose students affectionately labeled "Crowfoot." Since old enough to think of such, Carolyn had her pick of handsome military cadets. The least my friend could do was share her largesse. She agreed and arranged for me a blind date. After considerable behind the scenes finagling, Ruel Wilson, (Buddy) from Wampee, South Carolina, located twenty-some miles from my Bug Swamp farmhouse, agreed to accompany Kim Wood, Carolyn's date, and escort me to the Winthrop choir concert in nearby Easley.

Always nervous before a performance, and now, excited about my date, I dressed in my new dress of powder blue. As a surprise, Uncle Hal and Aunt Aline had mailed me a navy blue suitcase, and enclosed in that, a twenty dollar bill, more than enough for my new dress.

The doorbell rang. Time for our dates. Poised at the foot of the stairs and gazing up at me as I descended stood a ravishingly handsome guy sporting thick, brown hair and ocean blue, beautiful eyes. The white of his block C sweater complemented his darkly, tanned skin. My heart raced ahead as I drifted down the stairs to meet my future. Of course at the time I knew naught of that. Buddy says he did, but he knows when to lie.

In Easley, scheduled to sing "The Laughing Song" from *Die Fledermaus*, I feared that, like my brother, this handsome cadet might wish to turn his pockets wrong side out, if he had ever heard of Grandma's remedy for silencing a shivering owl. Apparently Buddy liked me, and, or in spite of, my singing, for he showed up at Winthrop the next weekend.

I met Buddy, March 10, 1953. A few weeks later, Hamp and Lucille Hardee, Aunt Molly's oldest son and his wife, drove to Winthrop. They shocked me. They said, "Billie Faye, Grandma's got little time left. We've come to take you home while she's still with us."

Grandma Nettie. Dying! Their news sent my world spinning. Grandma was as much a part of my life as breathing. She was my sleeping buddy. She baked tea cakes. Always she doctored my constantly skinned knees; she kissed away hurts, real or otherwise. She excited my imagination with tales more interesting than any I'd seen on any big screen. With no Grandma, my personal world could shatter. *Lord, Please!* I prayed. *Help my grandma! Help me!*

I went home and stayed a week. Locked into the final stages of arthritis, Grandma suffered terribly. I could rationalize away none of this.

Easter weekend over, Mother said, "Billie, you've no choice. You have to return to your studies."

How could I leave my sick Grandma?

In that era we had no phone. Lucky for me, Buddy and a fellow Clemson classmate drove by my house on their return to Clemson. They offered to drop me off at Winthrop. I knew this was out of their way, but I accepted.

Time to leave. Accompanying me into her bedroom, Buddy met Grandma Nettie for his first and only time. She lay propped on pillows. Plaited and tied with pink ribbons, her scant gray hair draped across her shoulders like a young girl's. I kissed her soft cheek. "Grandma," I said, "Meet my friend, Buddy Wilson."

Grandma extended her hand, the bones in it twisted by arthritis. Her voice sounded weak, but she managed, "I'm right pleased to meet you, Buddy Wilson."

I said, "Grandma, I have to go back to school; but, I'll see you soon."

Afraid I wouldn't, I needed to get out of there before bursting into tears. Grandma beckoned me near. Blue eyes twinkling, she whispered in my ear, "Little Bushy, I'd rather you marry *that brown boy* than anybody you ever dated."

---Hmm.

Buddy wore a chestnut brown shirt, and like always, for he was an Ocean Drive Beach boy, his skin looked darkly tanned.

The next weekend Carolyn drove the two of us to Clemson, and with Buddy and Kim, Carolyn's beau, we attended a campus production of "The Student Prince." Back at Carolyn's, Mrs. Tarrant met us at the door. Her eyes spoke before she did. "Billie, your grandma's with Jesus."

I have decided that God weaves humor and purpose, sometimes both, amidst sorrows as well as life's pleasures. On March 10, 1953, I met Buddy Wilson. A month and eight days later, having stated that she preferred I marry Buddy over any other, Grandma Nettie died.

I John 4:8 shares with us, "God is love." I take John's statement as "law and gospel!" I believe that Father Almighty maneuvers His creations to their inter-twinings, sometimes in ways mystically humorous. A long line of ancestors, Hamiltons, Holmes, Todds, Williams, Royals, Allens, McNabbs, Hardees, Mansfields, La-Pierre's, all brought me a love of singing, and without that, never would I have toured with the choir to Clemson and have met my future husband. God set us both into the same time and space. With one foot already in the beyond, Grandma saw Buddy and me in our possibly predestined niche, and she told me, "Marry that brown boy."

After graduating from Winthrop, then teaching English for a year at Wampee, South Carolina, and after Buddy fulfilled his two-year service obligation to Uncle Sam, on Sunday, August 21, 1955, I married "that brown boy," and I'm glad I did.

Grandma drew her last earthly breath my junior year at Winthrop, and, biblical or not, after her Good Hope funeral service, I felt she returned with me to school. For so long Grandma had been unable to attend church, certainly none of my performances. At school I had sung in Minotti's opera, *The Telephone*. Mother and Daddy drove to Winthrop for that, but not Grandma Nettie. Bedridden for some time, she missed our Winthrop Choir's Georgetown and Conway performances. After Grandma died, on Winthrop's next musical agenda was our Alumni May Day festival. Watching performers dance around a May Pole, I whispered, "Enjoy this, Grandma," confident that swaying with me and singing along to our group's "Welcoming May" songs, Grandma's smile would stretch so wide her gold tooth gleamed. I felt dear Grandma Nettie's presence until early summer brought me home.

That first night, after visiting with Mother, Daddy, and Jack, I crawled into Grandma's feather bed. Alone. I still felt blessed. Closer to heaven. How could I not, with Grandma there?

That same spring, 1953, Buddy graduated from Clemson College and I met his mother, Ople Bell Wilson. I rode to Buddy's graduation with him, his mom, and his friends, Ray and Anne Morton. Later, at the Clemson library, Mrs. Wilson said, "Let's go up to the balcony."

I followed her. We stopped before a sixteen by twenty inch picture similar to a half dozen others decorating a wall. She pointed. "Is there anybody up there you think looks a bit like Buddy?"

Shaking my head, I gazed at all of them. These men belonged to some other century. Still, one fellow had a nice, pleasant face, looking, not unlike Buddy might have that age, wearing the habit of the era. Actually their eyes looked similar.

I picked the right man, but I didn't tell Buddy's mom. She said, "This gentleman is my grandfather, my mother, Maggie Bryan's dad. His name was Lucien Dillard Bryan. After The War Between the States, he represented our county in South Carolina's state government."

I said, "You mean after The Civil War?"

Mrs. Wilson said, "Not on your life. I speak of *The War Between the States.*"

"Oh," I said.

That summer, thank the Lord for Ray Morton. He lent Buddy his car to take me on dates.

Besides Buddy's graduation, in 1953, another blissful event took place. Mother's brother, Mace, ex-German POW, his wife, Louise, and their son, nine year-old Roger Dale, welcomed a baby girl into their family. This was the first child born into Papa Todd's clan since 1944, while World War II busied itself playing world-havoc. I couldn't wait to see our new baby.

Buddy drove Ray's car into our yard. "Let's go," I said.

"Go where?"

"To see my new cousin. This'll be a treat. Babies in my family are all beautiful."

We drove over to Adrian, for Mace, Louise, and Roger Dale lived with Papa, Mama Todd, and Randall.

We coasted into Papa's yard, the one dotted with huge trees, their four-inch high roots meandering over the place like "ever'-which-a-way" intruders. I jumped out and sped up Mama's kitchen porch steps. Buddy followed sedately.

Mace exited Papa's central passage doorway. I asked my uncle, "Where's the baby? Where's little Bonnie?"

Mace said, "In there." He indicated what, in the past, was Papa and Mama Todd's master bedroom.

"Come on," I urged Buddy.

From the kitchen Louise joined us. She led us straight to a frilly pink bassinette. Inside lay a darling little dark-haired, brown-eyed baby girl. I picked her up.

Buddy reached for my bundle. "Gimme." I discovered that if ever there were a baby-lover born in this world, it was my husband-to-be.

A year after Buddy's graduation from Clemson College, in June of 1954, I graduated from Winthrop. One would think that a great occasion. Certainly I was happy to have completed my four year degree.

However, standing in line, wearing a robe and mortar board for my second, and probably last time, I gazed at classmates. Before me were three girls with whom I'd spent so much time at Winthrop, especially our senior year: Carolyn Tarrant, Anne Moore Sisler, and Rhoda Spears, my room-mate and suite mates. They made college life especially memorable. How could I accept parting with such close buddies? On numerous weekends Anne took me home with her to Charlotte. I adored her mom and her dad, a retired railroad man, and, "Wow!" How I enjoyed eating Mrs. Moore's angel food cake with cream cheese icing! Anne took me to the only night club I'd ever entered, which I left in thirty seconds. That place was brimming with smoke! Anne introduced me to Chinese fried chicken. I could go one and on.

And Rhoda. Thank goodness she was a fellow Conway High School graduate. Back home certainly she and I could get together, as long as Rhoda didn't move away to Timbuctu. She and I had both worked at Adrian for Misters Purley and Kelly Thompkins. A true friend, back in high school she nominated me for "cutest girl in our grade" for our year book. No way did I win that tribute, but I did appreciate Rhoda's gesture.

Then there was Carolyn Tarrant. That she introduced me to Buddy Wilson said plenty about my roommate. Parting with these friends symbolized drastic changes piling on me at once. That summer brought me a sense of completion; but, it also left me perplexed about a future over which I had limited control.

My last year at Winthrop, Buddy spent at Ft. Hood, Texas. Furloughed in early summer, he was soon shipped over the Pacific to South Korea. Army officials said he'd be away for no more than a year, which sounded like forever to me.

Home for the summer, missing Buddy, I pined. I lost my appetite. If Grandma were still around, she'd have said, 'Little Bushy, see Hal!'"

That year it seemed like everyone in Horry County was dying off. About once a week I found myself at the funeral of some friend, relative, or acquaintance. Within twelve miles of our home were Good Hope Baptist, Poplar Methodist Church, where my aunt, Leatha, was buried,

Maple Baptist, Aunt Sally's church, Bayboro Baptist, Aunt Laura's church, and Cane Branch, the church Aunt Molly's family attended.

At one of those funerals, Mr. Heyward Goldfinch, Conway's funeral director, asked if I'd allow their funeral home to sponsor me at Conway's Chamber of Commerce's first tobacco festival contest. Somewhat insecure in the "looks" department, I gave him a resounding "No Sir!"

Mr. Heyward persisted. Probably at the sixth funeral, having little social life and missing Buddy, I gave in to Mr. Heyward's urges. He entered me into Conway's newest, Conway Chamber of Commerce contest, where, for some unknown reason, I became our town's first tobacco queen. My Winthrop singing mentor, Miss Pfohl, derided girls who vied for such titles, and while I appreciated the honor, I wondered how short, stubby Billie Faye placed higher than thirty-five other girls, all prettier. About a month after the contest I discovered that two of the contestants turned out to be students in my new Wampee High School English class!

Miss South Carolina, Rankin Suber, Billie, Conway Tobacco
Queen, Marha Dean Chestnut, Miss Conway, 1954

Walking through Conway, occasionally I imagined people giving me "the eye." I thought they might be thinking, *who picked her for any kind of queen?* But, to be crowned by Martha Dean Chestnut, beautiful Miss Conway, while Columbia's Miss South Carolina, Rankin Suber, stood at my side, I needed to pinch myself. That girl came in second in our country's Miss America contest!

Mother and Daddy said I had worked hard enough in our tobacco fields, I deserved the title. Twice.

Part III

And all thy children shall be taught of the Lord;

and great shall be the peace of thy children.

Isaiah 54:13

All Grown-up

Chapter 16

A New Career, a Sharp Memory

Upon graduating from Winthrop College, I signed a teacher's contract with Hartsville City Schools. My future husband talked me into breaking that contract to teach at the school he attended five years earlier. Two doors from the school, his mother wanted a boarder, and across the Pacific in Korea, Buddy would feel happier knowing his two girls looked after each other.

Twenty miles away, my parents said little about my Hartsville or my Wampee job. They hoped and prayed for the best.

After Buddy left for overseas, I felt lonely. And fearful. Here I was, a twenty-one year-old college graduate expected to fill the shoes of a grownup. How could that be? I still felt like Grandma's Little Bushy.

But Winthrop College declared me an adult. They presented me with a diploma. They said I knew enough to inspire younger minds to learn.

I tried to bolster my confidence. *Girl, you did well, practice teaching. That says something about your readiness.* No amount of appealing to my ego amounted to a plug nickel. If I had to, I'd fall back on "acting." I'd act the part of a teacher, and with the help of Our Good Lord, I'd turn into one, hopefully, a good teacher.

Early on when asked, "What do you want to be when you grow up?" I sometimes answered, "A singer," or "An actress." Mother liked it when, more realistically, I said, "A teacher." A teacher scribbled with snowy chalk on a shiny blackboard. She sat at an impressive desk decorated with an adoring student's apple. She supervised others performing tasks she devised. Like my teachers, I wanted to purse my lips, look down my nose, and say, "Certainly, Philip. You may be excused. Number one, or two?"

If this "number question" sounds puzzling, when I attended Good Hope Grammar School, holding up one finger or two indicated how long a student should take for his or her *outhouse* so-journ.

Growing up just before and during World War II, thanks to pious parents, every Sunday I ensconced myself into a polished mahogany pew at Good Hope Baptist Church, the religious and cultural center of my youth. Ladies in our church possessed at least one trait in common. No civilized woman past puberty pulled on a dress until she had struggled into a girdle, my mother excepted. I marveled that Sister Sadie McBride could somehow manage to bend her knees and plop into the Amen Corner pew without bursting right through the seams of her sausage wrappings. But Clarissa Wright's armored, bean-pole body experienced Sadie's self-same problems. (These names aren't real!) Whether Olive Oyle slim or rain-barrel-rotund, females of our species attending church crammed unyielding bulks into torture garments so binding, neither animal, vegetable, nor mineral could guess what lurked beneath. Some girdles contained vertical strips of whale bone sewn into unforgiving fabric rendering free movement next to impossible. Every Sunday dear Grandma Nettie laced-up her hundred and eleven pounds into just such a thing-a-ma-jig.

The following incident took place at Buddy's Wampee High School where I spent my first year teaching ninth, tenth, eleventh, and twelfth grade English to some students more sophisticated than their teacher. That year all of my classes proved special; but, on the first school day, the eleventh grade class presented me with ...

A Sharp Memory

Here I was, Monday morning, fall of '54, a college graduate "acting" the part of the only English teacher at Wampee-Little River High School. For sixteen years I had prepared myself for this day. *I am all grown up; I can do this,* I told myself, for wasn't the inner-tube-like contraption I wore today the epitome of adulthood? I remember powdering its insides, stepping into the girdle, then tugging, yanking, until, finally, the aggravating retainer settled into place, rendering all softness *almost* impenetrable.

Superintendent Brown kept new teachers in his office, explaining procedures until the bell for first period sounded. Teachers should never be tardy on their first day! I rushed to open the class room door, instantly aware that thirty-two pairs of young eyes pinned me to the black board. Carefully I placed my books onto an apple-less desk. A thought struck my brain. *If this were five years ago, Buddy Wilson could be sitting in that front row seat.* I desired nothing more than to bolt for the door.

Lord, help me now, I thought. From somewhere came *you're the teacher!*

That day I wore my impenetrable, inner-tube girdle beneath a pleated, pink plaid skirt. Steeling myself for a session with a group most likely preferring Myrtle Beach's pearly strand to this classroom, I smoothed my skirt and sat down at my desk.

The name heading this eleventh grade roll book: "Bob Anderson!"

"Here," a hoarse voice erupted from a wee lad, his nose supporting spectacles that dwarfed his face.

"Addie Bass!"

"Present!" I glanced at Addie, an older looking brunette who looked like she'd prefer being some-place else.

"Betty Cox."

A diminutive blonde sang out, "Here!"

That's when I distinctly felt something pierce my derriere. The jab wasn't painful, just sharp, like a slight pin prick. I moved in my chair. The prick became prickier.

"Leonard Dawsey."

"Here, teacher." This tanned, shaggy-haired young man grinned from ear to ear. "You feel good today, teacher?"

"Fine, Leonard. Thank you."

"Hazel Gore."

"Here."

What a pretty girl. Dark, curly hair, hazel eyes, like her name.

"Teacher!"

"Yes, Leonard!"

"You sure you feel okay?"

When I failed to answer promptly, he arose, paper in hand. "I got a poem to read."

How strange. "Later, Leonard."

All enrolled students had answered "Present." In my new teacher voice, I instructed, "Everyone, get out paper and pencil. Your first assignment: write a one page autobiography. Tell who you are, how you spend your time, your favorite books, and your future aspirations." Earlier I had written those topics on the board.

The second lad sitting in the first row raised his hand. "Teacher, what's an aspiration?"

I shot a glance at my roll book. "Tony, an aspiration is whatever you wish to be, to do, or to become. Is that clear? Twenty minutes from now, pass each paper to the front."

Leonard Dawsey stuck up a finger. "You said I could read my poem later. Is now, later?"

I shoved back my chair. Pain definitely jabbed my bottom. "Okay, Leonard." I squirmed, seeking a different sitting angle. "Read your poem."

Lily Sellers volunteered, "Leonard writes one for every occasion."

Leonard grinned, shuffled from one foot to another. He read:

There once was a teacher brand new.
She may have bit off more than she can chew.
She came to the beach
Said here she would teach.
She didn't know our school was a zoo.

"Thank you, Leonard. You've written a limerick. A five-line poem."

"It's got five more lines." Leonard continued to read from what looked like a bare page. That boy was composing on the spot.

The teacher that's with us today
Deserves all she gets for her pay.
I don't know her yet,
But I'm willing to bet,
She's got very thick skin.
I'll say!

Half the class howled, slapping their thighs. Certainly I knew why. In the chair seat beneath my bottom I felt for the tack. Packed to the hilt, it had plunged all the way through my girdle, into me. Smiling, I surreptitiously removed Leonard's surprise, slipping it into an open drawer.

"Good job, Leonard." I hoped he thought I meant the poem.

The students wrote their autobiographies, complete with aspirations. Hopefully most of them became first class citizens. Young Leonard grew up and by now has probably retired from the popular beach golf club he spent his life managing. I wonder if over the years, he composed lines to messy divots, odes to sweeping greens, maybe limericks to neophyte golfers.

For me, my memory of the tack incident could have been much sharper (shades of weatherman, Al Roker) if not for my *nearly* impenetrable girdle!

Later, hearing about shenanigans Buddy Wilson and his school chums played on Wampee's hapless teachers, I felt blessed that my guy was two years older than this old gal, for my fashionable girdle hadn't risen to its height of fashion until the year before.

Part IV

Genesis 2: 24

Therefore shall a man leave his father and his

mother, and shall cleave unto his wife . . . .

Chapter 17

In the Beginning

On Sunday, August twenty-first, 1955, Rev. Robby Crooks preaches a stirring sermon on commitment. Afterward, Ruel Wilson, locals call him Buddy, and I stand before Good Hope Baptist Church's altar, and vow to each other our lasting commitments. We are the first couple married in Good Hope's beautiful, new sanctuary.

Daddy, Mother, Buddy, Billie Faye,
and Jack, after the wedding

After a brief stop at my Maid of Honor, Bobbie Hamilton's home for pictures and refreshments, Buddy leads me to his car. I kiss my sad mother and dad goodbye, settle into the car, and look straight ahead. "Whew!" I breathe.

"What's wrong with you?" my new mate asks.

"I just wish Mother and Daddy could be happy for me. It's not that they don't like you. For some reason they just hate to see me married. Actually, it's Mother. She always has wanted me to be 'a career woman.'"

"You're not sorry you married me, are you?"

"No way, Hosea!" I feel a decided lift in mood.

My new hubby and I head toward Ashville, North Carolina, where we spend our first night as man and wife at The Hamiltonian Hotel. Wonder why we chose that spot? Next morning we head for The Skyline Drive. After a night or two spent in tourist cabins along the way, and a day spelunking, about two a.m. the following Thursday morning Buddy and I end up on the Washington D.C., National Capitol's steps.

Where are America's citizens? On our pre-dawn visit in 1955, General/President Dwight D. Eisenhower's Capitol building, seemingly is reserved for just us two. We marvel. Besides Mr. and Mrs. Ruel Leston Wilson, Jr., no other beings are in evidence, not even security guards.

A week or two after returning home an old married couple, to Buddy's '53 Chevy Bel Aire, he and I hitch a trailer packed with everything both would hold, and take off for upstate Clemson College. Buddy is beginning a graduate program with Clemson's Agriculture Department, and I have signed a year's contract to teach at the nearby town of Seneca, South Carolina.

That afternoon finds the two of us following a car driven by Buddy's new faculty advisor, Dr. Cecil Godley. He leads us via a back road connecting Clemson to South Carolina's historic town of Pendleton. Parts of the drive are paved; other sections a mixture of fly-away dirt and crushed rock. Above our heads trees make leafy contact. In and out of vision, South Carolina's Oconee River meanders between red banks of clay.

I slide to the center of our Chevy Bel Aire's wide, front seat. Cozying up to my new mate, I gaze at his straight nose, his strong hands on the steering wheel, his left hand's little finger, missing from a tractor accident occurring years ago. He has told me, on our first date my nonchalant reaction at seeing his hand missing a finger impressed him.

Our car emerges from the woods. A cloud of dust obscures any view.

Dust settles. Eyes wide, I lean forward. On a slight incline beyond the gate, a white doll house claims its site amidst green pastureland. Beyond the house looms a silver barn, fences, a herd of wooly sheep.

Wide eaves shelter a cement front porch. Windows return our gaze. Trees invite us closer. Through a side door Dr. Godley leads his new college shepherd and me into our first home together.

Though on that day I lack the gift of foreknowledge, for the next seven years I'll greet my husband at that door, when he returns from work, from classes, maybe from an afternoon of golf. Our first two children, born here, will rush to the door at the "clop-clop" his feet make, stomping red, Piedmont clay from work boots, before he steps onto a linoleum floor I insist be waxed weekly. Never mind that Clemson Tigers play football games on Saturday. Never mind our hectic schedules, his as graduate student and college shepherd, mine as a seventh and eighth grade middle school teacher. The sheen on that floor is hard to maintain!

As we enter the side door of our 27' by 27' cottage, I won't know that one day in the not-so-distant future, my husband will yell at me louder than that door slams. His aqua eyes smolder. "What is it you want from me? A divorce?" All because I need to spend my Saturday "football" afternoon waxing black and white asbestos tile, and he is determined we'll both cheer his precious Tigers to a victory!

Back to that day of Moonlight and Roses: Dr. Godley tells us we're lucky to be the first residents of Clemson's sheep herder's cottage. "This house is my baby." Pride lights his eyes. "I designed it and I supervised its construction." Through the side door, he leads us into a hallway, blunted on the end by a minuscule bath. To the door's immediate right an unenclosed coat-closet awaits. On the left wall, doors open to two bedrooms, one about 10' x 12', the other smaller. Between the bedroom doorways another open closet, that of shelves, awaits towels and sheets.

The opposite half of our new home consists of living room and kitchen. Mostly kitchen.

Soon, we've unloaded a hand-me-down maple bed-frame, dressing-table, and clothes chest, all painted ivory, *brush wielded* by my new mother-in-law, "Mrs. Wilson." We place these pieces, together with an old-fashioned bedspring and WPA manufactured cotton mattress, *stitched by* Mrs. Wilson, into the smaller, green room. Our luxurious foam mattress lies on the floor of the master bedroom. I call out, "Buddy!" listening for an echo. My voice ricochets off walls and hard tile floor like in a canyon.

When we finish unloading the trailer, every room but our bedroom is complete. Hopefully the remainder of our furniture will be shipped in a few days.

Before we marry, to finance this momentous life venture, Buddy mortgages his green Chevy Bel Aire for $900.00. With that cash we eke out our Blue-Ridge Parkway-Skyline Drive venture to Washington D.C., buy a couch, refrigerator, stove, and blonde Honduras mahogany bedroom suite. The studio couch opens into a creased-in-the-middle bed, which Buddy and I share when we have company. We allow guests to sink into our receptive, foam mattress. Buddy's Great-Uncle Tom, on an expedition through South Carolina and Georgia visiting various Primitive Baptist Churches founded by *his* Uncle Tom, raves about his night's rest on our foam bed till the day he dies.

Covered in tiny red and yellow flowers, our couch presents a cheery look. Enhancing the room's brightness, I buy white sheers for the space's single window as well as for the front door window. Concocted for me by last year's Wampee/Little River High shop boys, a tiered bookcase, slanting south, lends a practical touch to our living area.

Inspired, I ponder Grandma Nettie's, now ex-peach-colored, Damask, story-telling chair, the one that sat beside the parlor window in the chimney jam' of our Bug Swamp farmhouse. Newly upholstered in flaming red herculon, Grandma's chair is a perfect match for the red flowers in our living room couch. An interesting maple chair adorned with golden beige Monks cloth completes our seating.

I still regret tiring of said maple chair and leaving it outside for a month, then hauling it to the dump. On learning this, my mother-in-law howled, "I loved that chair!" Years later, I clearly understand her feelings.

"Fix us some lemonade, Honey?" Today my new mate dares me to act domestic. Tired after unloading our furnishings, he and Dr. Godley relax in our built-in dining nook while I slice lemons we brought in a cooler. About an hour ago the men loaded and plugged in the refrigerator. Obligingly, it has frozen its first ice.

Popping cubes from a tray, I'm unaware that five years from now I'll wake up one morning to discover our precocious eight-month old baby boy, Jimmy, atop this refrigerator. It isn't tall, and a table sits beside it. Once again he has climbed out of his crib. Jimmy laughs and drums pink heels against the door. Another morning I awake to find *no* baby boy in the house! Through the window I spy "Li'l Swee' Pea," drawstring nightie, trailing. He's climbing the gate separating us from our sheep neighbors. I race to save our peanut before old Ralph, a frustrated "checking" ram, finishes the assault on our child for which Ralph's body language intimates he's preparing.

Ralph may be frustrated because Buddy and his cohorts employ the ram to detect ewes in estrous. These graduate students and their advisors are the first scientists in the world to inseminate sheep artificially using frozen semen. They've rendered Old Ralph impotent; but, ignorant of this in mind and body, he thinks himself God's barnyard gift to ewes.

Sorry. I digress. Back to fall, 1955:

Sipping his lemonade, Dr. Godley beams at cabinets painted white, and counter tops crowned with a substance resembling dark, felt paper. (Not my taste!) He says, "I am proud of this kitchen. We got a lot of cooking space from our shoe string budget."

"Yes," I nod enthusiastically. Blinded by newly-wed bliss, I'm convinced of his magic, except for those counter tops.

The first month Buddy and I sink into our new mattress on the floor, because our "blonde Honduras mahogany bed room set complete with bookcase headboard," (salesman's title) takes its time arriving. We stash underwear in kitchen cabinet drawers.

On the day we arrive at Clemson's sheep farm, I'm unable to see our future. Although I have high hopes, I prefer, and mostly get to wear, rose-colored glasses.

My new husband looks after myriad sheep, and I keep a shiny-floored house. Buddy reports to work at Clemson's agricultural department, and I motor over to Seneca, South Carolina, with Margie Tilley and Gene Langdale. All three of us teach seventh and eighth grade core subjects at Seneca High School.

"How many kids do you want?" Buddy asks me.

"Two," I say, not in a hurry for any. I'm still a kid myself.

He says, "Let's have six."

Well, six must be an operative number, for six months after we wed, I find myself "in the family way," my parents' terminology for what is happening.

(Pregnancy belongs in past tense)

Luckily I wasn't one of these expectant mothers who puke before breakfast. However, I had gained more weight than necessary before becoming pregnant. My doctor said, "We'll fix that," and he put me on a strict diet. Saddling me with pills equivalent to today's "speed," he also prescribed seventeen daily vitamins to replace milk, necessary protein, carbohydrates, etc. I lost weight.

Three months before our baby was due, our telephone rang. "Billie, can you come home for a few days?" Mother's controlled voice said something was amiss.

I said, "What's wrong, Mother?"

"Honey, Sally died. One minute she was alive, walking around her kitchen, the next, well, she died."

I was silent long enough to gather my thoughts. "How is everybody?"

"Everybody's sad. Can you come?"

"I'll try. I need to talk to Buddy."

Early next morning we left Clemson for Aunt Sally and Uncle Homer's Maple Swamp community.

For years Daddy's sister had suffered diabetes along with its many debilitations. Her kidneys gave her problems. She developed diabetic neuropathy in her feet and legs. Gangrene in her toes became a worry. Finally, Aunt Sally's heart joined other parts of her body in protest against old sugar diabetes.

In 1953, the same year I met the fellow Grandma Nettie referred to as "that brown boy," Grandma died. Now, three years later, Aunt Sally had succumbed to the disease her mother always feared for her first born.

That day, puttering around in her kitchen, Aunt Sally walked over toward the side front door. That quickly her heart beat its last. If people who said, "Hamiltons fall dead," were still alive, they probably would have tagged Aunt Sally with that same trite statement. In spite of my aunt's heart failure, we knew the real culprit was diabetes, trailing after her since little Sally Hamilton couldn't keep her hand out of her mama's brown-sugar jar.

Still in the era when bodies were brought home so relatives could "sit up with the dead," Aunt Sally lay in her casket in her own living room, in the same spot the family placed their always beautiful Christmas tree. I ventured over to her side. So white, so still, she looked too much like Grandma before her burial. Like every dead person I'd ever seen, with her head flat against the pillow, gravity spread out her face slightly wider than usual, though she still looked like my Aunt Sally, the cheery aunt who made the best of every situation. Her color appeared normal, and soft gray curls framed her face. Goldfinch Funeral Home people were expert makeup artists. I touched the cheek belonging to Grandma's first baby. I whispered, "I'm so sorry you're gone, Aunt Sally. I wish you could be here to see my baby. I'll miss you." I whispered more softly, "I love you, Aunt Sally." Softer still, "I sure did enjoy your creamy grits."

I could have added, "Give Grandma my love." I didn't. Grandma already had my love.

I dreaded seeing Frances Marion. So much sorrow. Of course Aunt Sally was also Leona and Geneva's mother. I hoped I'd never lose mine.

A Bad Lesson

Papa Todd's older brother, Uncle John Frank Todd's daughter, Liza, lived at North Conway with her family. Liza's daughter, my cousin and fellow Winthrop classmate, Jo Frieda Sellers, married and became Jo Frieda Rabon months before Buddy and I tied the knot. After Aunt Sally died, riding down Conway's main street I said, "Buddy! Stop at the next house. I want to see Jo Frieda."

Screeching his brakes to a halt, (Thank goodness no car trailed behind us.) Buddy turned into the driveway of a substantial looking house boasting a full front porch. I jumped out of our car, ran up front steps, and knocked on the door. Jo Frieda, answered my knock. "Billie Faye!" she said, giving me a one arm hug. Her other hand held a spoon.

"Is it a bad time for company?" I asked.

"Not if you don't mind watching me feed my offspring," Shortly, Jo Frieda pushed onto her porch a high chair occupied by a precious, hungry little boy boasting a mop of hair and anxious for his food.

"How's your hubby?" I asked.

"Busy. Like usual. What are you two up to?"

I said, "Can't you see? We're having one of those!" I pointed to her number one fellow."

"When?" Jo Frieda asked.

I said, "In about three months."

That's when her young lad banged on his tray, his way of demanding, "Food!" His mom loaded a spoon and started toward his mouth. Buddy, rubbing his tummy, said, "Mm. Good."

Jo laughed. "Are you hungry too? Maybe we can share."

Watching the young fellow eat, Buddy approached Mother and son. I knew my husband was thinking about our future child. My grown man knelt before Jo Frieda's lad. Grinning and shaking his head, Buddy pursed his lips and blew. So did Jo's little whipper-snapper, and his mouth was packed with food. Cereal, bananas, and whatever else masticated flew straight into Buddy's face.

Jo Frieda popped out of her seat. "I'm so sorry!" She reached for a near-by washcloth.

I said, "Don't be sorry. Just hope your baby boy hasn't learned something new he'll repeat." I added, "Buddy, you got just what you deserved."

On our drive back to Clemson Buddy said, "What're we having, a boy or a girl?"

"One or the other." Not wanting to sound flip, I added, "Grandma said if you're having a girl, you'll have heartburn when you're expecting. Well, I had no heartburn. Does that mean I'm having a boy? Would you like a son?"

"Honey, I want a fine, healthy baby. Boy or girl, I'll be happy."

Three Months Later

What a sunny Saturday morning! Buddy, home for the day, tended his sheep. Old Ralph, his "checking" ram, acted ornerier than usual, and Dolly, a favorite ewe, looked about as ready to give birth as yours truly. Graduate student, college shepherd, and assistant professor, Buddy was busy earning all our living. For months now, I'd skipped teaching, enjoying my "baby" sabbatical.

Buddy spied me hanging out sheets. He shouted, "Billie! The mailman just went by. Go see if my check's in the box."

Our mailbox rested atop a post about as far from our sheep farm home as Grandma Nettie's box was from our Bug Swamp house. The difference was, I could see our Clemson, really Pendleton mailbox across open pasture, while back home, trees took over.

A baby Coming Somehow Pops Me into the Present!

Halfway to our mailbox, I stop short. Grab my belly. Carefully I continue on. No check today. Returning, I wave to Buddy. "Come home," I yell. "I think this is **it**!" Inside the house I tell Mrs. Wilson, "You'll soon be a grandma."

She says, "I already am."

I know that. Four months ago Buddy's sister, Ramona, gave birth to cute little Kenneth Wayne Earnest. Anticipating our baby's arrival, Mrs. Wilson, has been with us all week.

As soon as Buddy gathers his wits, and I perform a few necessities, he picks up my already-packed suitcase, and he, his mom, and I take off for Anderson Hospital, about seven miles from the sheep farm.

I end up on third floor, in room 315, in the bed nearest the door. Nurses pop in for preliminaries. They ask my doctor's name.

I say, "Dr. Hunter."

The nurses eye each other. Shake their heads. "Sorry, Honey. You're out of luck. Today Dr. Hunter is in Maryland with Clemson's football team."

Buddy is a total Tiger fan. At least *he* should have remembered. On football Saturdays Dr. Hunter belongs solely to those Tigers. He's their team physician. Why had I picked that man for my doctor?

Shortly, in comes a brand new face. White clad, Dr. Griffin must be my guardian angel. Mrs. Wilson, seeking to make me comfortable, plumps my pillow. She breathes, "Thank goodness."

Meanwhile pains increase in strength; times apart shorten. "Where's my husband?" I ask a nurse.

"Next door. He's watching the Tigers and the Terrapins." She quips, "Between that game and the baby, I fear we might lose a father."

No laugh from me. Mrs. Wilson finishes my back rub. I barely remember going into delivery. Between pains and whiffs sucked in from some sedative bracelet a nurse buckles onto my wrist and says, "Breathe this when you hurt," I knock myself out. The first voice I hear, Mrs. Wilson says, "Billie Faye! Open your eyes! See this baby!"

I open eyes heavy enough to need a prize pole.

"Isn't she sweet? Look at all that hair. See that pink ribbon?"

Such commotion! I crack my eyes. Everything blurs. Someone's baby. Whose? Mine? Mine!

Mona's Illness

Our baby, Mona Lynne, grew. She became a fifteen month old little girl. "It's time I weaned this child," I told my husband.

His answer, "Past time." In those days (and possibly today?) to hasten the weaning process, doctors gave Mothers a male hormone.

A few days later our baby girl grew listless. Refusing food from any source, she needed a doctor. Dr. Griffin showed me inside her mouth. Administering treatment, he said, "Mona Lynne has what we call a fever blister spread. This bismuth should take care of her problem."

It didn't. A couple of days later, when I called and told him Mona seemed worse, Dr. Griffin sounded urgent. He said, "Meet me at Anderson Hospital."

Immediately, he evaluated her kidneys and ordered fluids administered. He informed us, "This baby isn't drinking enough for proper kidney function."

By morning Mona Lynne seemed even more listless. Fluids given last evening filled her thighs. Icy cold, they looked like overblown rubber tires.

Dr. Griffin took us aside. "In my opinion you should take this baby to Emory University Hospital in Atlanta. Right now they are doing the most extensive kidney disease research in the nation."

My eyes sought Buddy's. My mind cried out, *our baby must be worse off than imaginable.*

While Buddy got together "stuff," I ran down to an empty hospital room. If ever I needed God's help, it was then. I knelt in that empty room and cried out to the only absolute source of help I knew. *"God,"* I sobbed, *"Please take care of our baby girl. We need You as our support. Guide us, Lord. Please don't let our sweet baby hurt. Don't let her suffer, and God, help her to live! In the name of Your son, Jesus Christ, I pray to You. Amen."*

Quickly we returned home for our over-night clothing. Packing lightly, we jumped into our car, and took off for Atlanta. Every minute seemed a count-down to our child's *survival.* I refused to believe otherwise.

We drove and drove. Finally, we closed in on Athens, Georgia. I knew this because we passed a motel called Bull Dawg Inn. City limits did nothing to curb our speed. A trooper's siren did.

"License, please," he stated. "Sir, this is a town, and you were speeding."

"Yes sir. I'm driving as fast as I can. I have to get my baby girl to Emory Hospital. Her life is at stake."

The trooper's face tightened. "Follow me." He jumped into his car and opened his siren full blast. This wonderful man escorted us through Athens, then waved us on. *"Thank you Lord,"* I prayed.

Fifteen years later, we chose Athens as our home town, and forty-two years later, at this writing, it still is.

Driving into Emory's parking garage, we discovered help at every corner. Doctors and nurses shouldered any further responsibility. They made us feel that with God and their hospital staff in charge, we had done our best.

Dr. Talbot, (not his real name) worldwide noted kidney specialist, put Mona into a Demerol induced, comatose state. Weighed twice daily, she received, via a medicine dropper, the exact amount of fluid she expelled through perspiration. For too many days Mona's kidneys failed to function.

Meanwhile nurses sought to make me comfortable. They ordered a regular hospital bed placed beside my baby's.

Sleeping one night, I awoke to panic. Gone. My baby. "Oh God," I breathed, "Let her be all right!" I rushed down the hall to the nurse's station. A vision! In a chair beside the nurse, my precious little Mona lay asleep on a pillow. The nurse said, "Mrs. Wilson, you looked so comfortable, and the baby was breathing so harshly, I brought her here with me."

Limp from fright, I thanked the nice lady and went back to bed.

Lucky for Buddy and me we had relatives in Atlanta. Buddy's cousin, Agnes, her daughter, Bobby Jean, and son-in-law, Bill, lived nearby with their two children. Buddy spent nights with them. Also he made daily phone calls to our parents. Mother was so stressed she developed a rash. Buddy's mom also was stressed to the max.

Meanwhile, in the hospital we met others there with loved ones. A rabbi lay comatose in the room across from ours. His two daughters visited us daily. Needing to let us know they cared, they presented Mona with soft, "baby doll" pajamas, a new style in that era.

Agnes's Methodist pastor, Rev. Charles Allen, renowned in Atlanta and author of many books, visited and prayed with us frequently. From back home at Good Hope, Hezekiah Hardee's research work sent him to Athens, Georgia, and he drove the extra sixty-five miles to Emory to look in on us. He reported back to Mother and Daddy that their granddaughter was resting, and that I looked in control; but, Buddy seemed pretty shook up. I was glad if that comforted my parents. Hezekiah was Grandma's deceased baby sister, Gertie's, son, also Elise and Genevieve's brother.

Meanwhile, my child existed in a coma. No change in sight. On Thursday Dr. Talbot told Buddy and me, "Never has dialysis been performed on a child this young; but if you two are willing, Saturday I'd like to try this procedure on your little girl. However, I still have another trick or two up my sleeve."

One of Mona Lynne's nurses, a young girl seemingly attached to our baby, told me that she had weekends off; but, if Mona were to receive dialysis Saturday, this nurse would ask to assist.

Friday rolled around, and I feared what next day might bring. Holding my baby, I dropped into her precious mouth the few drops of fluid she received each day. I bathed her. I combed her hair. I dressed my limp Mona Lynne in her new baby doll pajamas.

Running out of clothes, I appreciated Buddy's cousin, Agnes. That day I wore a gray, sateen, shirtwaist dress she sent me. Buddy had stopped by a garage on the way over; so, he wasn't with me at the moment. Comfortable and clean in a new dress, I lifted my sleeping baby off her pillow, cradled her in my arms, and prayed that God would take care of her during dialysis next morning.

Suddenly, what in the world? My lap felt warm. Wet. I lifted Mona. On my sateen lap, water glistened. Standing, I raced up the hall to the nurse's station. "She did it!" I cried. "My baby soaked my dress." We made so much noise, people ran out of their rooms. They gathered around us.

It seems Dr. Talbot had given Mona an antidote for bismuth poisoning. Hallelujah! That unlocked her kidneys. Never again have those organs given the child, nor adult Mona, problems.

Saturday arrived with no need for dialysis. Her nurse came anyway. She said, "I need to see my baby."

After seventeen days in a Demerol-induced coma, sudden removal of that substance from Mona's system brought on seizures, frightening us and her physicians. Immediately they re-administered Demerol, gradually tapering her off that medication. What a relief to see our baby on her way to recovery. Only a few more days of strengthening, and doctors deemed our little girl able to return home.

Mona's illness brought Buddy and me fear and dread greater than either of us had experienced. Her doctors told us our baby had less than one chance in a million of recovering from her renal shut-down. However, that scary time also granted treasure. It strengthened our faith, not just in God, but in people: doctors, nurses, clergymen, fellow human beings. Our church family, Clemson Baptist, helped us pay Mona's hospital bill, for in that day we carried no insurance. Our little family felt, and was, truly blessed.

After being so sick for so long, Mona forgot how to walk. Thankfully, she soon remembered. Then, each afternoon after work, as sure her daddy stepped onto our side porch and scraped his feet before entering, Mona's baby feet pattered down the hall to greet him. "Dad-dy!"

Easter, 1957, we loaded up Buddy's Chevy Bel Aire and headed for Bug Swamp. We hadn't been home since Christmas. Pulling up underneath Grandma's double peaked cedar tree, we found no one in sight. Quietly, Buddy and I walked up Daddy's front steps, opened their never locked door, set Mona Lynne onto her feet, and she walked through the house on her own.

Suddenly, we heard "Mona Lynne!" Mother sounded like she might have a heart attack. "Where did you come from? Where are your mommy and daddy?"

"Here we are, Mother," I said, "right behind our daughter."

Resting a while, we took off for Wampee, to see Mrs. Wilson. Twenty minutes later we turned into the yard of the remodeled church where she lived. She ran outside before we could open a car door. Grabbing our little girl into her arms, Mrs. Wilson looked at neither Buddy nor me, not until Mona kicked her feet, squealing, "Mammy!" Finally Mrs. Wilson raised her head. "This baby sounds as good as new!"

"She's fine," Buddy says. "We told her not to call you Mammy, but she'll do it or bust."

"I like 'Mammy.' That's what I called my Grandmother Belinda. I'm just glad my baby is well. Let her call me anything she pleases."

In the parlor we watched Mona Lynne explore her new environment. Mrs. Wilson said, "What an awful time, our baby so sick. Uncle Tom has been going through his own torment. His grandbaby was too sick to live. He told me, 'Ople, here you are, praying for your grandbaby to live, and I'm praying that mine can die easy.'"

After we visited and had a bite to eat, we took off for Adrian, straight to Papa Todd's. Mace and Louise still lived with Papa and Mama. Louise gave birth to Roger Dale in '44, just before Mace joined World War II at Normandy, and for nine years, Roger remained an only child. Then, beautiful, brown-eyed Bonnie graced their lives. When Mona was three months old, Louise gave birth to her second daughter, and Gail Todd was a beauty. What a contest. Instead of beautiful brown eyes like Bonnie's, Gail's looked jet black! And I always envied people with dark eyes.

Actually I thought my Mona Lynne and her blue orbs just as beautiful.

On this trip Mona and Gail got acquainted over a basket of toys. I've never been more thankful to see my baby alive, healthy, and enjoying her cousins. Bonnie was old enough, she kept peace when both little girls wanted the same baby doll.

Always when we visited home, we had two destinations, Good Hope and Wampee. On Easter we streaked over to Wampee, picked up Mrs. Wilson, and brought her back to Good Hope. That way we could be with her, my parents, and go to church. Afterwards we took Mrs. Wilson home, visited Buddy's grandparents, spent the night with Buddy's mom, then next morning, returned to Clemson. Visiting two families and trying to please both on trips home could get mind-boggling.

Visiting Buddy's grandparents, I also got to see his "younger than Buddy" aunt, Loy Ree. I met Loy Ree before knowing Buddy existed. His second to youngest aunt, Doris, in business school at Winthrop, sat at my dining hall table. When Loy visited our school, Doris made sure I got to meet her beautiful sister. Later, at Wampee High, I taught Loy Ree eleventh grade English.

Having zero friends my age in the area, Mrs. Wilson's young half-sister, became a true companion. When my mother-in-law went to Pennsylvania for the birth of her daughter's son (Mrs. Wilson's first grandchild, Kenny) Loy Ree spent nights with me, or I with her. I was scared to stay in Mrs. Wilson's house alone. Also, Loy Ree, another high school student, Joyce Lewis, Sibyl Thompson, a local young married lady, and I sang trios and quartets at various churches in the area. Joyce's brother, Russell, played our piano accompaniment.

Our Second Blessed Event

God gave us Mona twice, once in 1956, and again in 1958. Two years later in 1960, as the Bible says, "heavy with child," I waited until Buddy returned home from Clemson's Agriculture Department. I knew he had arrived when I heard feet scrape on our side porch steps.

Mona jumped up from coloring a caterpillar, purple. "Daddy! Daddy!" She ran into his arms.

At this stage, I was slow arising. Carrying a happy daughter, Buddy approached where I sat in our small living area. "You okay?"

We both considered *the time* close at hand. "I was waiting for you. I figure a walk around the pasture may help."

Buddy said, "Probably won't hurt."

"You and Mona care to tag along?"

"I'm tired. We'll just finish this purple caterpillar. Okay by you, Sugar-foot?"

Mona ran for her coloring book.

Outside in a far corner, Buddy's sheep herd had gathered. I walked to where pasture collided with pines. A warm day, this mid-August Monday afternoon, fleecy white clouds against an ultramarine sky rivaled, they surpassed the white of our sheep. I took a deep breath, immediately feeling a kick somewhere near my rib cage. I had hoped my baby had dropped lower by now. Too close to a grounded covey of quail, I jumped at their rush overhead.

Why couldn't we always have pretty weather, not too hot, not too cold, everyone and everything at peace. Even the drone of a small plane in the distance sounded tranquil.

The drone drew nearer. It hiccupped. It choked. Hand to forehead, I scanned the sky. Fast approaching, ever lower, a small, silver plane touched down between me and our house. I held my breath. Ever lower, that misplaced silver transport continued rolling, way past the sheep barn. Diagonally opposite my stance, across the far range, the plane halted. A man climbed out of the cockpit. He headed toward our house. I got there first.

Holding Mona, Buddy waited in the yard. I grabbed his arm. "What in the world?"

The pilot walked through our gate. "Hello," he stuck out his hand. "I'm Jon Gates. My plane gave out of gas."

We introduced ourselves. "There's a rather large airport at Anderson," Buddy told the man.

"I tried for that, but this pasture looked closer. I was afraid I wouldn't make it to Anderson."

Buddy asked, "Are you from around here? What's your business?"

The fellow yanked off some kind of skull cap. "I'm from Hollywood, California, flying to Florida. I deliver film."

Interesting, but not how I'd planned this day.

By now we had reached chairs near Mona's sand box and swing set. I left the men and took Mona inside, for there were just two chairs beside Mona's swing.

Soon Buddy stuck his head through the doorway. "Be back in a little bit. I'm taking Jon to a motel. He needs to make phone calls."

As if in protest my inner child kicked. Hard.

Next morning, before Buddy returned to his Clemson workday, our phone rang. Answering, Buddy said, "That was the pilot. He needs me to pick him up and go after gas."

"What about your work?"

"I've alerted Dr. Wheeler I may be called away. You know. Your condition."

Before too long Buddy and Jon Gates motored across the pasture in Buddy's Clemson pickup. I watched them gas up the plane.

Jon revved the plane's engine, circled around farther from the nearby grove of trees, stopped the plane, and beckoned to Buddy. They looked to be draining gas from the plane's tank. Again, as far from the trees as possible, the plane re-circled, then, motoring in a straight line, increased its speed. Almost brushing tree tops, it rose into the sky. I let out my breath. Goodbye Jon Gates.

Joining Mona and me in the yard, Buddy said Jon was afraid he had overfilled the plane's gas tank, making it too heavy to take off in such close quarters. Buddy stashed two full gas cans in a corner of the sheep barn, a token of the first excitement happening that Monday, August 15, 1960.

Last night while Buddy helped Jon, I called Mother and Daddy. I told them my time was near, that they should come today. Early evening Mother and Daddy drove up. Mona Lynne would need them when we left for the hospital. My parents settled into our spare bedroom.

About ten thirty that night nature warned me, "This is truly *the time.*"

We called Dr. Griffin. He was out of town; but, young Dr. Hellams became my doctor's substitute. So be it. At Mona's birth I'd met a new Dr. Griffin when he took Dr. Hunter's calls.

Thankful that Mother and Daddy were with us, I kissed my baby girl and said, "Honey, be good for Muh. I'll see you soon."

Mother patted my cheek. She said, "Everything's gonna come out all right."

I said, "You're funny, Mother."

Eyes shiny, Daddy said, "Bye, Little Chu."

Fifteen minutes after entering Anderson Hospital, nurses wheeled me into a room. Shades of Mona's birth, I ended up in the same room, 315, in the same bed, the one closest the door. Deja vu all over again.

In labor with Mona I had sedated myself with that wrist band contraption. After tonight I might have no other babies. I must not miss a second of this miracle.

They wheeled me into delivery. I looked around a room that could have been a shiny kitchen complete with cabinets, tables, and a sink. A harsher pain finished off that thought.

The nurse took my hand. She said, "Push."

"No. Don't push," the doctor said. "I'm putting you to sleep."

I protested. "I don't want to sleep. I want to be wide awake having this baby." Another pain cut me short.

"You won't sleep long. You need an episiotomy."

In no time I'd landed into another world, all around me black, except for a large wheel taking up two thirds of the space. I was the black, the wheel, the space.

The wheel spun. It contained a million spokes, each spoke, the former's opposite. One spoke was black, the next white. Another was good, the following, bad. Next came hate, then love, and so on, for every existence and its opposite in the world. This seemed to continue forever.

Suddenly, "Wake up Mrs. Wilson."

"What? Oh yeah. The baby. What was it, girl or boy?"

"Neither yet. You were under just a couple of minutes. Now, push!"

I pushed, till I felt veins pop out on my forehead. Still I pushed.

"Here it comes," said a nurse. Then, I heard, "Waah!" And the doctor said, "You've got you a boy."

The next instant, beside my bed a tiny body dangled, heels held by the white jacketed deliverer. And did that doctor ever spank my precious baby! I said, "Doctor! You can spank him. Don't kill him!"

"Nurse, get me a clean jacket," the doctor ordered.

I thought, *just because you've delivered my baby, you want a clean jacket?*

I watched as the doctor took this jacket and wrapped it around my baby, still wearing everything that clings to a newborn before he's bathed. Dr. Hellams opened a door close at hand, and I heard him say, "Mr. Wilson! Greet your new boy."

From the time I reached the hospital at close to 11 o'clock Tuesday evening, only two hours and twenty minutes passed before I gave birth. This fortuitous event took place on Wednesday, August 17, 1960, at 1:20 a.m.

Back in the same room and bed as with Mona, I took into my arms my new son. He seemed hungry, gnawing on his small fist; but, today I had nothing in my breasts for the poor thing. Soon the nurse brought him a bottle of water. I hoped sucking on that made my sweet little tyke feel better.

Already I was in love. I examined my boy from head to toes, counting all ten, also his fingers. No mama had ever been more blessed. His perfect little head looked like he had been to a barber, and I was used to seeing newborns wearing so much hair they already needed a haircut. I looked into his bright blue eyes and thought, what *is your* name, little one?"

James. James sounded substantial, even dignified. But I wanted to tack on something belonging to me.

Buddy pushed open the door. "Here's your son," I said. "Say hello to James Hamilton Wilson."

Buddy held the baby close, then farther away, eyeing him. "Hey there Jimmy," his dad said.

Later, nurses changed shifts; here came a new nurse with my boy. She placed him in my arms.

I eyed this baby. He looked different. I couldn't help disappointment descending. That's when the woman behind the curtain in the room's second bed said, "This baby's not mine!" She pushed the button for the nurse.

I checked my baby's bracelet. "This baby's not mine!" I told the woman, "Looks like the nurse gave me yours."

So that's how babies got mixed up in hospitals.

Friday was going-home day. Mother, Daddy, Mona Lynne, and Buddy drove up to the hospital's exit. In a wheel chair, waiting in a grassy side yard, I cuddled my baby boy. My nearly four year-old little girl popped out of our car. She raced over. I pushed aside blankets, revealing Mona's brand new baby brother. She touched his cheek, and smiling big, said, "Hey there, Peanut." For a while, that name stuck.

Before going to the hospital Mother had cooked a pork roast. Back home, we deposited a sleeping Jimmy into his bassinet and sat down to dinner. "Mona," I called, "Come eat."

I heard a grunt. In the doorway stood our baby daughter, arms filled to overflowing with her "Peanut."

"Take him," Mona gasped. "Quick."

Our son, Jimmy, came into this world, September 17, 1960, also the birthday of his Grandma Ople Wilson's beloved younger brother, O.J. Bell, Jr.

Part V

Chapter 18

Memories, Heartfelt

Memories carefully stashed can slip through crannies, emerging on butterfly wings and warming the heart, or they can bam the noggin like a whack from a sledge hammer. Remembering Mother's last Christmas brings on an especially painful blow from that hammer.

In 1962, when our baby boy, Jimmy, was two years old and our daughter, Mona, six, we moved to Blacksburg, Virginia. In 1965, we again relocated, this time to Bowie, Maryland. A year earlier, by Jimmy's fourth birthday, Mother's doctor visits sky-rocketed. She complained of pain, of fatigue. Because of her kidney ailments, physicians said she should lift nothing weighing over ten pounds. That meant, when we visited home, she was not supposed to lift her young grandson.

Normally on our visits home, Mother delighted in motoring her grandchildren around their Bug Swamp farm on Daddy's John Deere tractor. She'd drive down the field road past Peter Rabbit's briar patch, home to several snakes; to Daddy's fish pond around which Venus fly traps grew. Mother and her grandchildren would seek out wild flowers to pick; maybe they'd spy some wild cat, peeking out from the edge of the woods. Sometimes, driving our children around on that tractor, she'd share with them Bug Swamp's wonders for over half a day.

Just before our first mid-sixties visit home, Mother called us at Bowie. She asked me, "Billie, do aches and pains normally come with age?" Mother was fifty-two.

A friend advised, "See a chiropractor." She did. Making a routine adjustment, the chiropractor cracked two of Mother's ribs.

By December, 1967, our family had adjusted to life in Maryland's relatively young city, Bowie. Forty thousand people populated this Washington D. C. bedroom-community. Commuters filled our highways, for our home sat in a hub, 17 miles from Annapolis, 17 miles from Washington D.C., and 35 miles from Baltimore. Studying early computer science and genetics at Blacksburg, Virginia, Buddy had completed studies at VPI. Now he worked as a biometrician at ARS's headquarters in Beltsville, Maryland. Jimmy, a first grader, and Mona, in fourth grade, attended Tulip Grove Elementary, a school directly across the street from our residence. Buddy's mom kept house for us, and while I taught middle school core subjects at Greenbelt, Maryland, a stone's throw from The University of Maryland, after school Mrs. Wilson looked after her grandchildren, Mona Lynne and Jimmy.

Finally, 1967's December vacation materialized. Our family packed up clothes and Christmas gifts, and took off for South Carolina. Between radio commentators' talks about ours and Russia's conquests of space, of Christian Barnard's recent transplant of a human heart, and of all the controversy over the Vietnam War, none captured my attention. My heart and mind brimmed with thoughts of spending Christmas with family.

Close to midnight, we arrived home. Next day I thought Mother looked and functioned much like usual. On our second afternoon, she nursed "a sick headache." All my life I'd lived through Mother's aggravating migraines.

Christmas morning, after our small breakfast snack, Mother sat around with the rest of us. We watched our children goof around with gifts from Santa, reminding us of our own Christmases past. Soon, Mother, along with other family members, finished preparations for our holiday dinner. Almost mid-day, while scrumptious food beckoned from the kitchen, twenty eager relatives, including Mrs. Wilson, Buddy and I, our two kids, Jack and Marcie plus their kids, Mother and Daddy, the whole Todd family, all of us dragged chairs, sofa, and stools into an oval circle. Jack and Marcie were there to exchange gifts, but were leaving afterward to have dinner with her parents.

By now our family had grown large enough, we drew names. Amid giggles, joking, and happy Christmas banter, Jack, Randall, and Roger Dale, Santa's elves, distributed an assortment of colorful gifts. Of course Mama Todd took longest opening hers, a blue and white flannel nightgown from Mother.

"Ready, everybody?" Our "band," this time Mace, Jack, and Randall, produced guitars. Grinning, Randall lit into his introduction to a Christmas tradition, our version of "The Twelve Days of Christmas," each with his or her own solo part. Mother chimed in with the rest of us. Her alto voice rang out sweet and true. Afterward, she and others spread the table with special goodies each brought along.

In their five-year-old bungalow, Mother's kitchen wasn't large enough to seat everybody. Filling our plates, we returned to our seats in the living room.

Tempted by roast turkey, dressing, sweet potato soufflé and "all the trimmin's," I could hardly wait "to chow-down!"

Mother's blessing was short. It went something like, "Thank you Lord for Christmas, for family and friends. Take care of us throughout the coming year. In Jesus' name we pray, Amen."

Echoing her "Amen," I said to Buddy, "I'm ready for some of that potato soufflé."

That's when I noticed our hostess leaning against the wall. I said, "Mother! Load your plate. Eat! This looks good!"

Mother took a deep breath. Letting it out slowly, she said, "Sorry, y'all. I have to lie down."

We looked at each other. I thought, *you worked too hard cooking this dinner. I should have known Mother shouldn't do this much.*

Our holiday vacation stretched from Christmas Day till January first, 1968. Most of that time Mother kept to her bedroom.

Usually Daddy was the poor-health person. He suffered ileitis, referred to these days as Crohn's disease. On this trip I noticed he barely voiced a complaint. Naptime the day before leaving for home, I pushed open his door. Wide-eyed, he stared at the ceiling. I said, "Tell me the truth, Daddy. How bad is Mother? What do you think is wrong?"

Daddy sighed, then met my eyes. "I don't know. Neither do the doctors." His mouth worked. Fear tinged his huckleberry blue eyes, so like Grandma's. "I'm scared, Little Chu." He raised up and sat on the bed's edge. "Forget I said that. Things'll work out. They have to. Remember? Ma always said, 'Don't borrow trouble. Have faith. Rest in the Lord.'" Tears puddled his eyes. "I sure as the Lord hope I can find my way to that place."

I hugged the original man in my life.

Imprinted on my brain is a vision of Mother the morning we loaded our car for home. Inside their front doorway, clinging to Daddy and wearing a short, tan and brown, amber striped jacket over blouse and skirt she created, Mother waved us a pale, teary-eyed goodbye. At that moment my mind snapped her image as plainly as would have a Kodak camera. I experienced a dread felt few times in my life.

The two miles from home past the county's chain gang prison camp toward our highway exit, I squirmed in my seat. Finally, I blurted it out. "I'm worried about Mother."

My husband stared at the road, never saying, "Don't be." And *that* worried me, for Buddy considered me an alarmist.

Back in Maryland, teaching seventh and eighth graders at Greenbelt Middle School, I continued to worry. At first I called home weekly, for phone calls cost money. Later, hang the cost! I called daily. I yearned to hear Mother say, "Sugar, I'm a lot better." She didn't. Somebody had to do something.

"Mother," I said, "Go to Florence; see a better doctor. You cannot go on like this." She had seen every physician at or near home. Sixty miles north, Florence Medical Clinic had the best reputation around.

Mother took my advice. About the time I expected her to return home from Florence our phone's ring sounded like a fire alarm. "Mother! What did the doctor say?" My heart drummed so loud in my ears I could hardly hear her answer.

"He says I have something called Multiple Myeloma."

At last! Mother's illness had a name. "What's that?"

"I don't know, exactly, but this doctor says I need to go to Charleston's Medical Hospital. They might can help."

The relief I'd felt vanished. *Might help!* "Why go there?"

"Now, don't you worry. I'll be fine!"

I dropped the phone and grabbed a medical book: *Multiple Myeloma. …Cancer…*

Cancer! I read ahead. Cancer of the plasma in Mother's blood.

First of all, the word, cancer, set off my alert gongs. And multiple meant many. *Many* cancers? *Oh Lord,* I prayed. *Don't let my mother die!*

So, after experiencing years of weird symptoms: anemia, loss of energy, aches and pains unlike any Mother had ever known, protein in her urine, fragile, broken bones, that's how her ordeal was identified.

For expediency, Jack and Marcie bought a station wagon and moved Mother and Daddy to their home in Savannah, Georgia. Once a week they loaded my sick mother onto a stretcher, placed her into the back of their station wagon, and drove her the hundred miles to Charleston. There she received radiation and chemotherapy treatments. Either the treatments or the disease immobilized her spine. Whichever, in a couple of months Mother could no longer walk.

My sister-in-law, full of her second child, was to give birth in April or May. That coincided with Easter vacation. Our family packed up and headed for Savannah.

I had just bought a soft, *brown*, cashmere overcoat. Luckily Georgia's weather was cool enough I could model it for Mother. Usually she made nearly everything I wore, mailing me a box of "Dottie" creations with each change of season. She would adore this coat. Her favorite color I liked least. *Brown.* But even I loved this coat.

The closer we got to Savannah, the sicker I felt. In my heart I knew a serious illness had mother in its grip; but, never in my wildest could I comprehend losing her.

We pulled into the driveway of Jack's brick bungalow. My six year-old nephew, blonde, curly-headed Jackie, was fast-pedaling his trike up and down the driveway. Daddy met us at the car. He looked drawn. I hugged him. "Where's Mother?" I imagined her looking like she had at Christmas.

"Inside." Daddy led us to the first bedroom on the left. I remember thinking, *the skylight overhead sure does brighten up this place*, trying to feel positive, anything but this stirred up sensation drying my mouth and pummeling my heart.

Mother lay propped on pillows, her dark hair carefully combed and her lips painted fire-engine red, probably her attempt to look cheery. This badge of courage failed its task. My mother looked different. Why? Later Jack said doctors had given Mother radiation treatments, put her on chemo pills, and prescribed a daily dose of Prednisone. That explained her puffy appearance.

I twirled beside her bed. "How's my new coat?"

"I like it. You bought *brown*."

Eyes glazing over with unshed tears, I said, "I bet you want to borrow it." Mother and I wore many of the same clothes despite our height difference.

Both of our children dashed in and hugged *Muh*, their name for my mom. That thought reminded me of Mama Todd's mother, my mom's grandma. Callie William's grandchildren called her *Mud*, their short version of "Mother."

While we were in Savannah, obligingly Marcie gave birth to their baby girl, Lisa Maria. Mona Lynne named her, insisting Marcie change the name on the baby's birth certificate from Lisa Mar*ie* to Lisa Mar*ia*. Unable to sit up and hold the baby, Mother cradled Lisa on one arm, admiring her adorable granddaughter's image in a hand mirror.

During our visit Daddy slept on a cot in Mother's room, caring for her immediate needs. I knew he needed our prayers, as did Mother, Marcie, and Jack. Every day they felt stricken by her illness.

Back in Maryland a peculiar situation kept me sane. At home I constantly worried about Mother. At school, Lloyd Singleton and Chris Barber (not their names) consumed much of third period's class-time. Troubled young lads, they used every technique known to "student-dom" to disrupt my class, demoralize me, and intrude on my teaching. They so filled my heart and soul at school I had little time to think about Mother. At home, consumed with thoughts of her, no way could I worry about them. God looks after his children in mysterious ways.

In Savannah Mother yearned for home. Since summer would soon be upon us, Daddy and I could take care of her there. Every summer my husband spent two weeks at Army Reserves camp, and our children's other grandmother, Ople, not far away, would care for them.

Rounding the curve where Great-Grandpa Bill Hamilton's hundred year-old farm house no longer sat, I moaned, "I can't stand to see Mother so sick." Nothing prepared me for realities. I opened our front door. A hospital bed hugged the spot belonging to Mother's beige sofa, and in the bed lay a woman I failed to recognize. This deformed-looking person had huge tumors, golf-ball size, all over her head, forehead, her face. God only knew where else!

Timidly, I crept to her side. "Hey, Mother." I stood helplessly, afraid that kissing her might hurt.

"You're here." She took my hand.

Seven year-old Jimmy stood on tiptoe at the foot of her bed. He could not hide his horror. "Muh," he choked out, "what's wrong with your face?"

"I don't look good, do I, Son?" Tears lit Mother's eyes. Later she told me she couldn't rid her mind of Jimmy's stricken expression.

Twelve year old Mona Lynne had gotten her first real haircut, ever! Recovering more quickly than her brother or her mom, Mona spun around, patting her bob, I thought, to cover her feelings. "Muh, how do I look with short hair?"

"Like me and Leath." Leatha, Mother's younger, only sister, died of Leukemia twenty years earlier. "You look just like we did back in the twenties."

Mona and Jimmy went home with their Grandma Wilson. Buddy took off for summer camp, and I stayed with Mother and Daddy.

Aunt Laura, Daddy's baby sister, along with friends and neighbors popping in and out, kept Mother, Daddy, and me company for most of the next three weeks, as the knots in my stomach cinched tighter. Performing vital household tasks, seeking to care for Mother and make her as comfortable as possible, at the same time worrying myself sick while missing sleep stressed my body mentally and physically. Then came the day Mother's pain escalated so drastically, nothing I did brought her relief. She moaned, "I can't stand this another day."

I thought, n*either can I!*

Ambulance attendants loaded Mother onto their vehicle and drove her back to Charleston Medical Hospital. Soon she and I were ensconced in a room housing two other patients.

Still stressed out beyond belief, at least now I knew when Mother could bear no more suffering, the right pain pills were available, and for the most part, we'd have time to talk.

Mother's words still could bring me up short. One morning after her pain lessened and before lapsing into sleep, she said, "Billie, let's plan my funeral. Here's what I want sung."

"Your funeral! Mother! You are not gonna die!"

"You know and I know: I can't go on living like this."

"But you'll get better. You have to!"

Eyes brooding, Mother lay silent. Then, she brightened. "That's a pretty dress you're wearing."

"Thanks. I made it." The dress was of a yellow, linen-like fabric.

"You *can* sew for yourself, can't you?"

"Sure, just not as well as you."

"I'm glad you've turned into a seamstress!"

"Don't pack away Great-Grandma Madora's old White Sewing Machine just yet," I chided. "I'll need a new suit this fall. Make me something blue. Not brown," I added.

She smiled, slipping off to wherever she went, bypassing pain.

I've never been a person to court controversy; however, watching Mother suffer, waiting for medication the nurses were late providing, I felt my "dander" shoot up. After three bouts of pleading for her medication, I yelled at a faceless, white uniform, "I hope what you were up to the last thirty minutes saved somebody's life. You sure are killing my mother!"

I could have sworn I heard a snicker. Frowning, yet laughing through her pain, Mother said, "I believe some of me rubbed off on you after all!"

While neither of the other two bed occupants in Mother's room suffered unendurable pain, both were seriously ill. The woman nearest the door had stomach cancer. "When you get to where you can't hold down an egg," she said, "that's when you don't much mind saying goodbye to this old world." She pushed herself higher onto her pillow. "Honey, will you roll up my bed, please? I'd call the nurse, but you know how long it takes to get one." As I rolled her higher, she patted my arm. "Don't you mind me none. I didn't mean what I said about leaving this world. I'm gonna hold on to my old life as long as the Good Lord gives me strength."

"I know you will." I poured her a glass of ice water.

The other patient lay beside the window. Miss Hattie, a Marion, South Carolina retired school teacher, suffered from a glandular disorder affecting every organ in her body, including her liver. Her skin as well as her eyeballs rivaled the color of a yellow lemon.

She looked toward her neighbor with stomach problems. "Humph!" she said, "so you can't hold down an egg. Try doing without your pancreas. With me, that's the last thing to go. Doctors said I'd never live this long. Here I am."

Some days Mother joined in those macabre conversations. She told her fellow patients how, a few years earlier, she'd been so fit, she could sucker a whole field of tobacco in half a morning.

During these days of pain, respite, sleep, and more pain, every time Mother felt free enough to talk, she'd say, "After I'm gone . . ."

I'd interrupt. "Mother, hush. You're going nowhere but home with me."

Suffering from his own illness, Daddy called daily. He visited on weekends, driven there by either family members or friends.

"Home is where your daddy belongs," Mother said. "He's too sick to sit by my bed."

One Saturday Grandma Nettie's niece, our fellow quartet member, Elise, drove Daddy to Charleston. "I want to talk to Elise. Alone, please," Mother told me. I knew what she had in mind. She wanted to discuss her funeral arrangements with someone who'd listen.

About a week and a half after arriving at Charleston's hospital, Mother and I sat quietly with Jack and Marcie. That Saturday I was glad Mother seemed relatively free of pain. Suddenly, nurses on either side of a stretcher pushed into the room a small, dark woman. They moved her into the room's fourth bed. When all but one nurse was called to the desk, Marcie went into action. She held the IV bottle while the sole remaining nurse administered drugs. She soothed the injured woman, wildly jabbering in Spanish. For the rest of the afternoon Marcie lavished tender care onto this poor lost soul, unable either to understand a word spoken, or to communicate with her care-givers.

"It's a shame. That's what it is," a nurse muttered. "That whole truck-load of migrant workers. Everybody's injured, and us short of help this weekend."

As far as I was concerned they were perpetually short of help. I bathed my mother; I brushed her teeth; I looked after her bodily functions.

During the three weeks of Mother's hospitalization I left her on two afternoons. Both times I visited Marcie's sister, Norma, who lived nearby. Both absences left me desperate to rush back to the hospital. I think I feared Mother would die before I returned.

Into our third week's stay, her temperature elevated. The doctor ordered x-rays. He took me aside. "Your mother has pneumonia." He looked serious. "In her condition, that's a blessing."

"How? Why is that?" I asked.

"I can treat pneumonia, but unless something takes her quickly, your mother can linger, just like this, for months."

"Please don't let her die, please," I begged.

This doctor, an older, balding gentleman with kind eyes, removed his glasses, and wiped them on his white jacket. He looked out the window, then back at me. Taking a deep breath, he shook his head and left the room. I remembered hearing Mother tell this same man, "Doctor, please help me die easy."

I felt deserted by every ounce of personal reason. I wanted Mother to live, but not like this.

For privacy, nurses moved Mother and me to a two-bed unit, one already housing a sweet old Gullah woman, also terribly ill. She died. Mother lingered.

All week long when young men and women, learning medicine, entered her room, Mother would plead, "Do something to help me." Praying people stopped by and she'd say, "Pray that I'll die. Soon." All told, this was the most depressing period of my life.

On the evening of July 10, 1968, Mother rallied. She talked more than I'd heard her since pneumonia struck. "You know I can't walk," she said.

"I know," I answered.

"When we go home, you earn us a living. I'll get me a wheel chair. I'll roll around all over the house. We'll have us one good ole time together."

She was completely discounting Daddy and my family, but I played along.

"Did you know I'm having a baby?" That captured my attention.

"What? *You're* having a baby?" I couldn't help a sick giggle.

"It won't be long now." Mother remained silent for such a while I thought she'd gone to sleep. Then, her voice lilted like a young girl's. "Let's bake us a cake."

Where was this coming from? "Okay," I said. "What kind shall we make?"

"Chocolate. I'll mix it up; but, you'll have to get me the ingredients. I can't walk," she reminded me. "Look in the refrigerator and get the eggs. Four big ones."

"Here they are; here are your eggs," I pretended to place them on an imaginary counter across her chest.

"I'll need sugar, butter, flour." She paused. "Cocoa. And milk."

"They're right here."

"Pour this batter into three pans. I like thin layers. And don't forget to grease the pans. Then, flour 'em. Dust 'em off."

"Mother," I said, "you think I've never baked a cake?"

It was then she grimaced. "Hurry, Billie Faye. Put the cakes in the oven. The baby's coming."

"Oh my!"

In her pain, we forgot our cake. "Ooh," she moaned. "I think it'll soon be here. Catch it! Catch the baby!"

Shortly, she gasped, "Is it a boy, or a girl? Let me see! Lookee! We've had us a boy!"

"Hmm," I said.

"See all that hair? My babies all have pretty hair."

She paused, apparently counting fingers and toes. "He's so sweet. I didn't think I'd have another baby." She looked at me. "This boy needs a name."

"What, Mother? What'll we call him?"

"Don't you know? His name is Bryan."

Shortly after that she lapsed into a coma. Frightened, I called the nurse. She took Mother's temperature. It registered one hundred seven degrees inside her arm-pit.

"Call the doctor! Do something!"

"Right now your mother's resting. Call me if you see any change."

Distraught, I called Jack. "Please come," I said, "I believe Mother's dying."

Hours inched past, her breaths rasping ever farther apart. About six A.M., July 11, 1968, Mother breathed her last. As I closed shut her slightly parted eyelids, a single tear ran down each of her cheeks. I kissed her. I whispered "I love you, my mother."

An hour or so earlier, Jack had joined us. He stood beside me. I looked at my baby brother. "Jack," I said, "We no longer have a mother." While my voice broke, I knew she was already at a far better place.

Three years passed. April 28, 1971, from our bedroom in Bowie, Maryland, I called my husband, at work in his Beltsville office. "Buddy! Guess what," I said. "The baby's coming."

I could hear excitement in this soon-to-be new papa's voice. "How do you know?"

"Trust me."

Chapter 19

Our third Blessing

After a quick trip to a nervous, Bowie, Maryland hairdresser for a "bouffant" hairdo, obvious in subsequent photos, I ran out to the curb, climbed into my husband's waiting car, and he and I motored through Maryland countryside over to Chevy Chase's Washington Sanitorium Hospital. Entering, my heels made loud, clicking sounds on a cavernous entrance hall's marble floor. I plopped onto the nearest couch while Buddy checked me into the hospital. As soon as a nurse hustled me away in a wheelchair, I figured he departed to parts unknown. I suppose Buddy joined other pacing, expectant fathers. Back then dads played an active role in just the initial birthing process. Me? I spent what seemed like hours in a narrow, single-bed labor room, alone, except for a nurse or two, a doctor administering my epidural, and occasionally someone, possibly a doctor, assessing my progress. Before I yelled "Oh! Ooh! Ouch!" too many times, a new nurse appeared. "Time to go." She pushed my bed down a hall, through double doors, and into the delivery room.

This room looked big. Bright. People milled around. The Asian man at my head seemed particularly attentive.

A white clad, masked man said, "Check her back."

I thought I hurt more than necessary. My epidural needle had slipped. Through the haze in my head I heard, "Push!"

Where was Dr. Offen? Like with my other babies, this doctor I had never dealt with before. Why, each time I gave birth, did God introduce me to a new doctor? Beside me the anesthesiologist re-adjusted the needle a second time. He said, "It won't be long now."

A shift in tense, for this feels like the present!
"Waah!"

I push up on an elbow, desperate to see my baby. They say he's a boy, but I never see him. Nurses whisk him away. To where? To a nearby sink. Looks like they're bathing him.

"My baby," I protest.

"Baby time later," says my new doctor. "Remember? I'm tying your tubes."

Stitched up, exhausted, and on the way to my room, I try to rise as the nurse pushes my stretcher before a glass window. She points, "See your baby? That third bassinet. It says "Baby Wilson.""

"Where?" My blurry eyes barely see shapes.

Seemingly hours pass. Finally, my room door opens. For the first time I cuddle in my arms blessed, soft sweetness, this new life entrusted to me. Like with my two other babies I count this one's fingers and toes. All here.

Pushing back baby hair, I say, "Sweet little bow mouth!" I gaze into his infant face. Huge eyes stare me down. Gray eyes. Almost black. My baby's eyes are so large, and piercing; so questioning, so intense, I shiver. I say, "You sweet little booger!" That nickname sticks for quite a while.

Meanwhile this baby's daddy joins us. Buddy picks up our child and holds him up to the light. He mumbles something. I say, "What?" He places our gorgeous little fellow beside me, sits down, and pulls in close. He says, "There's you, me, Mona, Jimmy, and baby makes five."

"You wanted six children. Remember? Too late now." That possibility the doctor ruled out this afternoon.

"With three as perfect as ours, who needs three more?"

Back to Past Tense

Next day my new son's dad came around for his morning visit, and our nurse brought us our "little booger." Busy oohing and cooing over our precious acquisition, finally we noticed the lady in the doorway. "Excuse me," she said. "I have birth records to complete. I need your baby's name."

My husband turned to me. "The lady's right. Our boy needs a name. What'll we call him?"

I tousled familiar curls, like those of all babies in our family. "Don't you know?" I said. "His name is Bryan!"

Ruel Bryan Wilson entered our family via the delivery room of Washington Sanitorium Hospital, Wednesday afternoon, about four P.M., April 28, 1971.

Recap:

August, 'fifty-five, Buddy and I marry, and in early fall of that year move into Dr. Godley's beloved shepherd's cottage. Mona comes to us in 'fifty-six and spends February of 'fifty-eight, sick in Emory Hospital. By Jimmy's birth we've been a family for four years and a month. Eleven years later, Bryan, mine and Mother's third child, completes our brood.

Standing before Good Hope's altar and proclaiming our wedding vows, my sweetheart and I think naught on wonderful or scary events awaiting us. With all four feet planted on our love plateau, we see nothing beyond that altar of ecstasy.

Deliberately corny, on our sun-struck wedding day, as my husband and I embark on our personal "sea of matrimony," I gaze at him. He smiles at me with what Cud'n Gen calls his "bedroom eyes," and blissfully I envision a lifetime of "happy sailing."

Nineteen Years Later

Forget any boat metaphor! At times that man I married makes me so mad, I want to chew nails. Like the afternoon he plays golf after I ask him not to. Nicely. I use perfect logic. We need to plant the dozen azalea bushes I got at a steal from Classic Nursery. Last night on the Eleven Alive weather report, Johnny Beckman predicted, as plain as day, a cloud-burst is coming. Soon!

All day I stew, thinking of the holes in our yard that need digging. And that man digging divots at Green Hills Country Club! Almost time for the father of my three children to return from the golf course, I stalk out the door.

He'll be sorry! After batting around all those golf balls, my lord and master will feel hot and sweaty. He'll trudge in through the back door. He'll sing out, "Honey, I'm home. How's about a frosty glass of ice tea." He'll spy my note. "Bryan and I are out of here, H*oney*! We're having *us* some good old *fun!*" Doing what, I haven't a clue.

Thus, my three-year-old son and I amble hand in hand down a hiking trail paralleling Barnett Shoals Road. We head for ... I am too aggravated to plan.

Bryan and I swing hands. We chase a blue butterfly, the color of my mood. "This is fun, Mommy," my son beams at me. That's when, on Barnett Shoals Road, a white Beetle screeches to a halt. An affable husband pokes his head out the window. He calls out, "Where are you two going?"

My mouth is a no-smiling zone. "Nowhere with you!"

Buddy whirls his car off the highway onto the trail.

Stalked on a sidewalk-wide trail by a man in a Beetle, what can a girl do? I climb into his car, and he chauffeurs the three of us to a nearby ice cream shop. I order vanilla.

Buddy's and Billie's three children, Jimmy, Mona, and Bryan

Grandma Billie, Niki and Jeremy, and Grandpa Buddy

Niki and Chad, A Wilson and Armstrong Family Wedding

Part VI

Proverbs 8: 17

I love them that love me; and those that seek me early, find me.

Chapter 20

Frances Marion and Her Family

All my life I knew Uncle Homer and Aunt Sally as close relatives. Once, spending the night in their old Powell family home before they built their own house, I slept as much as Uncle Homer allowed. Never before or since, have I heard snores loud enough to raise the roof; but, his could have raised the rafters.

Shades of Grandma Nettie. In their bedroom lay a stack of quilts, mounting to the ceiling. Aunt Sally told us that one icy evening in January, she woke up, cold. Grabbing a heavy quilt, she threw it atop their other covers. That night Uncle Homer squirmed. He moved here. He moved there. Next morning Aunt Sally opened tired eyes. She shrieked. Atop their covers, head raised, eyeing her intently, lay her restless companion, not Uncle Homer, but a huge snake, all of three inches in diameter and over four feet in length.

One Saturday at this same residence Aunt Sally washed their laundry. Beneath her black, iron wash pot, hot ashes smoldered. Frances and I ran around, playing in their back yard. I never saw anything more powdery, more inviting that those soft, white puffs around Aunt Sally's wash pot. With both bare feet, I jumped into that white hot ash. For weeks I couldn't walk. However, Grandma's poultices of clay, dampened with vinegar and applied daily, eventually remedied that.

We never knew when Uncle Homer and Aunt Sally would dart in for a visit. One night eating supper, our family sat around Grandpa Hampie's table. In walked the Powell family. Well, three of them anyway. Uncle Homer pulled up a chair. Not to eat. To talk. He said to my baby brother, "Jack, let me show you a trick." Taking a dime from his pocket, he tossed it into the air. Smiling wide, Uncle Homer drew the coin from behind Jack's ear. A second trick, tossing the dime into the air, Uncle Homer stood beneath the coin, mouth opened wide. Taking a huge gulp, he smacked his lips. "Jack," our uncle rubbed his belly. "Umm! That was good."

Uncle Homer presented Jack with the "magic" dime, then left for home.

"Look, Mama!" Jack threw the dime into the air, caught it in his mouth. He gulped. Jack grinned.

"Where's that dime, Jack?" Mother demanded.

Jack rubbed his tummy. "Here."

It took Mother almost a week of searching through "you know what" to uncover Uncle Homer's dime.

Another night he and Aunt Sally came while we were eating collards and cornbread. I never liked collards, but I did like collard liquor with my cornbread. Uncle Homer put up with my way of sopping bread into liquor as long as he could. He pulled over my plate. "Look," he said, crumbling up Grandma's skillet delicacy. "Here's the way to eat cornbread and collard liquor." He spooned liquor all over my bread. "Now eat this.'" I always credited Uncle Homer with my love of what Grandma labeled "Homer's dog's mess."

I loved my uncle's stories. He said that one summer evening after supper, his mama, "Leanner," (She was Leanna White Powell, wife of Francis Marion Powell.) pulled off his clothes in the kitchen and gave him a bath. They heard visitors in the parlor. His mama said, "Stay here, Homer Boy. I'll get you your pajamas." Left alone, not to mention, naked, little Homer thought, *I'm goin' after my Mama.* He reasoned, *If I can't see people, they can't see me.* Stitch-stark naked, eyes clinched shut and yelling "Mama!" the four year-old little guy raced through the room. He wondered, *Why did them people laugh so loud?*

As a young girl, I felt lucky to have a passel of girl cousins. Of course Leona, Lena Bell, and Geneva, Grandma's elder granddaughters, were too old to be my friends. Not Frances Marion. Two, maybe three years older, she never pulled "age rank" on me, possibly because she passed first grade, advanced first, and second grade all in one year.

So did I. However, Frances continued her skipping craze. Her second year she completed third and fourth grades, entering fifth grade in her third year in school. That young'un was smart as well as nice to me. Mother said, "Once in a while, let Grandma visit Sally alone!" I couldn't. Back home my bed would have been too empty without Grandma. Besides, I loved going to Aunt Sally's. Frances always found fun things to do. We ate. I've said before, I loved anything Aunt Sally cooked. We played cards, which I couldn't do at home. We sat at Geneva's dresser and combed each other's hair. We painted fingernails. We visited neighbors. At one time I knew Frankie's neighbors as well as my own.

By this time Leona had married Dicky and was a home demonstration agent for Horry County's lunchrooms; however, Geneva still lived at home. One day Genny told Frankie and me, "Let's go to the store." We climbed into Geneva's car and drove just beyond Maple church to a "Jot'em Down" type store. Geneva rushed into the place and came back with large Pepsis for herself and Frances Marion, and as requested, a six ounce Coca Cola for me.

Just as we leaned back for swigs of our drinks and were munching on peanut butter nabs, up drove that Lee boy, Geneva was seeing.

Geneva panicked. "Give me your drink!" She traded my small Coke for her Pepsi. She didn't want that young man seeing her sip from a big old drink bottle.

In 1920, when Grandpa Hamp died, Leona had been his first grandchild, but already Aunt Sally was expecting Geneva. She became Grandma's only namesake. Aunt Sally named her second baby daughter Nettie Geneva Powell. When anyone asked, "Little girl, what is your name?" Genny answered, "My name is Genettie Geneva." Grandma loved that answer almost as much as she loved her beautiful granddaughter.

All three of Aunt Sally's girls, like their cousin, Billie, attended Winthrop College. Three years older, Frances paved my way to Winthrop. Once there, I felt more comfortable in new surroundings, having met many of Frankie's Senior Hall buddies, especially her roommate, Katie.

She and Frances ushered me out to the main street located in front of our school. They showed me how students caught rides to town, to church, to movie theaters. Simple. We lined up on Oakland Avenue's sidewalk. Cars stopped; people opened doors; we ran and sat inside, free taxi service. We met interesting people that way.

During my senior year something untoward must have happened to someone hitch-hiking at Winthrop. Afterward, "bumming rides" was forbidden. Shucks! Now if we went to church, to town, or the movies, we walked. Only seniors were allowed cars, and those rich enough to own one were few and far between.

While I was still in college Frankie met Brice, and before I knew much of anything about that relationship, they married. By then she was teaching, I believe, at Homewood Elementary, and I was dating my future husband. Buddy had asked that I join him in Columbia and visit his Aunt Leethard Bell Bessent for the weekend. I'd already told him I couldn't. However, Brice had some important business at Fort Jackson; so, Frances said, "If you want to go to Columbia, come with us."

Shades of my mother. I never dreamed my cousin could be such a prude! All weekend long she demanded a running commentary on everything my boyfriend and I did. She said, "My cousin is not getting a bad reputation on my watch."

While Marion taught school, Brice worked for an insurance agency. I loved their brick bungalow located down the street from her parents. I thought her one lucky girl.

Then, I heard. My cousin and her hubby were in a nasty car accident. Marion had to be pried from the wrecked car before taken to the hospital. For the next few months, now married and living on Clemson's sheep farm, I kept calling home, asking about Frances Marion. She must have progressed, for suddenly, Mother told me she was pregnant. I already had my little girl, Mona, and her brother, Jimmy. Not to be outdone, later that year, 1960, Marion and Brice presented Baby Jeff to our family. Like Frances Marion and I, growing up, gave each other presents, our children traded Christmas gifts with blonde, cutie-pie Jeff. In the latter sixties, Frankie and Brice's delightful, blue-eyed Julie joined their clan. She had such sweet little cheeks.

Meanwhile, Dicky and Leona's sparkly-eyed baby girl had left babyhood. Leona, naming her daughter after her mom, had tacked a cool "e" onto "Sally." Excellent musicians, both Sallye Beth and Jeff played the piano. How Aunt Sally and Grandma Nettie would have enjoyed these, Aunt Sally's grand, and Grandma's great-grandchildren.

Grandma Nettie gave God credit for every day she lived. Ripping open sugar sacks to make drying cloths, she'd sit across the table, pausing now and then to stare into her mind's eye. Then she'd turn to me. "Little Bushy, do you know how blessed we are, just to be born? To be able to sit right here in this kitchen and look out the window at them beautiful crape myrtle blooms?" Her blue eyes shared her truth. "They say heaven is perfect. It is; but, some days I feel so blessed just sittin' in my own kitchen, it plumb scares me." She'd ponder some more. "There's one reason, though, that I dread dyin'. I'll want to know what's happenin' to my chillern, left here on this old earth."

This very minute, could Grandma and Aunt Sally be lounging on some big, white cloud, peeking through mist at their grandbabies and palavering together? With the Good Lord, if he so ordains, anything is possible.

Chapter 21

Tab and Sis, the Todd Family

Callie Williams' off-spring called her Mud. They called George Williams, Dad. Every Sunday morning Mud, her carpenter husband, and their children climbed up wood steps leading into Bethlehem Baptist. Time was, when Callie and George filed into church, trailing behind came five offspring. This Sunday, following them were only Berry, called Bud, and Sis, who told no one her real name. Bud and Sis were younger than Bertie, Ida Jane, and Nancy, who, these days attended Bethlehem Church with their husbands.

Last Sunday, from her front row seat beside her husband, Nance, now Mrs. Sam Gore, turned. She grinned at her younger sister. Yep, Sis was practically sure. Nance knew Sis's secret. She liked Tab Todd; but, never would Sis admit that to pesky old Nance. That girl was a born tease.

Sis couldn't help her feelings. Didn't want to. Tab had the sweetest smile.

Church was about to begin.

Just like his admirer, Tab sat in an aisle seat, except his was two pews up. That boy looked so handsome in his clean, blue overalls and starched, plaid shirt. Why he rivaled everyone else at the service, including the preacher. An hour later Mud's baby girl couldn't have told a soul the preacher's text; but, she knew exactly how Tab's lips curved up, smiling. And that fellow smiled every time he turned around and caught Sis looking. Then his head flew back like a shot. And his neck blushed fiery red.

Leaving the church, Sis accidentally (?) brushed against Tab's arm.

That boy didn't miss a beat. He grabbed Sis's hand. He pulled Neighbor Callie's daughter all the way across the church yard, clean to the artesian flow.

Sis's thought: *Is Mud seeing this?*

Tab's next move cinched the girl's feelings, igniting two hearts with a flame not doused for eternity.

"Want a drink?" He asked.

Sis shook her head. "Not from a glass everybody else uses."

Beside the flow lay a pile of shells, possibly intended to cover some loved-one's grave. Tab picked up the largest, the pinkest shell. He washed it carefully, and filling it with sparkling artesian water, offered it to Sis. Sis drank deeply, all the while gazing into the face of young love.

Todd Family Realities:

Before the girl destined to be my Mama Todd turned nineteen, Talbert Decal Todd married Cleva Felisha Williams, known by all as Sis. A year or two of wedded bliss brought forth another treasure. February, 21, 1913, my mother, Baby Dottie Lee, blessed their lives. Three years later the mama of one became the mama of two. Her second daughter, Ivey Leatha, joined the troop, soon followed by Little Mack. Poor thing, at three and a half, he suffered a disease shortening lives of many post World War I children. Colitis stole away Mama Todd's baby boy. In his absence the smell of lemons lingered. Lemonade was all Mama could get her sweet little sick man to swallow.

In 'twenty-one, before Little Mac's death, Mama Todd knew she'd soon deliver another child. She and Papa named their last baby Victor Mace. Destined to fight in World War II, captured by Nazis, Mace walked a "death march" across frozen Germany. Released after a declaration of Allied victory, Mama's second son proved aptly named "Victor."

A slew of rewarding years were filled with giant "ups," occasionally by depressing "downs." Mother always said she never wanted to die before either parent. They'd suffered enough grief experiencing the deaths of Little Mac, then Leatha, living to adulthood before dying with Leukemia. Despite Mother's wishes, July 11, 1968, in Charleston Medical Hospital, Dottie Lee Todd Hamilton breathed her last, *three months* before Papa Todd, and *nine years* before her mother.

Months earlier, encouraged by friends and relatives, Mama Todd and her mate of fifty-seven years moved into a trailer, leaving behind their silver-painted house with its many friendly porches. Adjusting to a new, smaller home, and heart sick, grieving over the loss of their eldest, the couple turned to each other for comfort. In a seeming eye-blink, a massive heart attack stole away Mama Todd's love. Desolate now, living alone, no Tab to cook for, no Tab to rub her sore shoulder when it hurt like crazy, what was left for a poor old woman to do? She reached for her broom. All the porch Mama Todd had left to sweep was a four by six foot deck where she greeted people. That was okay. In a dozen or two broom strokes, she could have done with it all.

For a while Mama missed Papa so much, she wanted to die. But she didn't. A few years passed. Then, something happened. Doctors said Mama underwent a "small stroke." Her general practitioner prescribed for her a dementia drug he thought worked for most. Now, Mama went truly crazy. Of course doctors didn't prescribe medicines that patients shouldn't take. Did they?

Mama grew so hard to manage, the family transferred her to a Marion, South Carolina rest facility. If anything, there she grew worse. Mama failed to recognize family members. She fought her nurses, and if her bruises were an indication, someone fought back.

With few alternatives, our family moved Mama to a different nursing center. Poring over his new patient's medical chart, a staff doctor questioned a drug his ward addition had received for at least a year, maybe longer. He directed his assistant, "Cease Mrs. Todd's present daily drug. Immediately."

Mama's change shocked everyone. She went sane.

Soon our family brought her home, and for the next two years our new, our old, our dear Mama Todd lived as well and happy as her station-in-life permitted. Greeting loved ones, she'd smile, high, round cheeks rising higher. She'd say, "Hey there. Smell my nose." At Christmas parties Santa's elves passed Mama her gift first, for like always, trying the patience of impatient grandchildren, she tore off wrappings inch by inch. Mama could never destroy pretty paper usable next year.

In 1977, again Mama Todd grew sick, this time inside a healthy-minded body. She had liked her second nursing home where the doctor restored her world. Returning there, Sis felt death approaching. Why not hasten the inevitable?

Mana struggled. Then she decided. Never would another morsel of food pass her lips. I know this is true, for I visited her. I tried to feed her mashed potatoes and gravy, apple sauce, vanilla ice cream. To every spoon of food offered, Mama clamped shut her mouth and shook her stubborn gray head.

July 18, 1977, a month short of eighty-six years old, Sis Williams, the teen-age girl drinking water out of Papa Todd's clam shell, Cleva Felicia Williams Todd, a hardworking, strong-hearted soul, wife of Farmer T. D. Todd, Mud William's baby girl, that mother's child breathed her last. Like she told visitors a month or two before death, "I have more loved ones to join," she pointed, "up there, than I have to stay with here."

We miss you, Mama Todd.

Jim's son, Jonathan, and Bryan's daughter,
Kayla, in an ancient tree at Dockside
Restaurant in Calabash, North Carolina

Chapter 22

Aunt Laura's Vision

Bryan came into our lives in Bowie, Maryland. A year later, Buddy's job as biometrician with ARS brought our family to our permanent home, Athens, Georgia.

Back in South Carolina, home in a hospital bed after suffering six years of post-stroke ailments, World War I poison gas victim, Uncle Murph Graham, Aunt Laura's husband, breathed his last. We were unable to attend his funeral, but as soon as possible we journeyed to South Carolina for a visit.

"I'm so sorry I missed Uncle Murph's funeral," I told Aunt Laura.

"I'm sorry too, Honey. I knew you wanted to come. 'Course I had Leona and Frances Marion. And Sallye Beth helped cheer me. Her eyes sparkle so, it makes me feel better just seein' her. Then, there were Molly's children. Hamp and Lucille came, Jack and Dotand, and Lena Bell. Since I have no kids on *this* earth, I always felt like Leona and Lena Bell were as much mine as their mama's."

I could identify with that. I felt like I belonged to Mother's sister, Leatha, as well as to Mother.

"Bryan," I called to my youngest child, just prying himself out of the car. "Come hug Aunt Laura."

Bryan dragged his feet up the front steps, not anxious to visit an old lady. He liked children for friends. However, as soon as Aunt Laura opened her arms and swathed him in a bear hug, then said, "You want to play with my choo-choo?" Our four year old son perked up.

"Where is it?" Bryan's blue eyes danced.

Aunt Laura opened a closet and brought out a train Bryan could ride, along with a black and white cow sporting a leather tail. She pulled the cow on a string. About every third turn of its wheels the wooden animal moaned, "Moo-oo-oo."

That made Bryan happy. Now, Daddy's youngest sister and I could visit.

"You've lost weight," I told her.

'When you've no one to cook for but yourself, a body won't eat as much." Aunt Laura sounded a lot like her mother, Grandma Nettie.

Grandma died way back in 'fifty-three, and twenty-two years later, I still missed her. Aunt Laura, Grandma's only living daughter, brought back memories.

"You know," she said, "sometimes I wish you hadn't give away Ma's old pump organ. I enjoyed playing that thing."

"I can still hear you. You entertained me with "Chewin' Chawin' Gum.""

"Yep, and you sang it."

"I did, didn't I?" We both laughed.

Aunt Laura had cooked chicken and dumplin's for us, hers an oven version. That day my husband, son, and I ate well. We especially enjoyed her moist, super delicious pineapple cake. Afterwards, catching up on family gossip, Aunt Laura and I washed dishes and cleaned up her kitchen. Bryan went back to play. Buddy stretched out in a recliner. Over an extended newspaper, he eyed a baseball game on television.

"Dotand and Jack came back to see me yesterday." Aunt Laura climbed onto a chair to put away plates. "Dotand's not quite as homesick as she was."

While serving overseas, Aunt Molly's Jack Hardee met and married his wife in The Philippines.

"Be careful! Don't fall, Aunt Laura." I helped her down from the chair.

"I'm always careful." She added. "Dotand's expecting."

"Wonderful! Pity Aunt Molly's not here to see all of her grandchildren."

"We need to treasure our every moment with people we love."

"Have you seen Leo lately?"

"Have I seen Leo! About ten o'clock most every morning Uncle Ott's baby boy walks through that door, bald head and all. 'Course the only time you get to see that bald head is if he eats with you. Even then sometimes he 'forgets' to take off his cap."

"Wouldn't you have thought a tree falling on Leo would have slowed him down a mite? It's a long walk over here from Good Hope."

"Pretty far, shorter if you walk up the railroad track. He's a good old Leo, though; and if he could hear a word you say, he'd be good company. He always was a bright boy."

"Aunt Laura," I laughed. "That *boy* must be fifty-five years old!"

"Try sixty-two," she made a wry face, "but he's still a boy to me."

We finished cleaning up, then sank into Aunt Laura's gray sofa. Opening the front of a corner table Aunt Rock always admired, my auntie brought out a picture album. We pored over photographs of Grandma, Aunt Sally, Aunt Molly, of Mother, all of them passed on to their next life. For six years after Uncle Murph suffered a stroke, in this same room he lay on a hospital bed. Aunt Laura had doctored him, bathed him, fed him, loved him, waited on him hand and foot. She lit him so many cigarettes, I remember Uncle Murph's "holding" fingers, the tarnished color of yellow mustard.

Aunt Laura fingered a picture of Uncle Murph in uniform. "What do people do who don't believe in God?" Her pretty face looked baffled. "If I didn't know my family lived on in a better place after this world, I don't think I could stand it here without 'em."

"Thank the Lord for your faith, Aunt Laura."

She leaned in close; spoke softly. "If I tell you something, promise you won't think I'm a liar?"

"I could never think that of you!" Where was she going with this conversation?

"I told this to Leona; but I never told it to another livin' soul."

"*What? What,* Aunt Laura? *Tell* me!"

"All while Murph was sick, he lay on a hospital bed, here in this very room."

"I remember."

"At night I couldn't sleep in our bedroom. Too far from Murph; so, I bought that little day bed you see in the corner. I slept on it beside Murph. Then, he died, and I sleep there right on.

"I don't know that you heard, but we've had several break-ins in this community. Down by the railroad tracks somebody broke into the Dawsey's house. The scoundrels stole a bunch of tools. In the other direction, one Sunday morning our Tyler neighbors left for church. While they worshiped God at Gurley, some man tore off their back window screen and broke a pane. He climbed into their house through the window. The Tylers got home to find silver missing, guns, and a collection of old coins dating clear back to The Civil War. And that thief had big feet. Police found his footprints.

"Now, I know I don't have much of anything a robber would want; but still, livin' here by myself, I've been scared."

"I'd be scared too, Aunt Laura, living by myself. Maybe you can get one of Uncle Murph's relatives to move in for a while."

"No, these days they have lives of their own. That's all right. I said I *was* scared. I'm not anymore."

"You're not?"

"I'll tell you why. Sunday night, a couple of weeks ago, I had just climbed into my daybed. I was feeling spooked, thinking of robbers, 'cause you know what had been happenin'. And, my house is so close to the road. People from all over travel this highway. That night, sayin' my prayers, I meant every last word. I prayed, *Lord, you know I'm scared. Please keep me safe. Please, Lord Jesus. Protect me.*

"Right about then, I heard what sounded like a *big* man wearing heavy boots, and he was walkin' across my front porch. I said, 'Lord, have mercy now!' I watched the door knob turn." Aunt Laura turned her sharp gaze on me. "Billie Faye, it really turned!"

"Hadn't you locked your door?"

"Yeah, but the knob did turn, and I knew, if anybody wanted to break in, that door wasn't made at Fort Knox! About then, my heart about stopped.

"That quick, I thought no more on any knob or any robber, for out of nowhere a figure appeared against the door. But wait a minute. Let me tell you. This here being didn't just pop into place. Oh, I don't know how to explain it."

Now Aunt Laura had my attention. I had heard of people seeing ghosts and things, but nothing like this.

"She, for she *was* a woman, she stood out from her background; but, right through her, I could still see the door. Seconds later I saw just a tall woman standing there. She looked as solid and real as anybody. I lay on my bed and thought to myself, *nobody's gonna believe this!* I couldn't believe it. I thought *who is this woman? Could she be Sally?*"

Aunt Laura was talking about Sally Rabon, Uncle Murph's niece. Like Aunt Sally Powell, Sally Rabon had diabetes. A few months ago, giving birth, Sally and her baby died. But for a while, she had lived with Uncle Murph and Aunt Laura.

"Billie, I couldn't see this woman's face. It was in shadow; but, I could see blonde hair, and the only person I knew with hair looking like that was Sally. Whoever, that woman standing in front of my door, she was my protector. The Bible calls such, guardian angels. Well, I tell you. She was mine."

I said, "Wait, Aunt Laura. I want Buddy to hear this."

She said, "Tell him later. I'd rather just talk to you. Anyhow, I stared at this woman just as long as I wanted. She wore a long, white dress, maybe a robe. This robe had a long collar. In front it draped all the way to her waist; but in back, it was pulled up, and it covered her hair. Like a scarf, that collar draped around her face, shading it. I squinted. I stared; but, in no way could I make out a one of her features. Just locks of blonde hair poking out from that pulled up collar. I will tell you this. I've never seen anything as white as that dress. It glowed. It gave out so much light, this thought dawned on me. The light outside our window, that one popping on when the sun goes down," Aunt Laura pointed toward the side window, "I thought it must be burned out. For just a split second I glanced its way. Then I looked back. That solid lookin' woman had started to fade. Soon, it was just like she'd never come. This room was dark, and that outside light was shining as pretty as you please."

"Oh, Aunt Laura! I'd have been scared to death."

"Actually, I've never in my life felt so safe. I pulled up the covers and slept as sound as a dollar the whole night long."

"What about that man on your porch?"

"I don't know. I've neither heard nor worried about him since. You see, somebody powerful's lookin' after me."

As far as I know, Aunt Laura's angel never returned. However, about a year later, routinely climbing onto her kitchen chair to put away dishes, Daddy's youngest and last sister suffered a stroke. She fell to the floor. An hour or two later, dependable Leo found Aunt Laura and called an ambulance.

Home in Athens I received a phone call from Frances Marion. "Billie Faye, brace yourself. Aunt Laura died this morning. She's with Mama and the rest."

Seventy-three years old, Aunt Laura died the same age as her mother, Grandma Nettie, and while I miss Aunt Laura's closeness as well as her chicken and dumplin's, I have no concern for her well-being. Wherever my dear aunt's spirit resides, she knows safety and comfort, for in death as in life, Laura Hamilton Graham has powerful connections.

Chapter 23

Pa's Party

After Jack and I left home and began adult living, Mother and Daddy moved Grandpa Hamp's old cypress farmhouse to the next-door field, referred to by Grandma as "The Julie Flower field." (Really yellow, Brown-Eyed Susan daisies.) In Grandma's house's stead, my parents built a modest brick bungalow. For five years they enjoyed their new home. Mother died, and for the next ten years, Daddy lived alone in his home amidst familiar oaks. Quickly Daddy learned to scramble eggs and butter toast. He stirred up a mean pot of grits. Sometimes I thought Daddy actually enjoyed his solitude.

Most summers my children and I spent a couple of weeks with Daddy, while my husband fulfilled his required reserve duty with the army. In 'seventy-eight, like every summer, Jimmy, Bryan, Buddy, and I rolled into Daddy's yard. Our daughter, Mona, wed at eighteen, remained in Athens. The first words out of Daddy's mouth were, "Billie Faye, I think I'm about ready to shut up this place and move in with you or Jack."

Jack and I, like Grandma's baby boy, Uncle Charles, both lived in Georgia, I in Athens, Jack in Savannah.

I hugged Daddy. He must have been struggling with this decision. He, Buddy, and I went into the house, while Jimmy and Bryan ran around to the pump house looking for snakes. Most of the time Jimmy could return in two minutes wearing a chicken snake boa.

"What's brought this on, Daddy?" I asked. "Is your health worse?" Daddy still struggled with ileitis.

"Billie Faye," Daddy moved in closer, like he knew a secret. "I've been hearin' things."

"In this house? What things? Not ghosts."

"Maybe."

I wasn't too surprised. Once while lying in a bedroom of this *new* house, I heard footsteps walk up the "old" house's back door steps, complete with the second riser's squeak. Whoever, whatever, it walked across an old porch board which creaked just like always. No, I wasn't surprised Daddy thought he might have encountered unknown beings. Actually God blessed our whole family with overloaded imaginations.

"Daddy, when you and Mother moved out of our old house, you said, 'Any of you spirits who want to, feel free to join Dot and me in our new home.' Remember?"

Daddy chuckled. "I did, didn't I?"

"So, what's new?"

"I am sort of ashamed of myself. But listen to the latest. At night, I hear voices. Aunt Freddie shows up. She gives me all kinds of advice; not that I see her. And Ma. Now you know I'm not scared of my own ma; but, when I hear these things and I can't see 'em, I don't like it!"

"Any time you want, Daddy, come live with me; and Jack's already looking for a new house in Savannah, he says one with an 'in-law' suite. We're ready for you when you're ready for us."

Daddy sighed. "About a month ago, my doctor gave me some new medicine. It may be affecting my mind. Sometimes I do get a trifle dizzy.

"One more thing. It seems I need to hold my tongue. Last Tuesday I walked over to the cemetery. For a while I sat down beside Dot's grave. Sadder than before I came, I said, 'Little Darlin', come home with me if you want to.'

"Well, I walked home, and entered through the side door. As soon as I got settled in this here rocker, the living room door opened. Then, shut. I said, 'Leo, is that you?' Nobody said a word; so, I got up and checked out the door. Nary a soul."

"Daddy!"

"I know what you're thinkin'. Again. I asked for it. I really must be crazy."

"I wish Grandma was here. She'd say, "When you're up against something you don't understand, call on the Lord!"

Daddy said, "I do. I say, 'Lord, please help me.' I guess I lack Ma's spiritual strength."

For years Jack and I worried about our dad; thus, prior to deciding he'd give up his home, we made certain he'd thought long and hard. Finally, Daddy moved his personal belongings into Jack's Savannah in-law suite, and when the urge struck, visited our family in Athens.

About every six months, that urge struck. On one of those visits, because of Daddy's abdominal pain, we made him an appointment with Dr. Gere, an Atlanta, West Paces Ferry Hospital doctor. The night before his appointment Daddy roamed around our house. Later he told us, "Several times I opened your front door, thinking, *where in the Sam Hill am I?* For years he'd suffered bouts of confusion. As soon as blessed Dr. Gere learned of this, he discontinued the "culprit" medication prescribed years earlier. Overnight our old Pa returned. We thanked Our Maker for sending us to Dr. Gere.

Daddy's Savannah and his Athens grandchildren grew accustomed to tip-toeing around their "Pa" at nap time. Nothing new. When Jack and I were little, Grandma Nettie drummed that law into us, along with others having to do with her perennial "boy's" comfort. Actually, like Grandma, Daddy hovered over his grandchildren. When Jack's teenage daughter, Lisa, started dating, Daddy grew especially protective. Luckily he liked the fellow she chose, an Alabama basketball player attending Armstrong University.

Always creative regarding children, Pa gave each grandchild a nickname. Jimmy answered to "George," and Mona to "Miss Lucy." Jackie, Daddy called "Joe." He called Bryan, "Wootus Brown," and Lisa became another "Miss Lucy."

Occasionally Bug Swamp friends visited Daddy. Every week, he wrote a check and mailed his tithe to Good Hope Baptist, his pipeline to God since birth. "I do miss Sundays at Good Hope," he'd say, staring into his past, "I miss Junior Brown."

Junior married Uncle Boss Hamilton's daughter, Bessie, and was Horry County's sheriff. Before Daddy left home, every Sunday morning Junior picked up my dad and drove him to Sunday School.

Leaving home, Daddy had rented out his bungalow. Visiting Bug Swamp, he usually stayed with Leona or Frances Marion. For a while, because of ill health and varied reasons, our dad had been stuck in either Savannah or Athens. Finally, he was returning home. Marcie and I put our heads together and decided we'd give him one humongous party. Most of Daddy's friends and relatives would be there. We hoped.

A lot had gone into preparing for this shindig. Marcie bought him a pretty, periwinkle blue shirt and reddish tie. They looked great on Daddy with his shock of white hair and his old beige suit. Even Daddy's great-grand children were present, proud in their fancy dress. Niki, Jeremy, and Tegan skirted "Pa." They peeked at each other, scampering in and out among party guests. Younger than my children, Jackie and Lisa, had given their pa no great-grands, as yet.

Who were some of these people? Certain strangers were recognizable because they carried in their genes particular Bug Swamp family traits like Roman noses, fat or lean body types, eyes like people we knew. The ten years Daddy was away, people changed. So had he. Unbelievably, my dad had become an old man of eighty-three. Time, like Rome's Mercury, definitely wore wings.

In came familiar faces, Uncle Dave and Aunt Lucy's daughters, Lena, along with her younger sisters, Leila and Reba. Daddy's cousins, they greeted everyone with smiles and hugs. Years ago when Daddy and Lena were teenagers, he had pulled her from an ocean whirlpool. He saved her life. Maybe that's why they remained close. Lena wrote him often, signing her letters, "the one who loves you."

Lena hugged me, saying, "Billie Faye, your daddy sure is looking good."

I smiled. "He doesn't look eighty-three, does he?"

Who in the world? The man standing in the doorway had shaved his head into a shiny dome. I peered. "Is that you, Hamp?"

Hamp Hardee was Aunt Molly's older son. And just who was this gorgeous young lady beside him? I hugged my cousin. "Hamp, introduce your friend!"

"Goodness, Billie Faye, we don't see much of each other. Meet my daughter. This is Janet Hardee, your cousin."

It seemed like everybody living at Bug Swamp and surrounding areas poured through the door. *Isn't that Miriam?* Why I hadn't seen Grandma's niece, Uncle Mack's daughter in ... it must have been twenty-five years! Back then Miriam had been a knock-out, a high school beauty. I could have kicked myself when I blurted out, "Miriam, you look just like Grandma!"

"What?" Miriam looked shocked. Well, what fifty-nine year-old woman likes to be told she looks like a fifty-five year-old's grandma!

I hastened to add, "You look just like I remember Grandma when I was a child!" Which was true.

Louise, Miriam's sister, probably made it worse. "Mickey, we were all young once."

Whew! I had little time to lament that social faux pas. Other people were pushing through the door.

Marden Dorman came with his son, Odell. Odell was the baby in his mommy's tummy that Mother said grew big because Ruby drank too many Pepsi Colas. (Mother was trying to break me of my Pepsi-drinking habit.) Marden, one of Daddy's oldest friends, made a beeline for his old buddy, just as had most arrivals. After all, Daddy was the guest of honor.

I didn't know everyone at the party, but we were home, and these were home folk. Elise, a singing cousin and her World War II veteran, science teacher, tennis playing husband, Fulton, appeared in the doorway. I ran to Elise, hugging her hard. She and Mother sang alto together in the Good Hope choir. She wrote to Daddy faithfully, telling him all community news. During our Bug Swamp stay I hoped to see more of Elise and Fulton. I'd heard that Fulton wasn't well.

Frances Marion and Brice arrived. During our last visit home, Buddy, Daddy, and I spent a few days with Marion and Brice, and they invited people over. One lady brought Daddy a chocolate cake.

Before he moved to Savannah, we accused him of being "sweet" on the woman. She called him daily. After one such call, when our smiles grew too wide, Daddy said, "That woman embarrasses me!" We thought he was secretly flattered by the attention of this spunky, widowed female.

I spied Marden across the hall, holding court. Whatever he said must have been interesting, for everyone looked entranced. I eased over and listened in.

"There I lay, flat of my back, hooked up to all kinds of machines. My chest felt like a load of bricks sat on it. A doctor and nurse hovered over me, and I was vaguely aware of my son and daughter. One of 'em, soundin' sad, asked, 'How much time does he have?' I didn't hear the answer, for everything receded: voices, heavy chest, my aching head. I felt wrapped up in a soft blanket, all black. It covered me like down, sinking into my every nook and cranny.

"Just when I settled into unbelievable comfort, in front of me swirled an opening. It started out a tiny pin-point of light. And that pin-point grew big, bigger. My whole being yearned for that light." Marden sighed. "A second, maybe an eternity passed. Suddenly the light grew dimmer. And with *Its* leaving, I sensed a presence. Whoever, whatever, that presence was as near all love as I can describe. Without words, it told me, *go back to your world. You still have work there.* Think of it! This old world had a need for *me*, Marden Dorman!"

No one spoke. I took Marden's hand. I kissed his cheek. "Marden," I whispered. "I'm glad you're back with us."

After returning from "the dead," Marden worked for the Gideons. He placed Bibles into hotel rooms.

Years ago, he and Daddy had some high old times together, for example, "the chicken incident."

Several young men at Bug Swamp formed a secret club, no females and no adults allowed. One night they decided they'd have a chicken bog. Enoch Hucks should bring rice, Marden, a loaf of bread, and Daddy, two chickens.

Daddy said, "Uh-uh." He knew his mother. She would kill him dead, if he stole her prize hens. Besides, Daddy hated deceiving his mama.

Marden said, "Don't you worry, Rassie. I'll bring the chickens. Your mama bakes really good bread. Bring that."

Next night, the chicken bog proved a huge success. Someone even pilfered a watermelon for dessert. Daddy especially enjoyed the meal. His conscience was as clear as rain.

Early the next morning, he heard Grandma Nettie in the kitchen. "Laura," she told Daddy's sister, "night before last something happened to my two best settin' hens. A fox, or somethin' definitely after chickens, it broke into my hen house, 'cause yesterday mornin', feathers were all over everywhere, and no hens."

That Marden. Not only had Daddy furnished their bread, Marden stole Grandma's prize hens.

People came; people went. This was supposed to be open house; but once here, many stayed, visiting with friends and relatives they hadn't seen for ages.

Jack crept up behind me. He whispered, "Billie Faye, who is that pretty brunette with Hamp Hardee?"

I said, "Jack, speak to Hamp and Lucille's daughter. That's your cousin, Janet Hardee."

My brother's eyes sparkled. He said, "Who knew there was anybody so good-looking in our family? Hamp's girl looks straight from Hollywood!"

"Maybe you should introduce them to Lisa and Jackie," I suggested. "Find Mona and my kids. It's a shame Grandma Nettie's grandchildren don't know each other."

Hamp was Grandma's first grandson, and I'd heard someone say Janet had just won a local Myrtle Beach beauty contest.

Leona and Geneva arrived together. They were Frances Marion's older sisters. Recently Leona lost her husband, Dicky. She seemed to be holding up well. Geneva looked cheery in her red wool suit.

Aunt Sally's Geneva broke quite a few hearts before marrying Robert. Together, they parented three, beautiful daughters, Linda, Betty, and Libby. Hadn't at least two of those girls been "Miss Conway" at one time or another? I would have enjoyed seeing them, but they hadn't come tonight.

Frances Marion's kids, Jeff and Julie, they came. Buddy feels a kinship with them. Jeff graduated from Clemson and Julie is studying there. Leona's daughter, Sallye Beth, also came with Frances. I hugged my cousins, thinking, *I wish you were here, Grandma. These kids, Sallye Beth, Jeff, Julie, Janet, as well as Niki, Jeremy, and Tegan, my children's children, all are your great-grandchildren.*

A few months ago when Leona's husband, Dicky, died, and we drove back for his funeral, I yearned for the past. Funeral service over, Jack, Daddy, and I parked in front of the home site we shared in another lifetime. From his passenger seat Daddy gazed into the distance, as though seeing the past more clearly than the present.

Some things never changed. In the driveway leading to Daddy's newer bungalow lurked that perennial, washed out hole. No matter how many times my dad filled that hole, washed-away sand gifted us with the same moon crater depression. Today it held a bushel of dry cedar needles. Growing up, we always parked beneath that cedar. Other trees, pines; moss covered oaks; Chinaberry trees; overgrown, ancient crape myrtles; Grandma's faithful pear tree that snakes fell out of; the mulberry tree beside Grandma's and Mother's wash house; all towered over the place as faithfully as when Daddy, then I, was a child. In fact a frayed rope still hung from a sprawled out oak limb. I wondered if it were part of my swing.

Fifty years ago Uncle Oliver Hardee gave me a beautiful, huge pecan. I thought it too nice and big to eat; so, I planted it … in the shade of our most massive oak. Lo, that nut germinated. It grew into *my* tree. Year after year I waited for that sapling to grow tall. My mistake: planting the seed beneath huge oak branches. Now, fifty years later, my plucky tree still strained to break free from its oak tree dominance. *Who knows*, I thought. *That sapling may survive the oak and grow tall yet!*

It didn't. That hunched-over tree reminded me of Daddy's younger brother. Still living in Ware County, Georgia, Uncle Charles couldn't come to Daddy's party. As a young man Daddy's brother stood tall, his future limitless. Later, like my pecan tree, Uncle Charles' body cramped into whatever direction rheumatoid arthritis induced, although he never allowed that nemesis to stifle his life. Unlike the fruitless pecan tree, my uncle's life produced progeny and accomplishments aplenty!

While Uncle Charles and Aunt Rock hadn't come to the party, their girls, Mary Jane and Sarah Anne, were arriving tomorrow. We'd see them before returning to Georgia.

Grandma Nettie and Grandpa Hamp spawned three daughters before Daddy, their first son, sprang into action. Aunt Laura regaled me with tales of "little" Daddy's antics. "Busy, busy, busy," Aunt Laura described him. One afternoon their mother had supper ready. She called, "Chillern, Hampie, supper's ready. Rassie! Where's Rassie?" No answer.

Enlisting everyone's help, Grandma searched for her baby. Soon Aunt Laura spied the two-year-old rapscallion astraddle the peak of the wash house roof like it was his hobby horse. The little fellow had scaled the thickly growing mulberry tree, the same mulberry tree I climbed as a child. He'd scooted out on a limb and advanced all the way to the top of the slanted roof.

Afraid to yell "Mama," and afraid to take her eyes off her brother, Aunt Laura called softly, "Rassie . . ."

Finally, she got Grandpa Hamp's attention. He climbed a ladder and retrieved their daring adventurer.

As Daddy's party wore on, I visited with one set of relatives, talked to other long lost friends, and reminisced about family members. I could see some younger children winding down. Even a few adults yawned behind their hands.

Since strangers had leased our Bug Swamp house, like usual, Buddy and I, our children and grandchildren planned to stay with Frances Marion and Leona. Jack and Marcie were visiting her parents. That left Daddy to spend the night with the party's host. We planned to return in early afternoon.

"Goodbye," I said to one after another. I couldn't help tears that threatened to spill. "Thanks for coming. We'll see you tomorrow. Have a good night."

Several wandered over wishing Daddy well.

Before leaving, Daddy's three great-grandchildren gathered around their "Pa." Four year-old Jeremy looked up at Heyward, Daddy's host. Jeremy said, "Mr. Goldfinch, "Can I see my Pa's legs?"

Heyward removed the mound of flowers. Opening the coffin full-length, he revealed Pa's legs.

Rassie Bryan Hamilton, our children and grandchildren's Pa, died Friday, September 11, 1988. Within view of our Bug Swamp farmhouse site, Daddy's body, not his spirit, rests beside Mother's earthly remains. To his essence, I say the same as to those of Uncle Bert, Grandma Nettie, Grandpa Hamp, my Aunt Leatha, Aunt Molly, Mother, Papa Todd, Aunt Laura, Mama Todd, Uncle Mace, Louise, Aunt Minnie: "Till we meet again!"

Chapter 24

The Magic Circle

At twelve I needed special permission to join Conway High's "teen" club. At twenty-one, I felt slightly awkward teaching English to high school students, some just three years younger than I. Then came the Sunday I stood before an altar and vowed I'd devote the rest of my life to the devotee beside me. Marrying at twenty-two, I became one of a couple, the important "other" in my life smart enough for the two of us. From that day on, I could relax and enjoy the love and companionship my dedicated partner provided.

Don't tell me. I know. "Ignorance is bliss." However, including inevitable life complications, with God's help, that joy continues boosting my strength until this day. However, a year and a half after saying "I do," with barely nine months' warning, the family created by Mr. and Mrs. Ruel Leston "Buddy" Wilson turned into three, and four years later, four. At final count, in 'seventy-one, our last child boosted our family's membership to five. By now my husband and I were so busy living, we had few moments to dwell on time's passage, nor on its predictable changes.

Years passed. Bryan, a year old when we moved to Athens, Georgia, would turn nineteen next month. Already our family of five had decreased in number, for Mona Lynne left us after her first year at UGA. Marrying Tim Wilkes, she continued her schooling and Tim surveyed land sites. They waited twelve years before presenting us with our third grandbaby, a darling little girl. They named Tegan Elicia Wilkes after a character in her mom and dad's favorite television series, "Dr. Who."

Younger than Mona, and wed later, Jimmy and his wife, Sue, summoned the stork years earlier than had Tim and Mona. First beautiful Nicole Anne, Niki, whose smile brought out the sun, blessed our hearts five years before Mona's busy little, danger-defying, two cute for words, Tegan became one of our nearest and dearest. Sweet-faced Jeremy Ruel, named for Papa Buddy, followed Niki by three years and preceded Tegan by two. Welcoming responsibilities granted us by our adorable grandchildren, Buddy and I still pursued life on much the same basis as usual.

Then came the day I looked into an *age-telling*, window-lit mirror. On a nearby wall hung a recent 1990's *calendar*. That's when my husband pushed open the door, saying, "Aren't you ready yet?" *I spied the color gray in the sparse hair atop his pate.* I think I screamed.

Always I've looked for "the good" in life. The same year I lost dear Grandma Nettie, I met Buddy, the man of my future. In 1968, my beloved mother died, much too soon. No good in that. Twenty years later, two years ago, Buddy's mother, Ople, died. Four months after that, Daddy departed this realm. Our parents' deaths the same year, a defining image of me in a bright mirror, plus other "telling" indications, probably aimed time's passage into hurtful focus.

On happier notes, Jeremy recently turned six, and in late fall Tegan would become four. Less than a month earlier, we welcomed into our clan Mona's second daughter, ebony-eyed Rachel. On this Sunday, March 10, 1990, for most of the afternoon that sweet baby slept in her mommy's arms.

And who was this growing-like-a-weed, blonde, brown-eyed super star, lounging in our Robin Rd. kitchen and eyeing her birthday cake? Nine years ago today, on a Tuesday in 'eighty-one, our first grandchild entered this world. Never could I forget Nicole Anne Wilson's birthday, for that serious looking baby girl was born on the anniversary of her Grandpa Buddy's and my first blind date a million years ago.

By five o'clock we had eaten our fill, sung "Happy birthday, Niki, and she had finished opening her stack of presents. Party over, Mona and Tim together with Jimmy and Sue packed up for home. Bryan scooted out for a date with Brenda, his girl-friend.

"Let's us spend the night with Grandma," Jeremy urged Tegan.

I said, "Jeremy, don't you have school tomorrow?"

He eyed his mama.

Sue looked skeptical. "Tomorrow is a school planning day."

Jeremy said, "Yeah!"

"Can I? Can I spend the night?" Tegan literally jumped up and down.

"What do you think?" That, from my daughter, jiggling her baby girl.

I said, "Let 'em stay."

Niki smiled. She gave me a good-bye hug. "Thanks, Grandma." That girl's voice always sounded throatier, richer than I expected. I wouldn't be at all surprised, someday, to see my granddaughter on the television screen, hosting the news ... the weather. Something special!

As soon as everyone else left for home, Jeremy began his usual mad dash trek around our house: through the family room, the living room, down the hall, and back through our family room. Behind him, Tegan, blonde hair half as long as her body, our four year-old called out, "Jawamy, wait for me! Wait for me, Jawamy!"

"What's on television?" I asked, hoping to settle down my two live wires.

"The Simpsons. Let's watch The Simpsons!" Jeremy turned the dial to my least favorite program. I'd managed to avoid it since its inception a year or two ago; but tonight, for a while it kept my darlings still. At its final scene I flipped off the set. "We'll find you a place to sleep," I told my grandchildren.

"No! Please! Five more minutes!"

"Five more minutes of what? Bart Simpson's over."

"Do we have to go to bed now?" wailed Tegan, eyes the color of amber syrup, a-brim with woe.

Jeremy's baby blues danced my way. "I know," he said. "Grandma'll tell us a story. Then we'll sleep."

"Well, I like that! Jeremy Wilson, are you saying my stories put you to sleep?" I ran my hand over blonde hair so spiky it felt and looked like finely-cut wheat. "I bet I know a story rivaling Batman."

On the word, "story," Jimmy re-appeared at our kitchen door.

"Hey Daddy," Jeremy said. "Grandma, I don't want to watch Batman. I like Scooby-Doo."

"Yeah," Tegan said. "Scooby-doo, Where Are You!"

I asked Jimmy, "What brings you back?"

"I left my wallet." He picked it up off the kitchen table. "Guys, Grandma's telling you a story? Boring. Let's turn on world news."

Tegan squeezed into my rocker beside me. "What story you tellin' us, Grandma?"

Jeremy plopped onto the carpet. Legs crossed, hand under chin, he eyed the two of us.

"I could tell you about the old woman, chased by a bear. Or the story about your Great-Grandpa Hamp's crazy gator. No," I put up the foot rest to my rocker-recliner, "I'll tell you about the time a snake bit my daddy, your grandpa."

Jimmy said, "Bye, you all. I'm tempted to stay and listen to Mom's story, but Sue says I should hurry home."

Without looking around, I said, "Drive home carefully, Son."

Jeremy and, hopefully, Tegan, remembered my dad. Jeremy had been four and Tegan two days short of two when Daddy died.

"Did you know, after that snake bit my dad, for the rest of his life, Daddy's blood was filled with jillions of …. No, I can't tell you what was in Daddy's blood. Not yet. That comes at the end of this story."

Suddenly, an epiphany struck me head on. Time had to be a magic circle. From the time I was born and set eyes on Grandma's Bug Swamp parlor, I was the grandchild. Grandma told me story after story. She'd begin, "Come here, Little Bushy. Sit in my lap. Have you ever seen a wild cat? Or a bear?" She'd smooth back my hair. Then she'd light into whatever tale, that day, struck her fancy.

Growing up in our Bug Swamp farmhouse, I begged for stories, my very life depended on Grandma's Nettie's story-telling. During The Great Depression era, we had no television screen to watch, no radio that ground out static. Grandma and any other human being within ear-shot, became my sole entertainment, other than nature's Venus-fly traps, doodle bugs, neighboring friends, books, etc. Tonight, Little Bushy still lurked inside this old grandma of four. At the same time, I was Grandma Nettie; well, really, Grandma Billie. Confusing to say the least.

With grandma batteries recharged, I prayed a silent prayer: *Thank you, dear Lord, for Grandma Nettie. Thank you for my sweet grandchildren.*

"Listen," I said, thrilled to entertain my offsprings' offspring. "After you hear all about how that old snake bit Daddy, I'll tell you about *The Old Woman and the Bear.* Bedtime's a long way off. In the morning you two can sleep just as late as you wish."

"Are you talking to me?" Buddy came in from our "bigger screen" room after watching the tail inning of some ball game.

"If you choose to walk in late for work tomorrow, sure I'm talking to you."

"Papa!" Jeremy jumped up and grabbed Buddy's hand. "You tell us a story."

"Yeah, Buddy," I said. "Tell them about the day you lost your finger."

All interest shifted from Grandma to Papa Buddy. Tegan sprang out of my chair. "How'd you lose your finger, Papa?" Tegan asked. "Did you ever find it?"

"Hey," I said. "Who would like some home-baked cookies and milk?"

Three people yelled, "Me!"

Buddy began, "I got up that morning with all my fingers on both hands."

"Then what happened?"

"Sit on the couch and I'll show you."

"Wait. Show me too," I joined the kids on the couch. I'd serve my cookies and milk at Buddy's intermission.

Info: Buddy lost his finger to an old Wampee, South Carolina, Farmall cub tractor.

Chapter 25

Lisa's Wedding

Summer, 1991, my brother, Jack's youngest, beautiful, blonde Lisa Maria, tops in her class at Atlanta's Bauder College, had just graduated, ready to run a business. In the wings, awaiting her next humongous event was Jim, a soaring basketball player hailing from Auburn, Alabama. All banners flew in Lisa's hometown, Savannah. Of course all of us arranged our lives around Lisa and Jim's upcoming marriage. Lisa asked my daughter, Mona, and Jimmy's ten year-old daughter, Niki, to be bridesmaids. Jimmy's and Sue's seven year-old Jeremy was to serve as ring-bearer. This would be our first such celebration since, fifteen years earlier, Mona married her love, Tim.

Certainly my mind flew to thoughts of Mother. In 1968, while she fought her losing battle with Multiple Myeloma, Jack's wife, Marcie, gave birth to Lisa. My family and I had motored down from Maryland to help with Mother. Unable to sit or stand, the day the new parents brought Lisa home, Mother lay propped on pillows. Jack found her a hand-mirror. She used this to view her prized new grand-baby.

Lisa was born in April. Mother died in July. And now, twenty-three years later, this baby girl would pledge her life to another. How Mother would have loved attending this milestone. After basking in the beauty and heartfelt import of Lisa's wedding, I thought to myself, *what if the Lord allowed Mother to witness this event!* The following projected from that thought.

Billie's Fantasy:
*Mother's "Fantastic" Voyage (Told in First
Person via Mother's Viewpoint)*

In heaven everyone is privileged; but surmounting my expectations, God was granting me, Dottie Hamilton, an honor. Gabriel, God's archangel, beckoned. His thoughts lent gold to my awareness. First I would need to coordinate my flow of energy with the heat bands of earth.

Earth. My home. That's where my people await God's calling!

My people. When dire pain rendered my earthly body unlivable, our Good Lord called, and I fled. Was that an eternity ago, or yesterday? I felt joy, fleeing the agony of human existence, to scoot up, up, out, away, until the silvery connecting cord gripping my mortal soul snapped, its burden thankfully left to enrich the world, to make leaves greener, flowers brighter, young cheeks rosier.

Pausing, I looked down at my son and daughter. For a moment I felt their sorrow. They gazed at my wasted body, their faces sad. Billie Faye told her brother, "Jack, our mother's gone. She's gone to the Lord."

I had little time to dwell on her words. Before me eternity spread wide. My focus, a brilliant light spread its joy. Nowhere was any room for sorrow.

Truth. Truth wore sunlit wings. It swept me forward. Truth knew no grief, no despair, no defeat. And with truth came balance. Death, a brief necessity for eternal existence, knew no effort, no stress, only peace, fulfillment, rewards spread out unceasingly.

Since in Paradise time proved nonexistent, happiness and being … just were. Suffice it to say, a moment or an eon had passed since Gabriel revealed to me God's gift, and that my translation to earth would be temporary. Of course.

As swift as thought, my spirit encountered Earth's outer limits, revolving as the sphere turned on its axis. Gradually I slipped through ions non-synchronous to my spiritual body. Overcoming those resistance bands left me free to travel anywhere on earth. I even regained certain human faculties. I grasped onto thoughts of earthly family. Readying myself for them, I should first re-experience the world.

Such a change from Paradise! A bombardment of emotions assailed me. I surrendered to a cacophony of love, hate, fear, dread, power. I swam, buoyed by care, deceit, desire, warmth, a dichotomy of human feelings. I could have been lost forever had not Gabriel's silent whisper reminded me of my pilgrimage.

I attained an immediate bubble of awareness. I was there; but where?

All around me this confinement of walls and ceiling appeared luxurious by human standards. Thick carpeting rendered footsteps noiseless. Walls rose up, up, up, to a ceiling looming skyward. On outer walls loomed windows, not to the outside world, because only light passed through those stained-glass panes; but such a light. Iridescent blues, pinks, lavenders, yellows, whites radiated into the hall's interior, blanketing all in a most "heavenly" glow. Trailing through a thick pillar supporting a beam, I became an invisible member of a colorful group.

Gabriel never revealed to me why I was here. Maybe this group was my purpose. I observed the assembly's turmoil. A beautiful girl in white, my old self sneaked in the title, bride. She dominated the scene. Why did her eyes speak to me? Blue, they looked familiar. An earthly past nudged my being. This girl's hair, shiny blonde, flowed to her shoulders. Something about the lines of her gown reminded me of a time I created like-lines … seams on a sewing machine! Her gown, white satin studded with pearls and rhinestones, hugged her body before swirling around her feet, its long, oval train, trailing.

The bride stood tall amidst a throng of beauties, all wearing deep rose-colored dresses. One young girl with eyes shiny like dark jewels, she claimed my attention. Such a pretty girl. Blonde curls encircled her face, honey-tan.

A tiny elfin sprite, gold-brown hair long and flying, dashed around the room, only to lean against and slide down into a corner. There, she sat and pondered. My heart wished to absorb that sweet face. She looked a bit like the bride. Who were these people? I needed this knowledge.

From around a corner strode a young boy clad in black. His outstretched arms held a pillow of white satin topped by a rose and two rings. The lad looked serious, his white blonde hair as shiny as any angel's halo.

Pushing a camera tripod, a determined young man halted before a plush couch. He reached over the sofa and removed from the wall a picture of some solid citizen. The fellow told the picture, "I'll replace you later." He beckoned the bride. "Over here, beautiful." An older lady busied herself with the bride's satin train.

More awareness arose from the past. This man was here to take pictures. Someone, I didn't know who, was marrying today. I had no memory of such luxury in my human existence.

The photographer positioned the bride onto the couch. He beckoned to the rosy maids, and they gathered around the bride. He said, "You, pretty blonde, move in slightly. And you." He said to the tow-head lad with the pillow. "Kneel. Face the bride."

The lad attempted a slight bend of both knees, then sensibly placed one knee onto the floor.

The photographer held hands parallel. He pointed to, "You! Pretty brunette! Move out a bit."

I was drawn to this young woman. Such a dear face. More strains of the familiar.

Gabriel's silent whisper intervened, transporting me into a candle-lit sanctuary. Flowers fashioned into crosses and hearts intermingled with white tapers, glowed in their candelabra. Crowning this beauty, organ music swelled, "Jesu Joy of Man's Desiring."

Handsome young men in formal black proceeded up the aisle. Mounting steps to the altar, one young man looked totally relaxed. He strode freely. He smiled, claiming his spot in the growing semi-circle. I loved that smile. Why?

Those lovely, rose-clad girls photographed in the hallway, they drifted up the aisle. My attention centered on the radiant young blonde and the pretty brunette.

Here came the ring bearer. He walked in beside a partner, the flower girl.

Music hushed. Abruptly the organist lit into "Here Comes the Bride!" My eternal spirit recognized the tune as "Lohengrin's March."

In time to music familiar to everyone who has ever wed or thought about marriage, a man entered through the sanctuary doorway; clutching his arm, the bride.

My son! My son, Jack, twenty three years older than that last glimpse above my sickbed. And the bride: Lisa! My granddaughter, Marcie and Jack's baby girl, born to Marcie not long before I ....

Memory intruded familiar pain into this moment of clarity. The helplessness I felt, my paralyzed body. Depression, pain, despair, the yearning I'd felt for heaven.

Yes! I'd waited for Marcie to bring home our new baby. Outside a car door slammed. She and Jack brought in our precious bundle. They uncovered her face.

Such frustration. Flat of my back, I couldn't lift my head.

Jack solved that. He placed Lisa beside me and gave me the largest hand mirror in the house. Propped onto pillows I viewed my grandbaby's every feature, from the top of her downy blonde head to the tips of her baby-pink toes. My daughter and I discussed the beauty and possible future of this precious addition to our family.

My daughter, Billie Faye. Beside me. I reached toward her hand, this older woman: my daughter, older now than I when I left this world. Together we watched her brother, my son, walk down the aisle beside his daughter. So beautiful.

The ceremony began. No longer just a shadow from Paradise, I felt myself a simple farm woman accustomed to simple fare, selling eggs to merchants. That way my son gained money enough to court his future wife. Rass and I, our greatest splurge in life was sending our two children to school, educating them so their lives would be easier than ours. Never could I have imagined this luxury.

I wanted to share with Rass, to call out to my Mama, to Papa, all basking in Paradise. To Rass's ma, Lisa's Great-Grandma Nettie, I'd say, "Look! Look, everybody! Would you believe such splendor could exist on this old earth? What decorations! And the bride! She's the vision every bride yearns to be. And would you believe Lisa's mama!" Marcie's off-white lace gown was lovely enough, she could have lent it to the queen of England. Marcie looked as radiant as her daughter!

'Course Grandma Nettie always knew how to take us down a peg. She'd say something like, "This wild spendin', it's got to be a sin. Without all this fol-de-rol, our sweet girl would be just as married. And a sight richer!"

The couple exchanged rings. My blonde ring-bearer frowned. He tugged on the Best Man's sleeve. The couple hadn't used his rings. The nice Best Man, the groom's father, stooped to reassure my precious grandchild. Lisa's handsome groom, Jim, patted the lad's shoulder.

Someone sang "The Lord's Prayer." The blonde bridesmaid, Niki, my granddaughter born to earth after I ascended, she fidgeted. In a sharing, eternal sense I felt her discomfort. Panty hose itched her legs, and her shoes pinched. After all, this was the first time Niki ever wore heels.

"I now pronounce you husband and wife," the preacher proclaimed. "You may kiss the bride."

Jim tipped up the face of his bride. They kissed. Lisa, turning toward the congregation of family and friends, pursed her lips. Widening her eyes, she silently mouthed, "Whew!"

Dual feelings descended. With one foot on earth and the other in heaven I felt Gabriel's presence. Wings spread wide, he hovered over the marriage altar. I scanned faces of my loved ones. If only they could see with my eyes. Gabriel was blessing the couple's union. I found myself thrust airily beside the archangel. He further opened my eyes. I recognized all my kin, gathered in this sumptuous sanctuary. I saw my son, my daughter, all of their children, and my children's children. I saw my oldest granddaughter, the child I held so dear. It seemed like yesterday that I broke into a rash when illness threatened her life. Mona Lynne was the brunette bridesmaid whose being spoke to mine. Her brother, my grandson, Jimmy was just eight years old at my death. He'd been horrified by tumors marring my face. All these dear ones, *mine*. Even the smiling groom's attendant, Jackie, another grandson. I hated that Jackie's stomach hurt so many nights when he was little. And the blonde ten year-old bridesmaid and her ring-bearer brother, both belong to Jimmy and his wife, Sue.

The little girl with long, golden hair, flying, Mona's sweet girl, Tegan. Where's their new baby? From on-high, a name drifted down. Through earthly mists I spied a tiny figure in someone's arms. Rachel! I memorized her dear, sweet face.

Above Calvary Baptist Church, amidst airy clouds floated two additional grandchildren. As of yet they hadn't arrived, but I knew them well: Kayla and Jonathan. Kayla would shine her light on Billie's youngest son, Bryan's family. Jonathan, Jimmy and Sue's afterthought, he would bring us great joy.

Above Gabriel a light appeared, growing in radiance. It drew the archangel; it drew me like air into a vacuum. Casting a loving eye onto the throng before me, I breathed, "Thank you, Dear Lord. Bless my family forever." *The Good Lord willing, in a flap of a wing, I'll see them again.*

Kelly, Sarah, Jackie, Jake, *Jack*, Jordan,
Marcie, Ryan, Landon, (*Jim and Lisa*)
Jack and Marcie Hamilton, their son, Jackie, his wife
and son and daughter, plus Jim and Lisa and their
three sons, years after those two were married in
"Lisa's Wedding." All are Jack and Marcie's family.

Chapter 26

The Waycross Reunion

A few years ago Uncle Charles and Aunt Rock moved their family from rural Waresboro to Waycross, Georgia. Since graduating from Clemson College in 1934, Grandma's baby boy spent each working day teaching agriculture at Waresboro High. Impressed by their Ag. Teacher's dedication, as well as his service to their community, Ware County drafted C. P. Hamilton as their Superintendent of Education. He and his family enjoyed their new Waycross home in its town/rural setting, abutted by their large pecan orchard.

On this particular morning Uncle Charles' heart clammered with confusion. Usually, he was the one traveling through two states to visit family; but today, plan was, they would visit him. Can't say he wasn't glad they were coming. He just didn't want anyone shocked. He'd failed a lot, in health and looks. In bed last night someone whispered, "You'll soon see your dear ones!" Dear ones had to be Ma and Pa, his sisters, Sally, Molly, and Laura, also Rass, his older brother. Maybe others. Seemed like the years hurtled through time since he'd been with so many close relatives.

While Uncle Charles yearned to see his folks, right now he felt like lying right where he was and doing zilch. For a little while, why couldn't Aunt Rock and his daughters, Mary Jane and Sarah Anne, stop hovering? He appreciated their love, their devotion, but from somewhere he had to drum up enough strength to enjoy tonight's get-together.

Charlie said, "Rock, you're so like Ma. You too, Mary Jane, wantin' to stay busy every minute of the day." He smiled at females he loved. "Not that being like my mama is in anyway bad." He stopped for a breath. "Plain and simple. Ma liked work and thought everybody else should. She'd dredge up something for us boys to do, (breath) whether at home, (breath) shelling corn for old Mary to gnash down on, (breath) or next door slaving away for Uncle Bert." He paused, closed his eyes.

"Are you okay, Daddy?" Mary Jane dragged her chair in closer.

Charlie sighed. "Just thinking."

About the time Mary Jane decided her dad was asleep, he mumbled something.

"What was that, Daddy?"

"I said, 'malingerin'.' Ma's word for laziness."

"No, Rock, I don't want that."

"Drink this orange juice, Charlie. You didn't touch your egg, or your toast."

Already laid up with rheumatism, Uncle Charles recently developed a respiratory ailment. "You know, Rock," he said, "I feel about as tired now as I did that summer I dragged tobacco for Uncle Bert. Let me tell you," Uncle Charles lay still, thinking and catching his breath. "From sunup on, that day proved a scorcher. I can still feel the heat from Old Mary's hide. And boy, were my legs sticky." Another pause. "By eleven o'clock that night, I think I'd swiped against every leaf in Uncle Bert Holmes' tobacco patch."

"Drink this juice. Stop your talking."

"Mama, let him talk." Sarah Anne pulled her chair in close, hoping to hear more about her dad's growing up in South Carolina's Bug Swamp community.

In Athens, Georgia, I heard that members of our family planned to visit Uncle Charles; however, my back "went out," and I missed the reunion. Thank goodness Mary Jane and Sarah Anne filled me in on talk that day.

Sarah Anne said Uncle Charles reached for her hand, leaving Aunt Rock holding his orange juice. Sarah Anne, their younger daughter, looked a lot like her dad with her dark hair, deep blue eyes, and pretty skin. He turned over her hand, tracing its veins with an index finger.

"I was just a kid, Sarah Anne, too young to work all day *and* all night. As soon as we got home, I slid off Old Mary. Ma caught me on my way down." Uncle Charles stopped talking and coughed into a Kleenex. "Ma half-carried me to the house. I flopped across that bed asleep before she could bring over a pan of water. She said she pulled off my clothes and washed me the best she could. That night I needed sleep more than 'cough, cough,' soapin'."

"Daddy, what was it like, growing up with Grandpa?" Sarah Anne's idea was to keep her daddy talking.

Uncle Charles took so long answering, Sarah Anne decided to tip-toe out and leave him to nap.

The man wasn't napping. He was thinking. "I always loved my pa, but I tell you girls, Pa could be one stern man. Many times he told me and Rass, 'Boys,' he'd say, 'If a thing's worth doin', it's worth doin' well!'"

Uncle Charles' laugh brought on a cough. "But I tell you, Pa was human." He coughed some more. "Rock, that orange juice."

Sarah Anne said she always got a charge out of her dad's chuckles.

He rallied, wiped tears onto a pajama sleeve. "Sometimes Pa was *too* human. This day Rass learned his lesson. He sure Lord picked the wrong time to laugh at Pa. Pa was a'hammerin' somethin' on the front porch, and smashed his thumb. One minute Rass was squattin' on his haunches watchin' the hammerin'. The next, that boy landed on the far end of the porch!"

Aunt Rock came back with a bowl of soup. "Somebody say something funny?"

"Take that stuff away, Rock. I'm talkin' to my girls." Uncle Charles broke into another coughing fit. That subsided and he talked some more. It was like he was wound up and couldn't stop.

"Girls," he said, "if you think Pa could be rough, you should'a seen Ma when she got riled. I tell you, she wore out Lutie and me the day she caught us playin' cards in the barn loft. The flat of your grandma's hand could feel more dangerous than any devil she said lived in those cards!"

Lutie was Aunt Tennessee and Uncle Furnie Harris's daughter, Uncle Charles' first cousin, and she lived next door.

"I'm about ready for my nap." Uncle Charles mumbled something else.

"What did you say, Daddy?" Sarah Anne thought he said, "It'll be good seeing ya, Ma."

Growing up on a Bug Swamp tobacco farm in the early twentieth century tried the valor of dedicated farmers. Charlie Palmer Hamilton, baby of the Hamilton family, possessed absolutely no desire to work the fields. He took little pleasure in balancing a plough facing a mule's rear end, or in expending energy performing ceaseless chores around a tobacco farm. In Uncle Charles' mind my dad was the son cut out of farmer's cloth. Rassie could stay on the farm with Ma. Uncle Charles yearned to get away, to discover his talents beyond the familiar horizon where blue skies kissed tobacco rows.

Despairing that he'd ever be anything but a Bug Swamp farmer, by the time Charlie Palmer matured to any decision about his future, Grandma's youngest had already goofed off through all of high school. One day, spring of 1930, Superintendent Seaborne announced to the senior class at Conway High, "Tomorrow I plan to meet with all seniors attending college."

"College!" The word clanged through Uncle Charles's mind like a dinner bell when he'd skipped breakfast.

He slept little that night.

Next morning, before leaving for school, the teen-ager approached his mother. "Ma, I want to go to college; but, I don't know how we'll pay for it."

Grandma Nettie cradled her young son's narrow face between soft hands. "Palmer," she stroked his brow, "if you want more schoolin', we'll find us a way!"

Still another obstacle loomed. When Superintendent Seaborne met with individual seniors to discuss future plans, he told young Charlie, "Son, stay on the farm. Forget school. You're *not* college material."

Uncle Charles regretted wasting his high school years, but he couldn't turn back time. "You're wrong, Mr. Seaborne," he cried, "give me a chance. I can make it at Clemson." He felt if he didn't go away to school, he'd be planted on the Bug Swamp farm like a hill of tobacco during a drought, and receive so few elements he craved, he'd wither and die there.

That very afternoon, Charlie went to see Uncle Hal Holmes. Grandma's younger brother, a local doctor, was a bachelor at the time, and financially comfortable.

Uncle Hal slapped Uncle Charles' boyish shoulders. He said, "Sure, Son, I'll lend you money for college. Wish somebody could have done that for me!"

As determined now as previously "lack-a-daisical," Daddy's young brother entered Clemson, complete with its well-known freshmen hazing and ROTC program.

Always Grandma served as the family's bank. She wore their money in a calico money-bag pinned to her petticoat waist-line. Most of the time Grandma had no need to worry about bulges. With money so scarce, when her son entered college, she sought to send her 'pride and joy' ten cents a week. Sometimes, she failed that.

Meanwhile Daddy married a pretty, young Todd girl, and a year and a half later, I arrived. That fall, after my birth in July, Uncle Charles hitch-hiked home. Stopping at a cross-roads store, my college junior uncle dropped a precious coin into a cigarette machine. He hit the jackpot! Out rolled streams of silver. Scooping up outlandish treasure, young Charlie Palmer arrived home with pockets loaded. He tossed his sister-in-law three whole dollars. "Buy our baby some blankets, Dot," he told her.

And she did; three of the softest, fleeciest blankets she could find at Burroughs and Company.

In 1934, a year after I joined the family, Uncle Charles graduated from Clemson with a degree in, guess what! The entire Hamilton clan celebrated. Grandma about burst through the bib of her calico apron, learning that her son finished college with a degree in agriculture, despite his feelings about Bug Swamp farming.

Waresboro, Georgia, the site of Uncle Charles' new, agricultural teaching career, to his Bug Swamp relatives seemed a continent away.

Their minds cloaked this bump in a South Georgia road in mystery as removed from truth as Bug Swamp from Egypt land.

I remember looking forward to Uncles Charles' twice-a-year visits, summers and Christmases. On one of those visits, he brought with him a tall, smiling, Georgia girl, his wife, Sarah. Uncle Charles called her 'Rock', short for her maiden-name, Roquemore. Grandma welcomed this new daughter-in-law, and breathed a sigh of relief. At last, Palmer had someone to look after him.

A couple of years earlier Grandma had given up matrimonial hopes for her boy after he and his beautiful, talented Good Hope fiancé broke off their engagement. So, Charlie Palmer. Married. Finally!

Later that year, just when life held great promise, Uncle Charles developed all over aches, pains, soreness. His doctor said Clemson's freshman year hazing probably added to this condition, which persisted. Aunt Rock nursed her husband. She fed him. She loved him. The doctor said, "I'm sorry, Son, but you're saddled with horrid old rheumatoid arthritis."

Uncle Charles suffered. His help-mate applied hot and cold packs. She massaged his pained body.

Thanks to Aunt Rock's care and God's mercy, tall, handsome Charlie Palmer, his bones tortured by disease, lived, but not without cost. His body bent forward from his waist, crowding his lungs and stomach.

When Grandma Nettie next saw her son, he looked thin and drawn, his shoulders hunched, and his head permanently bowed, but never his spirit.

In spite of Uncle Charles' chronic illness he tackled his position as Ware County teacher of agriculture with a fervor matched by few.

Life rewarded him and Aunt Rock with a beautiful, blonde, blue-eyed baby girl. When Aunt Rock's delivery date grew near, we Bug Swampians paced our farm house floor. Finally, Uncle Charles' tantalizing telegram arrived: "Features like father, fixtures like mother."

Not quite three years later, Aunt Rock gave birth to a second child, dark-haired and dimple-chinned. Again Uncle Charles telegrammed us, this time, "Fixtures like mother, features like father.

Years passed. The Waresboro couple gave themselves to their family, their work and to their community. They honored others, and in return, received honor from those they served.

To further his career, for years Uncle Charles and his family spent summer vacations at the University of Georgia. There they boarded with Mrs. Birchmore, a wonderful woman who became third grandma to Mary Jane and Sarah Anne. Aunt Rock took courses, earning a teaching degree; although years prior to this degree, she taught at Waresboro High School. Meanwhile, Uncle Charles sweated his way through graduate school.

What kind of time spin took Uncle Charles and Aunt Rock so quickly from newly-weds, to parents … to grandparents? "Before their very eyes," Grandma Nettie would say, they discovered both daughters, grown-up and married, Mary Jane to Tommy, and Sarah Anne to Frank. At reunion time Uncle Charles and Aunt Rock's "children," Bert and Jane, belonged to Mary Jane and her husband, Tommy. What special gifts from God!

Old Mary's tobacco-drag partner satisfied his ambitions with his final status. Charlie wished he could look Mr. Seaborne in the eye. He'd say, "Remember me? The boy you said wasn't college material? Well, Mr. Seaborne, let me tell you something. Before I retired, I became Superintendent of Education in Ware County, Georgia, same position you held at good old Conway High."

Mary Jane came in from the kitchen. "Sun in your eyes, Dad?" She let down window blinds.

"I'd never have thought it," Uncle Charles said.

"Thought what?" Mary Jane picked up the book she'd been reading.

"Just talkin' to myself." Her dad beckoned her nearer. Never had his eyes looked bluer. He whispered, "Mary Jane, they'll be here soon."

Aunt Rock joined her family. Uncle Charles raised his head. "Look, Rock," he pointed toward the door. Surprise lit his face. "Sakes alive, Ma! You're here!"

"Golly!" Behind Ma his whole family piled in. "Sally! Is that you? Laura! Well, I'll be blessed, Molly, you're here too! Where's Rass? Hey, Rass! You brought Pa. Hey, Pa!

"This is great! Just great! I didn't know we'd have our reunion right here. Gather around, you all, let's entertain Rock and the girls. We'll sing us a song, just like used to! Ma, you sing the high part. Rass, you sing bass."

Surrounded by his mother and father, sisters and brother, Uncle Charles serenaded his wife and daughters with a breathless, "Amazing Grace, how sweet the sound."

Just for Ma, always after "Palmer" to memorize scripture, he recited the twenty-third psalm. He started in on "The Lord is my shepherd. I shall not want . . ." He paused, reaching for his mate of nearly fifty years. She took his hand. "Rock," he wheezed, "this talking is wearing me out." His eyes drooped shut.

Aunt Rock squeezed his hand with both of hers. She kissed his forehead. "Rest well, my love."

Mary Jane says, in her mind's eye she saw her dad rise from his bed. He stood up arrow-straight, following his father, mother, brother, and sisters to a larger family reunion, a reunion which one day Mary Jane, Aunt Rock, and Sara Anne would attend.

A day or two later, a second reunion took place. Charlie Palmer Hamilton's family put his body to rest on a hill in Cordele, Georgia, Mary Jane and Tommy's home town.

I yearned to be with them all. In Athens, I bade a long distance farewell to a beloved family member. *Happy sailing, Uncle Charles. Enjoy your homecoming.*

Chapter 27

Changing of the Guard (1993)

An Early Family Saga

Each year our family is thrilled to honor our forefathers who made living in these United States of America, "Land of the Free and Home of the Brave," possible. Many years we load up our car and join other Athenians at or near Bishop Park, watching a plethora of splashy, sky-spangled eye-pleasers accompanied by their popping and bursting "sis-boom-bah's."

Our family adds a further dimension to July fourth. My husband, Buddy, popped into this world on the birthday of his Uncle Sam. During our children's "home" years, after fireworks at Bishop Park we'd return to Robin Road, break out presents, sing "Happy Birthday, Dear Daddy, Buddy, or Son," if his mom were with us. Then, we'd, gobble up birthday cake and ice cream.

In a blink it seems, our children marry and create their own family traditions. Thus, Buddy and I gravitate toward other "empty-nesters." Hosted by Don and Lois Shackleford, Archie and Dixie Hyde, and Warren and Marcia Trotter, Buddy and I begin a new tradition. We celebrate both Uncle Sam's and my husband's birthday, boating, eating, and socializing at Lake Hartwell, Georgia.

One day our daughter, Mona, says, "Mom, this year let's have a birthday party for you and Dad. You can still go to Lake Hartwell for the fourth. We'll have our party the sixth. Can we manage that?"

My birthday falls on July eighth, four days after Buddy's Fourth of July shindig. We'd just split the difference. Mona says, "I really want us to do this."

Anytime our family can get together, that's fine with me. Buddy and I drive off the main highway onto a short dirt road, leading ... where? It isn't that I don't visit my daughter; but I always get the feeling of an adventure, passing houses on either side of a road ceasing where my daughter's tree-studded yard begins.

Mona, her husband, Tim, Tegan, their seven-year-old daughter, and Rachel, their four year-old baby girl, live at a place called Devil's Pond. July 4, 1994, stepping out of our Mitsubishi, I think, *Devil's Pond. What a misnomer.* To get to the front door, shades of "The Wizard of Oz!" Buddy and I tread up a yellow brick "walkway." Our imaginative son-in-law calls this walk he planned and executed, Mona's "yellow brick road." Nestled amidst a forest of dogwood trees, their home reminds me of an enlarged version of "The Three Bears" house, the one invaded by Goldilocks. Another eye-grabber: A second-floor, diamond shaped window frames a glamorous girl wearing long tresses. Tim has placed Mona's Cosmetology manikin for intruders to see, and think, *somebody's watching us!*

Father Time: a finger-snap ago I was the child, Grandma's Little Bushy. Always ready with some task for my brother or me, Grandma was also quick to hug and wipe noses. Now, I tell stories, kiss and hug; sometimes even referee a fight or two.

While we're still out front, Jimmy and Sue drive up. Goody! We'll get to see our newest grand-child. A little over a year ago our son and daughter-in law took a trip to the hospital and returned with this second baby boy, Jonathan. Before they leave, their doctor says, "Anybody got a magic marker? I need to paint a mustache on this kid. Then he and his dad will be twins."

At Mona's, Buddy and I jockey for positions nearest the door. "I get him first," I tell my husband, as I reached for a blanket of sweetness. That sweetness is in no blanket. Wearing shorts and a tee shirt, he runs ... not to me. He runs straight into Papa Buddy's arms. Shucks! Children always like him best.

Niki, and Jeremy climb out of their car. They eye Tegan and Rachel. I whisper, "Niki, get everybody together. Find them something to do."

She calls out, "Hey, kids, let's play school. I'm the teacher." Probably Niki would rather spend her time with a phone glued to her ear, talking to Anne Cox, Allison, or Amanda.

Two years separate Tegan and Jeremy. When they were close to four and six, those kids raced around and around through our house. Tegan, her foot-long hair flying, trailed after Jeremy, older and a foot taller. "Wait for me Jaramy!" I never knew why they ran. It wasn't like they had anywhere to go but the den, the hall, the living room, and once more, the den.

"What smells so good?" I ask anybody who will answer. Buddy and I sit side by side on the couch. Everybody else looks busy. Buddy still jiggles Jonathan on his knee. I ask, "Where's Tim?"

"He's outside, barbequeing ribs." Mona pours tea into a pitcher.

Sue says, "Shall I top off this salad with dressing, or wait for people to pick their own?"

Mona says, "Let 'em choose their own."

I ask, "Can I help?"

Both girls chorus, "No."

"Humph." It is rather nice, sitting here, smelling all these goodies and waited on hand and foot. Definitely a change.

Tegan sits beside me. She reaches a finger toward Jonathan's cheek. "Hey there Cuz."

Jonathan smiles at Tegan, slides off Papa's lap, then dashes to his mama.

Tegan shakes her head. "Jonathan doesn't like me."

"Yes he does. That's one reason he ran away. He likes you too much. Now. I want to hear about you. Your mama tells me you've been breaking board after board at Tae Kwan Do. Which do you like best, martial arts or soccer?"

"I like both. Did you know that Rachel is our soccer team mascot?"

"I saw her riding on different team members' shoulders."

Recently I attended Tegan's soccer game, and heard the players call Rachel, "Sammie." Wonder why they called her that?

Maybe that's what Mona's talking about. She says Rachel will sit in front of a mirror and comb her hair to the side. She'll say, "Now I'm Sara."

One day I noticed the name "Toni" on Rachel's bedroom door. I asked, "Who's Toni?"

Mona said, "That's what Rachel calls herself this week. Some days she's Sport."

"Why Sport?"

"Sport, from Harriette, the Spy. Mama! Really. Who is my daughter?"

I tell Mona, "She's my spirited little black-eyed granddaughter, and her name is RACHEL!"

Jeremy runs into the room. He says, "Grandma, you've seen me and Niki and Tegan play soccer. When are you coming to my soft ball game?"

Buddy asks, "When do you play next?"

From the side porch Jimmy pipes up, "Five o'clock Thursday at Satterfield Park. I'll pick you up."

I've always thought Jeremy should play baseball, or, in this case, softball. He's a ten-year-old bat wielder if I ever saw one.

Sue, placing a colorful salad on the table, asks, "When is Bryan coming?"

Tim's hands are filled with a platter of ribs. He tells Sue, "Bryan can't come tonight. It has something to do with Brenda's family. But he says maybe we can all get together next week."

I hate that Bryan and Brenda couldn't come. Bryan called me this morning and said their Golden Retriever, Danger, had been killed; run over by a car. I haven't said anything, for I don't want my family sad. Kayla should be here tonight, visiting with her cousins. She and Jon-Jon would have fun together. Four months older than Jon-Jon, she's a little whirlwind.

Niki puts down the hall telephone. "I asked them to play school, Grandma, but they were too busy running around. She turns to Tegan, "How about you? Are you ready to play school?"

Sue asks, "Where is Jeremy?"

"He went to the bathroom. Here he comes," Buddy tells her.

Jeremy comes over and picks up his baby brother. "Hey Grandma. Do you think we favor?"

I say, "A little. You both have blonde hair and blue eyes. One birthday after you had lost three teeth, you ran around singing, 'All I want for Christmas is my two front teeth.'"

Jeremy said, "I didn't want the third one?"

I tapped him on the rear end like Grandma Nettie did me when I "smart-talked."

That's when Tim says, "Listen up, everybody. Let's eat!"

By the time I felt full enough to pop, Sue said, "You two, gather around this cake."

Buddy and I bent over the beautiful carrot cake our South African daughter-in-law baked, iced, and topped with two candles, one for each of us. I shouldn't have been surprised she did such a perfect job with that cake. Her mom, Priscilla, is a great baker. She taught Sue well.

My wish for my family is that we get together more often, and for Bryan, Brenda, and Kayla to be with us at our next get-together.

Niki walks me to the car. I put my arm around her waist. At fourteen she's already a good four inches taller than her short old grandma. I say, "Thanks, Niki, for trying to help with the kids."

Niki shakes her head. "They don't listen to me."

I tell her, "It hasn't been that long since you were their age. Do you remember the night you, Papa, and I went to get ice cream and I tried to show you the man in the moon?"

Niki says, "No."

"Well, I do. I never could get you to see that moon-man, just like my daddy never could get me to see him."

Niki smirks. "I've seen the man in the moon, Grandma."

"You have?"

Niki nods. "Not in person, but Neil Armstrong's picture was in one of your old National Geographic magazines."

Just like, earlier, I swatted Jeremy's bottom, now I swat Niki's. Jimmy and Sue's kids remind me of their old grandma, just as smart-mouthed as I was eons ago.

Riding home I stay silent so long, Buddy asks, "Cat got your tongue?"

"I've been thinking. You and I are so blessed. No one ever had a better daughter. She's not just my daughter; Mona's my friend. I could say a ton more, but I won't."

Buddy reminds me, "You know, we do have two more kids."

"Yep," I say. "All our children are special. That Jimmy makes me almost jealous."

Buddy says, "Now you sound silly."

I tell my husband, "You don't know? Our son has a second Mama. He tells me he traipses out into the woods and sits against a tree until he feels a part of it. He likes old Mother Nature more than me. I'll bet you a silver dollar."

Oops, Grandma, I know I shouldn't bet.

I don't say that aloud. Buddy would *know* I'm off my rocker.

He says, "I hate it about Danger. You could have told me. That was one sweet little pup."

Buddy had ridden to Atlanta when Bryan's wife, Brenda, drove there to purchase their doggy. My husband had cuddled little mama-less Danger all the way home.

"You know, Buddy," I say, "I'm glad we bought our card and gift shop, if for no other reason than it taught Bryan how to deal with people."

Buddy agrees. "You mean it taught him to sell."

"Yep. It gave him a trade. Our boy was born to sell, anything, from birthday cards, to cars, to double wide trailers pretending to be houses. Why he told me the other day, "Mom, don't be surprised if I turn out to be a millionaire."

Buddy says, "At least he can dream."

I add, "You never know."

Tonight, Buddy and I have rounded a bend in our lives. We are able to look farther down the road to where he and I pass our baton to the next generation, our off-spring. I'm comforted, assured that this baton will land in the hands of capable, sensitive human beings, and, God willing, their children will pass on our family's banner into a successful, non-ending future.

I have great hope.

P.S. (Turn of the Century, Year, 2000)

Bryan, Brenda, and Kayla, all three have become Calabash citizens. Six years ago, the year we celebrated our birthday at Devil's Pond, Buddy retired, and we moved to our Calabash River cabin. Two years ago Bryan and Brenda built their own home on a next door river slough. Our sweet little neighbor, dusky-skinned, blue-eyed, seven year old Kayla, has two cats. She calls them Myrtle Beach and California. Her Golden Retriever, who chases raccoons in the marsh, answers to "Tango." Tango is Golden Retriever number two. Sadly, they buried number one at Union Point, Georgia, their dear, loving dog, Danger.

Since living at Calabash, Kayla's sapphire blue eyes alone are enough to captivate Grandpa Buddy, not to mention Grandma Billie. On the phone she says, "I love you, Papa." That's when he melts, jumps to his feet, and races next door.

In Athens, Jimmy and Sue live in our home, along with Jeremy and Jonathan. Niki has just finished her sophomore year at Florida State. This summer she's occupying Bryan and Brenda's upstairs and waitressing nearby at Captain John's, here on our river. I bet she gets good tips. Viewing that girl's brown eyes complemented by golden hair, is worth all of twenty percent per meal! Niki's one sharp girl, and, Grandma's intuition: whatever her future, our granddaughter will rise to the top. Already I'm nostalgic for the years she brought over her friends and entertained them at my house. Time's moveable beacon: it beckons from both yesterday and tomorrow.

Four months younger than Kayla, Jonathan is a blonde whiz. He especially likes to sit on Grandma's lap and get his back scratched. He and Jeremy have a black and white dog named Jessie. Niki's dog, Bluebell, named such because she has one blue eye and one that's brown, also was mama to a sweet little pup named Lazy. I say "was," because Lazy was attacked by a mad raccoon and is no longer with us. Neither is the raccoon. Niki is also mama to a kitty cat, oft times hiding beneath our coffee table. He "meows" to the name, Henry.

Oh! I've just heard something about Jeremy Wilson I don't like. A big boy for his age, Jeremy is playing football for Clarke Central's Gladiators. I'm sure Jeremy's happy, but I don't like the idea of big old football players roughin' up Grandma's boy. Another thing I'm leery of: at sixteen, Jeremy has his own car. Drive carefully, you hear me, teenager? 'Course that boy of mine, he's washing dishes at a Creole restaurant to pay for his car. I'm proud of him for that, and for a jillion reasons; but what thrills me most: while Jeremy drives, he pops in a tape and sings along with his music. Listening to Jeremy sing, I feel almost back at Bug Swamp. Sometimes I join in.

Tegan, four years younger than Jeremy, is a rising eighth grader. Unlike certain of my grandchildren, Tegan loves books. She and I have read all thirty-five (I think) books in K.A. Applegate's "Animorphs" series. Tegan buys a book, reads it, then passes it to me. She also paints with me when I'm in Athens. Actually, she's better at painting than her grandma. At the moment my second granddaughter plans to be a veterinarian. Oh. Now that Tegan's a second degree black-belt, she's my body guard.

Rachel and Jon-Jon attend the same school. Rachel is a fourth grader who loves socializing and singing. When Barnet Shoals School interviewed Rachel for admittance to kindergarten, our five-year-old stayed inside so long her mother went to fetch her. Recently Rachel had fallen in love with "The Lion King." Those interviewers asked the little girl if she liked singing. Miss Rachel said, "Yes. Want to hear me?" My granddaughter, true to her heritage, by the time her mother returned, had sung almost every "Lion King" song: "The Circle of Light," "Ha Kuna Matata," "He Lives in You," "Can You Feel the Love Tonight?" Rachel also writes poetry, one, on a door length poster dedicated to her "black belt" sister, her heroine; and Rachel paints great pictures. She and Tegan are parents to three dogs, three cats, and a bird.

Kayla, a second grader, attends Union Elementary near Calabash. Her beautiful eyes say it all; but she won't let the world in on half her secrets. She and Grandma, living next door, swing in the yard and watch squirrels swing through the trees. Kayla knows how to be a little lady. However, she can be a sweet little mess. At five years old, she brushed Tango's teeth with Grandma's toothbrush. (I knew it tasted peculiar.) Later she put Tango to bed in Grandma's guest bedroom. When I opened the door, covered to his doggy chin, Tango turned his head and looked at me, as at home on my embroidered pillowcase as any other houseguest.

On several momentous occasions Kayla slipped behind Papa Buddy and tipped him over backward in his easy chair. She thought this hilarious. So did Papa Buddy. He didn't the time she snipped off his hair in a place or two. I treasure those memories. I also remember watching and re-watching with Kayla the movie, "Air Bud." We sat through that movie together at least a half dozen times.

Last season Kayla took lessons in karate, and at the moment she's enjoying some kind of dance instruction at the town of Little River. She especially wanted to play soccer. Bryan and Brenda bought her a soccer outfit, but, sad to say, her team failed to materialize.

Like her grandma, Kayla paints pictures. She likes painting fish, and water. At about five, she drew an unidentifiable Mr. Somebody on a surfboard, chased by a shark. She said, "Can I sell this Grandma?"

I asked "How much money do want for it?" Kayla said, "One hundred dollars." I wrote *$100* on a scrap of paper and she copied at the bottom of her painting, 001$, (backward). I framed it, and today Kayla's surfer dude hangs over my Calabash kitchen table. I guess I owe my granddaughter a hundred bucks.

Back in Georgia, that blonde headed second grader, Jonathan, loves puzzles, has since six months old. Before he could walk, he'd "sit alone" in his crib or on the floor, and put together big-piece puzzles. Right now Jon-Jon collects keys. When I "visit" home, and lose a certain key, if anyone can produce that key, for some reason it's Jonathan. Also our youngest is fascinated by what he creates with Lego blocks. Buddy, seeing Jonathan's "Lego city" on the family pool table, says, "This boy has the makings of an architect." We'll see. When I come home and haven't seen my boy for a while, arms out-stretched, Jon-Jon rushes toward me. He says, "Gra-a-a-and-ma-a-a." I love that.

All my grandchildren interact well with people, do great work in school, and love their grandparents. What more could a grandmother ask of her children's children?

Well, that's quite enough palaverin' about family. I know what Grandma Nettie would tell her *great-great* -grandchildren if she could: "Chillern, be kind. Treat others like you want them to treat you, and love the Good Lord with all your heart, mind, body, and soul, for He made you!"

You said it, Grandma. I hope I've passed on your banner. I'm trying.

As Tiny Tim said in Dickens' *Christmas Carol,* "God bless us everyone!"

Our granddaughter, Kayla, graduating from kindergarten, with her mother, Brenda, and her dad, Bryan

Mona, Tim, Rachel, and Tegan Wilkes

Part VII

Romans 9: 28

And we know all good things work together

for good to them who love God …

Chapter 28

Coatless In December

Fall of 'ninety-four, my husband retired from his job as biometrician at Athens' Richard Russell Center. Dazed by time's "here today, gone tomorrow" swiftness, this morning, like a string of others, we awake to a day minus dread. From our bedroom windows we see fish jumping. In the trees next to our house, chattering squirrels leap from branch to branch. Buddy and I feel truly blessed. Our home away from home rests on the tidal banks of the Calabash River, not too far from where Dr. Stone assisted my mother-in-law in delivering the infant son who would become my husband.

During the early part of the 1900s, local people didn't believe in building next to the river. Buddy's Aunt Ellen said she couldn't stand its glare.

Her glare became our delight, as well as that of our son, Bryan, and his family. The river, an inlet from the ocean, permits us perennial, pleasant breezes; it bestows a tinge of salt to the air. We're privy to the song and sight of every coastal bird imaginable, to the sounds of wings flapping, the sight "of swans a'swimming," like the lyrics our family sang each Christmas. I could extol the wonders of our riverside haven "till the cows come home," Grandma Nettie might say.

Today, Friday afternoon, late November of 'ninety-nine, peace floods my soul. Outside, occasional puffs of air stir tree branches separating us from the river. Leaves flutter to the ground like multicolored snowflakes.

"Buddy," I tell my spouse. "You would never guess it is so close to Christmas!"

On this evening I have reason to claim peace. In less than ten years Buddy has suffered a heart attack, survived congestive heart failure coupled with quadruple bi-pass surgery, endured a vital lung operation, and, as an afterthought, had his gall bladder removed. Finally, he's out of the woods. I cross my fingers, then chide myself. Of course he'll be fine. Doctors say he will.

From the radio Bing Crosby's voice resonates throughout our small home-away-from-home. Although my soprano singing voice of the past has turned into a sixty-seven year-old croak, I attempt to blend my voice with Bing's. "I'm dreaming of a white Christmas…." From the looks of our weather, dreams of snow are all we'll have. Just as well. In a few days, motoring home to Athens, we won't need icy roads.

Buddy calls from the kitchen: "Billie! You ready yet?" We're eating out tonight.

"Soon." I'm entranced by the river. I've glimpsed the Calabash just as the tide turns. Except for leaves floating on its surface, the nearly motionless tidal river, like a lake, reflects sky and clouds and birds. I call to Buddy, probably snacking on something that'll spoil his supper. "Look outside. Every heron in North Carolina must be flying home."

Still gazing at the watery scene, and dressing before friends arrive, I pull over my head a black jersey blouse. This will be our last Friday evening together before Buddy and I return to Athens.

In settling the blouse my arm brushes against … What is *this*?

A knot the size of a bantam egg pokes from the side of my left breast. Forgetting our peaceful river, I fumble cold finger tips over my intruder.

"Buddy, come here!" I place his hand on the lump. "What *is* this?!"

"Hmm." He avoids my eyes; not before I see worry in his.

For two years, ever since a mammogram looks suspicious of an abnormality, I religiously examine my breasts.

Back to that mammogram:

Nervous, in spite of the North Carolina technician's chit-chat, I submitted to pulling, tugging, and positioning inherent to the procedure. Afterward, she showed me enlarged negatives back-lit on a wall. Her next statement froze my blood: "The doctor will surely ask for an ultra sound when he sees *this* mammogram!" I stared where she pointed. My shadowy breast appeared empty but for a small network of tangled, white webs. Terror prevented me from asking, "Is this what cancer looks like?" The technician took several more x-rays.

Waiting in the car, Buddy asked, "How'd it go?"

"Okay." My lips felt too wooden to elaborate.

All afternoon I sat on what I'd learned. If I told my husband, he'd worry, and from experience, I knew: *worry begets worry.* That night fear completely over-rode the movie we attended. In *Midnight in The Garden of Good And Evil*, instead of Savannah pseudo socialites partying and murdering, I imagined myself the star of a CANCER horror flick. I cared not a whit who went to whose citified party. Angry, I felt acutely aware that life as I knew it might be shattered. That unethical x-ray technician held a special place in my hall of contempt. Never should she have shown me the x-ray. What a nitwit.

That night in bed I turned. I twisted. "Lord," I begged, "please take away this fear!"

And He did. He stripped away my gut-wrenching paralysis. I slept the rest of that night as well as every other night of the two-week period I awaited my mammogram report. When no report came, I called my doctor. The nurse said, "Just a moment." She left the phone for an inordinate length of time. However, returning, she blessed my heart. "No cancer, Mrs. Wilson. Don't you worry about a thing."

And now, two years later, December 1999, a lump! Was my anger misplaced? Possibly that presumptuous technician knew more than her co-horts.

Our friends arrive. I switch off "Let it snow, Let it snow, Let it snow," and coatless, we exit into a seventy-three-degree December evening.

Ordering quesadillas and swapping small talk, my mind grapples with a gnawing worry. *How can a lump grow this big, so quickly?*

After a restless weekend, early Monday morning I call St. Mary's Hospital in Athens. "I found a lump in my breast," I tell them. "As soon as you can schedule it, I want a mammogram!"

The faceless voice frustrates me. "We're booked till February."

We bid our Calabash children, Bryan, Brenda, Kayla, (and Tango) farewell, wish them a Merry Christmas, and arrive home a week before that holiday. Immediately I'm ensnared by last minute shopping, gift wrapping, cooking, celebrating. Beneath hectic holiday preparations swims a sea of dread, which, through necessity, I attempt to ignore.

The night before seeing my family doctor, lying in bed, I stare at nothing. "Are you still awake?" Buddy asks.

I swallow tears. "I'm remembering all those days you were sick. And now you're better. Why do we have to worry about me?" I hope he doesn't hear I'm crying.

"You'll be fine. You will."

I always believe my husband … unless I'm wide awake worrying and it's two o'clock in the morning.

Next day the doctor I see refers me to a capable surgeon. Dr. C palpates my lump and arranges an immediate mammogram. Later, he shows me the growth on black and white film.

Dr. C's kind brown eyes turn serious. "Mrs. Wilson, you need a biopsy."

"Here? Now?" I'm fearful, but anxious to put behind me at least *one* dreaded procedure.

Using a thin needle, Dr. C deadens my breast. Thank goodness, for the biopsy needle looks long enough to poke through a mattress. He drives this projectile straight into the lump, pumping the needle vigorously for sufficient study material. Wonder of wonders, no pain!

As I await biopsy results, our world enters a new millennium. Between New Year's Day celebrations and disposing of Christmas decorations, I almost forget my Damocles' Sword, hovering.

A couple of days later I re-enter the surgeon's office. Avoiding his examining table, I sit in a chair. I'd love a miracle. Dr. C taps on the door. His face speaks volumes. "I'm sorry, Mrs. Wilson. You have cancer. *Poorly differentiated infiltrating ductal carcinoma.*"

Gulping, I ask, "What is *that*?"

"You have plain old breast cancer."

I could have spent the rest of my life without those words. Still, hearing *cancer,* I feel a weird relief. *Cancer,* I address my intruder, *you're inside me now. Just don't you bother to unpack your bags!*

I opt for a lumpectomy, which the surgeon calls a partial mastectomy. "We'll take out just the tissue necessary," he tells me. I understand *necessary* to mean the cancer and a small area of tissue free of malignancy.

From the time I learn that cancer resides in my body, I experience moments of near panic. Multiple Myeloma declared war on Mother. Her sister died from Leukemia, and Daddy suffered squamous cell cancer, metastasized to his liver. This eventually took his life. I know the wiles of this enemy, setting sites on me. I pray for courage and strength to face treatments ahead.

Although never in a million years would I have chosen this path, at times I feel somewhat excited. I'll see inside operating rooms, meet patients afflicted with cancer as well as other diseases research seeks to eradicate. I'll encounter souls much braver and better than I. What an experience this can be!

The following Tuesday morning, with the interloper excised from my body and on its way to a lab, I wake up to a left breast swathed in gauze and tape, and as pointed as that of Madonna in an early stage performance. A drainage tube ending in a clear Jackson Pratt bulb is anchored to my blouse. At home my brother, Jack, and sister-in-law, Marcie, have come to see me through this operation. I tell Marcie, "If things get no worse than this, I'm home free."

Two days later fluid in the bulb runs virtually clear. The surgeon removes the tube and makes me an appointment for axillary dissection, a proper name for lymph node removal. I tell him, "Let's get this business out of the way."

Then I'm tempted to stop treatment. I say to my daughter, "Mona, the cancer's gone. No cancer, no problem. Right?"

Mona, tells me about a friend of hers in a similar situation. When the doctor removed her lymph nodes, three were cancerous.

"How did they treat her?" I ask.

"She's had six months of chemotherapy and is about finished with radiation. Her hair's already a quarter of an inch long."

Hmm. I'd forgotten. Chemotherapy makes you bald. "Maybe I won't need chemo."

Before dawn Tuesday, lymph node removal morning, I step into the shower, thinking, *today I'll see the operating room.* Following lumpectomy I had no memory beyond a line-up of supine patients awaiting knives to fall.

Like the morning of the lumpectomy, I kiss my spouse, suffer the nurse to search for an elusive vein, and await euphoria. Propped on pillows, I observe the corridor-like space. A man wearing a dark beard looks my way. Opposite him, a young woman's eyes remain half closed, scare lines tracking her forehead. Me? I forget to worry. With a soothing IV dripping into my hand, I could be on a field trip.

A double door pushes open: *inner sanctum.* Sporting so much stainless steel, this sacred space looks like a kitchen! Beneath dazzling lights doctors and nurses amble past. At least three other patients lie in beds or on tables. "Where's my doctor?" I ask the nurse beside me.

"There," she points to a masked man on a stroll. *My* surgeon? He laughs, conversing with a robed compatriot.

"Slide onto the table," I'm told.

I scoot from my bed to the operating table. A nurse reaches for my arm.

"Are you putting me to sleep?"

I never hear her answer.

Not until I find myself in a hospital room do I truly awake. Buddy's there. And Mona. "I'm going to the bath room," I mumble. Someone rushes to help. Afterward, I say, "Where're my clothes?" I'm told I can stay in the hospital overnight. By two that afternoon I'm ensconced in my own home bedroom.

Unlike after the first operation, now I feel considerable pain. Earlier the doctor told my husband he took "a pound of flesh" from my armpit.

I rest that arm on a pillow, shuddering to think of poor souls who, during one operation receive double mastectomies with lymph node removal from both arms. For most of the week I alternate between sleeping on the bed and in a near-by recliner.

A tube leads from the sutured incision in my armpit to a stab opening in the side of my breast. A JP bulb to catch fluids draining must remain compressed and be emptied at intervals.

In about a week, I return to Dr. C's office. For the first time the surgeon beams.

He says, "Your cancer has spread to *no* nodes. Not one of the thirteen nodes isolated shows metastatic carcinoma!"

I feel weak with relief.

He checks the fluid in the bulb. "Too pink."

The next Wednesday I return. Dr. C removes a blood clot from the tube and says, "Come back next week and I'll take out this baby whether or not the fluid's clear."

The third week I brace myself for pain. Before leaving home I take a couple of Tylenol, and in the Doctor's office, scrunch my eyes. My voice quavers. "When are you removing the tube?"

"This tube?"

I haven't felt a thing! Into the trash the doctor tosses a hose, big and long enough to water petunias. He says that because my cancer was large, three and a half centimeters at its greatest diameter as well as being "poorly differentiated," I'll need three months chemotherapy followed by three months radiation treatment.

I console myself. *That's half the length of Mona's friend's treatments.*

A week after last seeing the surgeon, my husband and I walk into the oncology center. Dr. W is no stranger. For several months he treated Buddy for low hemoglobin. "On the scales," the nurse instructs my spouse.

He points at me. "She's your patient!"

Dr. W examines me, saying, "You really do need chemotherapy." He refers me to an assistant for blood work, a routine continuing every three weeks for the next three months.

I go to *The Pink Room.* Awaiting various procedures, patients sit at what could be school desks. An attractive young black man, looking completely out of place in this "sick" room, rolls up a sleeve, and at the sink runs hot water over well-defined biceps. He continues this for quite a while.

"What's wrong with your arm?" I ask.

"Small veins," he says. "Hot water helps 'em stand out."

My nurse takes me into a private cubicle containing monitoring equipment, a comfortable recliner, a straight back chair, a sink, and a television.

"Turn on the TV," I tell Buddy. "Let's watch ONE LIFE TO LIVE."

Vicky, the star, has breast cancer. Unlike me, I tell everybody, Vicky hides her cancer.

The nurse interrupts my viewing. "Let's see. Which vein looks best?" She eyes the roll of blue atop my hand.

I point out that the vein at the bend in my elbow works just fine.

She says "The drug they're giving you is dangerous. Seeping into flesh, it can cause you to lose a limb; or, if I use these veins, only a hand.

Hmm . . .

Searching and thumping, the nurse says, "Small, but this vein will do." She draws blood, runs a test, returns, and begins my first chemotherapy treatment. "Tell me if you feel any burning," she admonishes. Beside me, the nurse personally administers scarlet, toxic Adriamycin, a drug capable of destroying good, as well as cancerous cells.

My first treatment proceeds routinely. A social worker says group counseling is available at the local Loran Smith Cancer Center. A nice lady breezes through with a bagful of hats made by volunteers. The turbans are for those of us who are, or shortly will become bald. I peruse her bag and pick out a couple of turbans. Maybe I won't need them. Not everyone on chemo loses his or her hair.

About an hour later, the IV bottle empties. I stand up, a trifle woozy. Buddy and I drive over to Five Points to a beauty shop offering the "Look Good, Feel Better" program. Determined to be ready for whatever, I leaf through a catalog and order a wig.

My chemotherapy consists of a saline solution containing Adriamycin, a less potent drug, Cytoxin, plus a steroid. The steroid is to keep me from feeling deathly ill. For two days it proves energizing. In the meantime I take a pill for nausea. The third day, after I've caught up with every chore possible, spent, I sit in a recliner. I have little appetite, and for that I'm grateful. Certainly I can stand to shed pounds. However, I read in one of Dr. W's booklets, some breast cancer patients gain weight. Shucks!

Near the end of the second week, I brush my hair and clumps plump the brush. Over the next few days I obtain enough bottle-blonde, permed hair to stuff a small pillow.

Wow! I've always considered my head flat, not this strange, bullet shape. Oh well, there's always my new wig. Before walking over to have coffee at a neighbor's house, I pull somebody else's hair across my almost bare scalp. Down the street Betty says, "I like your new hairdo."

Three weeks after the first treatment and at three week intervals for three months, I receive therapy. "Really, chemo's not that bad," I tell friends. As time wears on, however, I grow somewhat weary. One day a needle stick brings me almost to tears, and I promise myself that never again will I allow anyone to poke a needle into the blood vessel located on the outside of my right thumb!

Finally, that phase of treatment ends. Dr. W thinks my sessions went well and makes an appointment for me three weeks thence at the Oncology Radiation Center.

Meanwhile I have a fiftieth high school reunion to attend. Wearing my fashionable wig exactly matching the artificially blonde hair I no longer possess, I greet class mates I haven't seen in fifty years. We reminisce and party, take a cruise down the Waccamaw River, reminisce and eat, reminisce and plan to meet again. Bald head (hidden) and all, I have a blast!

Buddy and I return to Athens just in time to begin the third phase of my cancer treatment. I'm becoming an old hand at this.

First day at the radiation center I decide I am in better shape than most of these patients. A woman in a wheel chair wheezes with every breath. A bed-laden patient, pushed down a hallway, disappears around a corner.

Multi-colored gladiola blooms decorate a counter. Religious music forms a soft backdrop for paper rustling. A graying, middle-aged lady answers the phone.

"Mrs. Wilson!"

That's me! A girl in street dress holds my folder. She leads me to a bright room overlooking a lawn edged in red and yellow day lilies. The girl smiles. "Dr. K will be with you shortly."

I look about. Paintings, possibly done by a child, decorate two walls. One painting depicts a rectangular white house with picket fence and walkway. A woman stands before the closed front door. Wonder what lies beyond that door?

Knock-Knock!

A smiling young man, hand out-stretched, enters the room. "Mrs. Wilson," he says, "I'm Dr. K."

My new doctor is Indian. He's personable and kind, and immediately I'm glad I chose this clinic. After a brief examination and blood work, we make the trek to the radiation wing.

"You may hate me after this," the new doctor comments.

He notes my alarm. "Oh, this won't hurt. You'll just need to lie still for a while."

"I can do that."

Dr. K and his assistant position me on a table. I lie atop a plain, black trash bag containing some kind of soft, form-fitting plaster. They guide my hand beyond my head. Ignoring extreme underarm soreness, I grip a stationary rod for an extended time, until materials inside the plastic bag harden into *my* shape. They call this cast a cradle.

The next day I return for my first radiation treatment. I lie with my arm and shoulder nestled in the cradle. On my chest, laser lights from overhead form a crimson cross. I'm instructed not to look at those beams. Hands tug on my body until I'm situated just where they want me. A technician, automatically positioning a huge machine above the cross of beams, says, "Breathe, just don't move. I'll be right back."

A buzzing begins, continues. I feel nothing amiss. In my head I count one, two, three, all the way to thirty-three before the buzzing stops and the girl returns.

"All done," she says. "Relax now."

We are finished?

I dress, return to my husband in the waiting room, and with our good friends, Don and Lois Shackleford, go to Peking for lunch. I love Peking's chicken curry!

Monday through Friday, I return for treatment. Dr. K anticipates scheduling me for twenty-eight to thirty treatments; but, after about two and a half weeks, a small blister forms on the perimeter of the treatment site. "Vacation time," the doctor says. Before my sessions end, I receive one more such holiday.

In a few days I return and continue for a total of thirty-two treatments, the last ten honing in on the exact spot of cancer removal. As I write this, my breast still sports a tan.

And my hair: about four months post-chemotherapy I've grown enough hair to brush, grayer than I remember, but wavy now. My sister-in-law, Marcie, says I look like Dame Judith Dench.

Discovering a cancerous lump alerts me to my mortality. I receive a "Pap Smear," my first in over twenty years. Results from this test read "negative." But the colonoscopy I dreaded proves necessary. Virtually painless, it reveals a pre-cancerous polyp removed during procedure. If I had procrastinated, eventually I might have found myself back in Dr. Ws' "Pink Room."

Soon my husband and I plan to return to our North Carolina hide-a-way. Grateful for Buddy's present good health, and anticipating no less for me, we'll relax on our cabin porch, past illnesses washed away by a symphony of marsh music.

Thank God for His ample blessings.

Part VIII

Psalm 102: 27

But thou art the same, and thy years shall have no end.

Chapter 29

Married, Forty-Six Years

Forty-six years, four states, four homes, three children, heart surgery, (four by-pass) and one breast cancer survival beyond our August, 1955, Good Hope Baptist Church wedding, on a sunny Sunday in 2001, Buddy and I return to the sheep farm. (You'll read about Buddy's by-pass surgery in my third memoir, *Bug Swamp, Calabash, and Other Family Legacies*.)

Taking the back way from Clemson, Buddy and I scour the roadside for familiar sights. I point, "There's the landfill! ... Over there! Look! Wonder if Willie Mae and Sarge Helton still live in that gray stone house." Willie Mae was organist in our Clemson Baptist Church, and Sarge was a part of Clemson's ROTC program.

"Ooh! There's the same light pole I almost crashed into. Remember? I was driving home from Clemson, Mona in the front, three-week-old Jimmy in back. For sure The Good Lord was in charge of that metal stake. Our car bent the stake double before we stopped a foot from that light pole. Whew!"

A mile or so further, I strain to glimpse the Oconee River.

Back then I loved the babble of the river, swamp willows weeping into their reflections, the flash of an occasional fish. Sometimes I sat on the Oconee's banks and told only *it* my secrets.

My first disappointment: just when I should spy the river sparkling beyond the next bend, a sign halts our progress. It reads, END OF

THE ROAD! An arrow points left, guiding us out the woods toward the Clemson-Anderson Highway.

"I wanted to see the house from the direction we first saw it," I wail.

"No way, Hosea." Buddy says, "Lake Hartwell swallowed up this part of the river."

I scoot over as close to my mate as Mitsubishi bucket seats allow. I gaze at his still perfect profile. His strong left hand with its missing little finger grips the steering wheel; his other hand reaches for mine.

Turning right just short of Pendleton, we approach the sheep farm from an angle opposite that of our original sighting.

"There it is! Our first home!"

Was it this tiny? The house still looks welcoming, although someone else's navy Pathfinder sits in our driveway. In a slight breeze, the trees our children played beneath swish greetings with their branches. "Sigh …."

The barn's still here, shining silver in the afternoon sun.

"Sheep! Where are the sheep?"

"Looks like our sheep turned into cattle." Pointing to a herd of longhorns, Buddy wipes something from his eye. Surely not a tear!

We never get out the car. I say, "Let's hurry. Maybe we can make it back to Athens in time for Tegan's soccer game."

"Jeremy's football team's playing Oconee County tomorrow evening."

"I hate to see those big brutes rough up my boy!" That's the truth!

Remember? Tegan and Jeremy are two of our six grandchildren.

Music from Scheherazade streams from the radio. My favorite symphony. I lean back and close my eyes, basking in Boston Pop's rendition of Dvorak's masterpiece.

"Find the Greenville station, will ya?"

Heaving a sigh,
I comply.

Poetic, huh?

"Who are you pulling for, Clemson, or The Dawgs?"

"Don't you know a tiger never changes its stripes?" My husband throws back his head and bellows:

> *Where the Blue Ridge yawns its greatness,*
> *Where the Tigers play ...*

He looks happy, murdering his alma mater!

"Our Dawgs'll get along very well without you," I tease.

Buddy raises his eyebrows. "You've gone over to the enemy camp?"

"The enemy!" *That,* from a Tiger who sired a litter of PUPS!

~~~

All told, I am happy that in 1953, on the tenth of March, I drift down a flight of stairs, straight into the life of a handsome young man. He sports a gorgeous tan, looks at me with lovely, blue-green eyes, and flashes an adorable smile. He wears a white, Block C sweater and waits for me. More or less, that's what he's been doing ever since.

P. S. Following this memoir, my third flight into the past will consist of tales, events, and legends impossible to omit from this old life story of mine: "Uncle Bill and his Crazy Quest" to become a witch, only to become the most Christ-like member of our family; "Bob Darby and his *Requited* Destiny;" "Fools, Digging for Gold;" "The Perils of Illicit Leisure;" "Zena, An Enchantress;" "Anna, A Snake-bit Woman from Florida," "Clabber and Whey, A'Workin' by the Day;" these and other stories cry out to be told, and will be, on Grandma Nettie's front porch, around our winter hearth, or from Grandma's peach-colored chair in the jam' of our chimney, all *Bug Swamp, Calabash, and Other Family Legacies,* the title of my third memoir.

Reading this third memoir, learn more about my indomitable mother-in-law, Ople Bell Wilson, her parents, her in-laws, their families. Visit Ople's Calabash, home to our Wilson patriarch, Great-Grandfather Jesse Wilson. For years the largest business in Calabash's town of many seafood restaurants has been Callahan's Gift Shop. In the eighteen hundreds that lot housed my husband's Grandpa Jesse's general store, also the local post office. Later, in the thirties, to feed and care for her children, Ople roasted and sold local oysters underneath branches of that lot's beautiful oaks. Two of them still stand.

The following people and their ancestry are human legacies to our family: the Hamiltons, the Todds, the Holmes, the Williams, the Allens, the Royals, the Wilsons, the Bells, the Lays, the Bryans, the Morses, the Randalls; each family group contributes a unique birthright to our present-day Wilson generation.

So, let's meet again. Any afternoon is good. We'll sit on the porch. Pull up a chair. I warn you, I don't dip snuff. But I do enjoy my glass of sweet ice tea.

Basking in the shade of Grandma's ancient, rosy crepe myrtles, listening to her mocking birds' happy palavering, we'll breathe in fresh, country air. If you prefer, we'll sit on the porch of our Calabash River cabin. We'll enjoy God's water-world while sipping our tea. Most important, we'll sit and palaver just as long as we please. I'm enough like Grandma Nettie, I enjoy talking. Still, I've no desire to monopolize any conversation. Tell me *your* stories. They're as priceless as mine, and I can't wait to share them.

Even better, write down life's highlights, exclusive to you and to no other living mortal. Your readers will be grateful, but definitely your children will inherit one of God's promised legacies.

Message: from children to parents:
1 Peter 3: 9 King James Version
. . . *ye* (children) *are therefore called, that ye*
(inserted, and they) *should inherit a blessing.*

Printed in the United States
By Bookmasters